THE
MANAGEMENT
TEAM!

The Management Team
© Copyright 1984 by Dorothy M. Walters

Royal Cassettes · Books · Speakers, Inc.
18825 Hicrest Road
Glendora, California 91740

First Edition

Library of Congress Cataloging in Publication Data in Progress
ISBN 0-934344-15-9

Printed in the United States of America

All those who know how to read have the power to magnify themselves, to multiply the ways in which they exist, to make their life full, significant and interesting.

—Aldous Huxley

Robert McFarland Soutter
The Inventor

Hanging in the office of Royal Publishing is a photograph of Dottie Walters' Grandfather, Robert McFarland Soutter, the inventor. Left. an orphan in London, his grandmother raised him and sent him to the church of the great speaker Charles Spurgeon. Temple Baptist Church was filled several times each Sunday, with thousands of people. Charles Spurgeon, the Billy Graham of his day, worked without a microphone. He was known as "The Prince of Speakers."

When Robert Soutter came to the United States in a sailing ship, he brought with him only a pack on his back and a letter of recommendation from Charles Spurgeon. That letter is now preserved and hangs with the photograph. Robert Soutter has many U.S. and Canadian patents for his inventions for railway trains.

DRIVE IT!

by Dottie Walters, CSP

My Grandpa was a Scot . . . an Inventor.
"Creating's just the start . . . You must do more.
You hammer out the train. You lay down the track
From here to the end of the world and back.

"My ideas built the cars, but without the load
There's no profit for the crew. First the cargo's sold.
The Engineers are drivers, but they cannot go
'Till Management has figured it. Then the whistles blow!

"Life is like the railroad. You have to use your head
Watch for signals coming. Check that green or red.
Get your crew all ready, then stand by to leave.
Master mind the system. Dream first, then Believe!

"Seize the wheels of commerce. Push them
                'round and 'round
Fire up your engine! Pull that throttle down.
Double check your switches. Light your super-beam.
You're the Manager, My darlin'

"YOU MUST DRIVE THE DREAM!"

—dedicated to Inventor Ted DeBoer
of the National Speakers Association

Gene Harrison

P.O. Box 6142
Bonsall, California 92003
(619) 758-5026

Gene Harrison

Gene Harrison has 28 years of hands-on leadership experience in both the private and public sectors, with a documented record as a motivator and innovative problem-solver. He has served on the faculties of the University of Florida and the University of Mississippi and held numerous combat and administrative assignments while rising from Private to Colonel in the U.S. Marines. His experience has ranged from leading 3,000 Marines in combat to managing a general merchandise operation of 1500 civilian employees with annual sales exceeding 70 million dollars.

Gene is Vice President of the San Diego Chapter, National Speakers Association and a member of the Board of Directors of the Golden Voice Chapter of the National Speakers Association. He is also a member of the American Society for Training and Development and International Platform Association. He is a full-time professional speaker/workshop leader who specializes in leadership training for managers and supervisors.

Prologue

by Gene Harrison

"Character is singularly contagious."
—Samuel A. Eliot

Character. What is it? According to Webster's Dictionary, character is honesty, integrity, self-discipline, fortitude and moral strength. Having spent my life looking in the faces of others, searching for character, I believe it is much more; it is that magic ingredient between members of a team that blends diverse person-alities and talents to enthusiastically pursue common goals and objectives. It fosters a spirit that makes it possible to overcome the most formidable of obstacles; it keeps the feet and hands moving when the head says it can't be done, and serves as a catalyst for men and women to transform their environment. It creates an environment of trust and confidence that makes everyone want to pull in the same direction. Character is the individual and collective heart of the successful management team.

For many years it has been my privilege to be sent to a variety of units and organizations to increase morale and team effectiveness. One of the most challenging of those assignments was to a remote village, in the jungles of South East Asia, which had been decimated by armed conflict. Basic facilities had been destroyed. Few families had not lost one or more members in the conflict. A feeling of despair and hopelessness permeated the atmosphere. I was taken to the village elder, a gnarled old man, advanced in years, who was known for his character and wisdom. He assembled a team consisting of the one remaining teacher in the village, a farmer and the senior military man, to listen to the plans for rebuilding. They listened patiently to the proposal, agreeing to most and modifying certain aspects of the plan to conform to the culture. My part in the endeavor was to provide advice and assist in acquiring materials. What a beehive of activity as they put their plan into action; farmers from the fields digging foundations, woodcutters from the jungle building, mothers with babies strapped to their breasts carried water, children carrying sand and materials, each doing what he could do best. A village, better than the original, rose from the ashes; spirit from the activity and a unity of purpose rose from their common need. That village stands today due not to technology or democracy but due to the character and spirit of the people who worked together with their diverse talents to pursue common goals and objectives.

What a marvelous challenge and opportunity faces the management team in this age of technology. An age when knowledge more than doubles every ten years; when a quarter inch chip of silicon has the capacity of the original ENIAC computer which occupied a city block. Yet our most formidable challenge, like that of the village elder, will be to effectively utilize the vast array of talented people of varied abilities and emotions to meet individual and organizational goals. The ultimate measure of our success will depend upon our ability to create a spirit that sustains a vision of excellence that challenges, energizes and enriches the individual and the organization. The keystone is character.

The following pages present pearls of wisdom from a wide range of successful managers and management consultants. Let them contribute to the spirit of your own management team.

"The miracle, or the power that elevates the few is to be found in their industry, application and perseverance under the promptings of a brave, determined spirit".
—**Mark Twain**

Activity energizes; inertia and apathy enervate.

—Harry G. Mendelson

Joe Batten, C.P.A.E.

Chairman of the Board
Batten, Batten, Hudson & Swab, Inc.
820 Keo Way
Des Moines, Iowa 50309
(515) 244-3176

Joe Batten, C.P.A.E.

Joe Batten is founder and Chairman of the Board of Batten, Batten, Hudson & Swab, Inc., Des Moines, Iowa, a 26-year old human resource firm engaged in creative management research, consulting, film production, and educational services. Joe is a renowned consultant, speaker, trainer, film maker, and author. He is known world-wide as the author of "Tough-Minded Management" (and ten other books) and such films as "Keep Reaching," and "Ask for the Order."

He has spoken over 2,000 times on motivation, selling and management. He is a charter member of the National Speakers Association Hall of Fame (C.P.A.E.)

Introduction

by Joe Batten, C.P.A.E.

If a diabolical force were to seek to plunge this nation, indeed the world, into chaos, confusion, and despair, the one best way to do it would be to dim or switch off the minds and abilities of managers and leaders.

It follows then that the *best* way to create a superior world, a world where rich and profitable relationships and enterprises can flourish, is to target *excellence* into the training, teaching, and practice of management.

The professionals who have contributed to this fine book have certainly addressed themselves to that goal with zeal, skill, and dedication. In my twenty-seven years as a professional practitioner of management consulting, it has been my privilege to work in tandem with some really magnificent people, my colleagues at BBH&S. They are dedicated to *excellence* in management throughout the world.

Allow me to proffer, in a very abbreviated way, some of the principal elements needed in the coming years if we are to indeed measure up to the awesome needs and challenges coming at us.

The basic definition of management which undergirds our teachings in thousands of seminars in North America each year is this:

> **Develop a clear and complete system of expectations in order to identify, evoke, and use the *strengths* of all resources in the organization—the most important of which is people.**

The precepts and techniques of *Tough-Minded Management* have now spread throughout the world. I'd like to share with you some thoughts directly from that book:

"Why should managers today expect more of themselves and of their people? Why is the quality of business leadership more crucial than ever before?

"Our abundant and opulent standard of living, our rights and privileges, are facing their most serious threat. How is this possible when, materially, we were never better off? Because with cold calculation, the forces of collectivism are exploiting our most obvious weaknesses throughout the world:

Weaknesses

- The worship of leisure
- The deification of recreation and amusement
- The pursuit of financial security only
- Fear of innovation unless it provides immediate returns in money and leisure
- The loss of hard-nosed individuality
- Refuge in mass thinking and collective movements; sheeplike behavior
- A tendency to talk rather than act
- Lack of awareness of the strengths of our own history
- Failure to take a strong stand for individual beliefs
- A tendency to view the future with trepidation
- Spiritual exhaustion

"The great need is for *purpose* and *direction*—for vitality, guts, and a positive approach. The principles of democracy as embodied in free enterprise do not have to be 'explained' or 'defended.' They must simply be *practiced* within a framework of dedication, the giving of self, and hard work. The times cry out for tough-minded managers, tough-minded men and women who understand the dramatic difference between 'hardness' and 'toughness.' Granite is *hard* and can be smashed by a hard blow. Leather is *tough* and can only be resiliently dented by a hard blow. Hardness is brittle, static, and weak. Toughness is supple, flexible, and durable."

Years ago, I had the privilege of sharing the phrase, "A tough mind and tender heart are one," with Martin Luther King. This became the title of one of his best known sermons and is the opening chapter in his book,

Strength To Love. Yes, love *is* the toughest-minded emotion in the world and when the toughest-minded leader—or manager—the world has ever known said, "Follow Me," he was presenting a beautiful example for all. The enlightened and inspired manager/leader of tomorrow will be committed to the following transitions:

From	To
Pushing	Leading
Telling	Asking
Hating	Loving
Directing	Expecting
Low expectations of self and others	High expectations of self and others
Adequacy	Excellence
Getting	Giving
Negative	Positive
Doubt	Faith
Expedient morality	Integrity
Competing with others	Competing with self
Preoccupation with weaknesses	Building on strengths
Role orientation	Goal orientation
Against	For
Destroying	Building

You will *enjoy* this book! You will find it useful and practical. It is in and on the heart and minds of *you,* the present and potential *managers,* that the future of our nation and world depends.

The *possibilities* on planet earth are enormous. Much

greater than any of us can currently perceive. The possibilities in the minds and spirits of people are truly the new frontier. Let us mine those riches. Let us dare to Expect The Best!

Will you?

Nothing left loose ever does anything creative.
No horse gets anywhere until he is harnessed.
No steam or gas ever drives anything until it is confined.
No Niagara is ever turned into light and power until it
     is funneled.
No life ever grown until it is focused, dedicated, disciplined.
                                        —**Harry Emerson Fosdick**

Our chief want in life is someone who will make us do what we can.

—Ralph Waldo Emerson

George L. Morrisey, C.P.A.E., C.S.P.

President of MOR Associates
P.O. Box 5879
Buena Park, California 90622
(714) 995-1244

George L. Morrisey
One of the top authors, speakers, seminar leaders and consultants in the field of management, George is founder and President of MOR Associates, a management consulting firm based in Buena Park, California. His background includes more than 20 years as a practicing manager and key specialist with several organizations in both the private and public sectors. He has personally served as internal or external consultant to more than 200 business, industrial, government and non-profit organizations.

George has written many management-related books including the best sellers, Management by Objectives and Results *(and its two later editions related to its application in* Business and Industry *and the* Public Sector) *and* Effective Business and Technical Presentations. *He is the author and producer of several audio and video cassette learning programs, all directed towards helping individuals and organizations become more effective and self-fulfilled.*

An active member of the American Society for Training and Development and the National Speakers Association, George received the national ASTD award for publications in 1973. He is a trustee of the international MBO Institute, a non-profit organization dedicated to advancing the state of the art in management.

Foreword

by George Morrisey, C.P.A.E., C.S.P.

What is a manager? A manager is not a title, not a position in an organization. A manager is someone who has responsibility for the use of resources. My definition of management is "the effective use of limited resources to achieve desired results." By this definition, virtually anyone is and should be considered a manager. Furthermore, we practice management in any area of our lives where it is important to achieve worthwhile results.

Management is both an art and a state of mind. There is no *right* way to manage. There are some methods that are more effective than others depending on the circumstances being faced. The exercise of good judgement on how and when to use various management tools and techniques is what clearly separates those who are successful in their managerial roles from those who are less successful.

The study of management is a journey, not a destination. Neither you nor I will ever be as good a manager as we might like to be. Furthermore, none of us is as good a manager as we already know how to be. We need to continually expand our horizons, looking for ways to increase our own effectiveness in this important part of our lives. The opportunity to examine the many fine ideas incorporated in this book represents the chance to build on those skills in which we are already successful and improve on those where improvement is desirable. Some of these ideas will be far more useful to you than others. Concentrate on those relatively few that you can take and put to use immediately and don't be concerned about those that are not particularly useful or that you are not able to apply at the moment.

Most of us practice at least two distinctly different professions, one which represents a technical knowledge or skill (engineering, accounting, sales, teaching, speaking, etc.) and one which is directed at getting things done both inside and outside of that technical field which, of course, is management. The real advantage in becoming skillful in the profession of management is that it is a much more transferable skill than is true in most of the technical professions we might choose to follow. Therefore, regardless of what you see as your primary profession, recognize that you are also practicing the profession of management. The more knowledgeable and skillful you become in that profession, the more effective you become in life.

THE
MANAGEMENT
TEAM!

C O N T E N T S

Those who persistently say that the job cannot be done should not interrupt those who are already doing it.
*—**Jerry Buchanan,** Towers Club*

Thomas J. Winninger, President

The Winninger Group
Box 1661
Waterloo, Iowa 50704
(319) 234-0761 • (319) 236-3174

Thomas J. Winninger, Business Leader

Pioneer in Consultant Selling and Stroke Management! *Thomas J. Winninger has been a pioneer in Consultant Selling and Stroke Management. Since the mid-70's Tom has personally worked with over 750 local and national business and sales organizations. His consultant skills and business building programs were developed for and in association with national franchise organizations, Fortune 500 companies, and independent business leaders.*

Practitioner, Participant, Consultant! *Besides consulting, speaking and writing, Tom is still involved in the day-to-day operations of Master's Management Group, Inc., Winninger Institute, Master's Marketing, and Winninger and Associates. His marketing programs have dramatically increased both the gross and net of numerous sales organizations.*

America's Most Unique, Enthusiastic Seminar Leader! *Tom personally spoke to 178 groups throughout the U.S.A. and Canada last year. 22,000 sales and business professionals participated in his conferences. Sales and marketing executives, association executives, and small business leaders hail him for his refreshing approach to business building.*

Author, Custom Training Producer! *Tom's inspiring articles have appeared in over 50 trade journals and magazines. His articles include:*
  "Success from the Inside-Out!"
  "The Persuasive Art of Selling!"
  "You Weren't Made to be a Duck!"
  "How to Eat an Elephant While Chasing Off the Monkeys!"
  "Who Are You Trying to Persuade?"
  "The 60-Second Silent Sell!"
  "What Are You Waiting For?"
  His video and audio cassettes are being used in Australia, South Africa, Canada and the U.S.A.

Who's On Your Team?
by Thomas J. Winninger

"Treat people as you want them to be, not as you think they are, and they will rise to the expectation you have of them."
—Thomas J. Winninger

Have you been trying to change people? If you have been in management, you realize that people rarely change! If they do, it's seldom because other people want them to change.

This and three other principles are ones management must adhere to in order to get people to work well on your team. Here are the principles:

#1 You don't change people. Behavior modification results when people adjust to circumstances.

#2 You don't motivate people.

#3 People are motivated for their own reasons, not for yours.

#4 People are re-active. They tend to give what they get. Fairness breeds fairness, support wins support, resistance fosters resistance, and lack of enthusiasm fosters lack of enthusiasm.

With these principles in mind, let's take a closer look at the four types of personalities on your team—Dan, or Darlene, the Driver; Ivan, or Irene, the Influencer; Stanley, or Stella, the Steady; and Clancey, or Clara, the Controller.

The Impatient Driver Personality

Dan, or Darlene, the Driver tends to be the impatient type. He wants your job. He thinks he knows everything you do, and he tells you he knows it better. Change and challenge are an integral part of a Driver's life. They are easily bored with a task. They're always in a rush, with a lot to do. You will find them working with their hats on, always threatening to leave. Early birds, up in the morning with most things done by noon, they shy away from crowds. They are competitive, wanting to win. Unfortunately, they equate winning with big—big offices, big cars, big houses. If there's one person they like to talk about more than anyone else, it's themselves.

If you are managing the Driver-type of people, don't be intimidated by their nature. Use their competitive attitude to the team's advantage. Challenge them! Help them set short-term goals. Because they're impatient, they will never reach long-term goals they set. Be sincere and give them plenty of recognition. Money is not their main motivator. Ego-satisfaction is more important. If you're involved in training exercises with Driver-types, be sure to keep the detail to a minimum. They'll figure it out for themselves.

The Influential, Social Personality

The second type is Ivan, or Irene, the Influencer, the social member of your team. They like people and tend to be groupies. They prefer planning the Christmas party and other social activities to working. Ivans are also name-droppers. Because friendship is of primary importance to them, they rarely tell you how they really feel because they fear losing your friendship. They want to be liked so much that they'll agree just to agree.

Unfortunately, they are hard people to find. They are often late for meetings and disorganized. They are rarely serious, and can't figure out why people hustle and bustle over objectives and goals. They prefer to talk about their golf game, bridge club, or luncheon date, rather than office goals. Therefore, you'll seldom find them at their desks diligently working.

The Influencer person is hard to manage since things offend them easily, but you can manage this team member by appealing to feelings. Create a friendly atmosphere and avoid arguments. Show personal interest in them; let them talk, but guide them with questions, keeping them on the main points. If they are late for meetings, talk about the things you know they'd be interested in early in the meeting, so they feel they've missed something. Because these people do not develop time-frames, establish tasks by time. Give specific, detailed directions in writing. Remember, Ivans can be fun. They look at the lighter side of things and don't take life too seriously.

The Consistent, Loyal Personality

The third personality type is Stanley, or Stella, the Steady. These people are consistent. They believe in the team concept to everything, but prefer to follow rather than lead. You'll enjoy their "get-it-done" attitude which is consistent, deliberate, patient and loyal. They're motivated by security, and shy away from a changing atmosphere. While a Dan the Driver is lying awake at night trying to figure out how to change things, Stanley the Steady is awake trying to figure out how to stop the change. Steadys become passive under pressure and are slow to react. They want to know all the specific benefits of their actions before going ahead. If you change the office furniture around, it will upset them to an abnormal degree unless the benefit for the change is thoroughly covered first. The family is the center of their life, so you will probably find pictures of their family on their desk.

If you have Stanleys and Stellas on your team (and hopefully you do), draw them out by showing interest in their family. Show them how their actions will minimize risk. Give them concrete examples of why something should be done. Be patient when you ask them to change. Give them all the facts, letting them know they are a cornerstone of the team, that they are as important as the Dans and Ivans to the ultimate success of the group. However, do not overwhelm them by talking about all the great things you think the team should be doing. Help them prioritize their tasks because they will usually start at the top of the pile and work to the bottom. They do not realize that many things on the bottom of the stack should have been done first. Steady people also need a lot of security, so they may act possessive and want to own you. You might even find they visit your office often after they have left your company's employment. But don't try to buddy-buddy them like you would an Ivan or Irene. Steadys develop relationships slowly, but once these relationships are cemented in place, they will last forever.

The Efficient Perfectionists

The fourth type, and at times the most difficult, is

Clancey, or Clara, the Controller. These people are perfectionists. Overly particular about things, they want to know why it is important to do something. They will question your directives and requests. They were wrong once in their lives, and their mothers never let them forget it.

It takes them a long time to do some things, including making decisions. They aren't slow, but they live by one philosophy—"If it's going to be done, it's worth taking time to do it right." Controllers are detail-oriented people. They are very efficient, but not necessarily effective. They base most of their decisions on figures, computer print-outs, and calculations. Recently, I was discussing with a Clancey why he had two calculators on his desk. Without a flinch, he said, "One of them might be wrong." They tend to be shrewd people, always finding a mistake in your work. They will put you on the spot, but avoid letting you put them on the spot. They're capable of turning the table on you.

It takes a strong management image to develop a productive team with Clancey and Clara, but it can be done. Give them detailed instructions, and always use logic and figures in your directives. Refrain from criticizing them in open, and appeal to harmony at your meetings and group discussions. When they have questions about why things are done, appeal to standard procedures. Help them prioritize. This type tends to become controllers and accountants of major corporations, and can be an integral part of the team.

Effective Management for Four Part Harmony

As you can see, to have an effective management team, it is important to employ all four personality types. While Dan the Drivers give directives, set goals, and fire up the group with enthusiasm, Ivan the Influencers keep everyone positive. Stanley the Steadys do the work, and Clancey the Controllers make sure the work gets done right. But heed this warning—each person's strengths can be as much a weakness as a strength. An overabundance of a strength becomes a weakness. A Driver who is too demanding, too competitive, and too aggressive, diminishes the team's motivation. A Controller who is too much of a perfectionist can stall the process. A Steady who is too security-oriented can keep the team from taking the risks that are necessary for ultimate success. And, the Influencers who are too socially-oriented and too impulsive become a weak link in the management chain.

What then internally motivates these people?

Dan the Driver has two motivators: (1) fear of failure, and (2) need of recognition. As a manager, you can appeal to Dan's desire to get results, while at the same time, give him plenty of recognition. Ivan, on the other hand, is motivated by the desire to be accepted by all. Stanley and Stella are motivated by a fear of losing security, and demotivated by an overabundance of unnecessary change. Clancey is motivated by a desire to get things done right, by numbers and by detail. All personality types can also be demotivated by too much criticism and disapproval.

To be effective, your team must be balanced. The three major management mistakes are . . .

(1) matching the wrong people to the wrong task;

(2) matching the wrong people to the wrong people; and

(3) assuming that people adjust to different tasks easily.

Mistakes

An effective manager is one who maximizes energy by minimizing conflict. Most organizations operate on 80 percent conflict and 20 percent task, rather than 20 percent conflict and 80 percent task. What is your team's conflict/task ratio?

As you work to build an effective management team, never lose sight of the fact that *you* are one of the four types. You, too, must adjust to your team players. If you are a Dan, you tend to be too impatient, too overbearing, too demanding. You won't appreciate that some team members are not like you. But, if you develop a team of only Dans, the team will not last.

Leadership Styles

If you are an Ivan, you must learn to set time frames for your goals. Spend more time talking about concrete examples with your employees. Do not be intimidated by the Dans on your team, and enjoy the fact that people are often more productive when they're having fun.

If you are a Stanley or Stella, you are a consistent boss. However, you do not take risks and often do not prioritize your work. You may not get the right things done in the right order. If you're a Clara or Clancey, you tend to be overly critical, a little too much perfectionistic and detail-oriented. There must be a balance in your life.

It has been proven through studies that having each team member understand the type they are and the role they play can help a team work together more productively and effectively. If you know what type you are working with, more things get done because there is less conflict.

The Management of Managers

There are four types of managers:

(1) Those that make things happen

(2) Those that think they make things happen

(3) Those who only watch things happen

(4) Those who do not know something's happening

Motivating your employees can be very personalized, and it all boils down to the fact that good managers tell their team what is expected, when it is expected, and how well the team members are doing. Four tools will help your team development . . .

(1) **Job Enrichment.** Help your team members see that they are important, special and a part of the team. This helps satisfy some of their inner desires to achieve.

(2) **Managing by Goals for Results.** Team members work to get to some point together. They can see themselves realizing a worthy goal step-by-step.

(3) **Participation.** Motivation comes when all team members know they are an integral part. They'll know they can tell you how they feel, share with you their goals and aspirations, and participate in decision-making.

(4) Job Rotation. On a limited basis, give each person the opportunity of doing something outside their area of expertise that challenges them to grow and make a new commitment to the job.

When working with individual members of your team, remember . . .

(1) Each of us have developed a distinct way of feeling, thinking and acting. Each of us have had different experiences in our life and have been brought up in a different situation.

(2) No two people see a situation exactly the same. The best approach management can use is to try to see the work situation from the employee or staff team member's point of view. Let staff members know that you appreciate why they might see a situation the way they do, even if you don't agree.

(3) You understand the behavior of others when you understand what motivates them. It is easier, for example, to understand Dan the Driver if you understand that he is results-motivated and very impatient.

(4) It is tough to see the other person's point of view. As a management professional, you must reverse this phrase and say, "Often it's tough for your team members to see your point of view."

Your employees will resist you for a number of reasons. The better you understand these reasons, the easier it will be for you to develop your people. The following ideas will help you deal with that resistance:

(1) Make all work purposes specific and clear.

(2) Consult employees before making a final decision.

(3) Do not appeal to them based upon your own personal reasons, but identify the benefits they will also receive.

(4) Give them concrete examples for changing things.

(5) Realize that staff members will also resist because they fear failing. Often, it's tough to accept new ideas because we're afraid that if we apply ourselves and it doesn't work, we will reap negative consequences.

(6) If there is excessive work pressure, your people will resist you. Let them know that you understand they are under pressure.

(7) Make sure the reward for making the change is adequate and based upon their benefit, not yours.

(8) They will resist you when they feel the present situation might be adequate, or that they are capable of putting up with it.

At the end of this chapter is a *Management Effectiveness Questionnaire.* It will let you evaluate yourself and the potential of your relationship with your employees. Be honest with yourself. Are you an effective manager? Circle "yes," "no," or "sometimes." On the bottom of the page is the key. Have your management team evaluate themselves. Then discuss it with them. To be an effective manager, it's important for you to appreciate your people for what they are, not for what you can make them. One of the greatest of all management principles is, "Treat people as you want them to be, and they will rise to the expectation you have of them." In other words, "Don't tell me I can do it, or that I have the potential. Treat me as though I am already doing it, and I will rise to what you want me to be." Concentrate on what people do right and not what they do wrong, and the wrong will diminish. Compliment team members for the right things they accomplish, and they'll work harder to do it right next time. Too often mediocre managers spend their time telling team members what they're doing wrong, or what they should improve on rather than concentrating on what they're already doing right and getting them to do more of it.

The future potential of your team depends upon you . . . your response to your team members, your ability to be pro-active, your ability to treat them as though they're already there, and your ability to adjust and treat each person as an individual. Treat team members for what they are, rather than trying to change them, and you will truly have an effective, results-oriented team.

DIAGNOSTIC TOOL "A"

"MANAGEMENT EFFECTIVENESS QUESTIONNAIRE"

The purpose of this form is to help us assess the potential of our company. We are looking for frank, honest opinions and constructive ideas from you. Please take a few minutes to complete and *anonymously* return this information. We hope to utilize this candid information to help us improve. (Circle "Yes" if generally yes, "No" if generally no, "Sometimes" if generally in between.)

Circle One

1. Willing to listen to my problems — Yes No Sometimes

2. Firm but fair — Yes No Sometimes

3. Lets me know he cares that I achieve success — Yes No Sometimes

4. Capable of providing sound solutions — Yes No Sometimes

5. Doesn't always agree with me, but I respect his opinion — Yes No Sometimes

6. Gets along with the group as a whole — Yes No Sometimes

7. Willing to help when asked — Yes No Sometimes

8. Honest, fair, trustworthy — Yes No Sometimes

9. Has a positive attitude — Yes No Sometimes

10. Helps create an atmosphere that makes me want to work — Yes No Sometimes

11. Appreciates my role as a member of the team — Yes No Sometimes

12. Generally knowledgeable in all aspects of our business — Yes No Sometimes

13. Communicates effectively on a one-to-one basis regarding specific work situations — Yes No Sometimes

14. Keeps me informed — Yes No Sometimes

15. Generally can be reached for help — Yes No Sometimes

16. I feel free to make suggestions to management — Yes No Sometimes

General remarks:
Please list constructive suggestions that might be utilized to help.

_____

_____

_____

_____

Results: *Yes* = +1;   *No* = -1;   *Sometimes* = +½;

In other words, for each *Yes*, give yourself a plus one. For each *No*, give yourself a minus one. For each *Sometimes*, give yourself a plus one-half.

If more than one person is submitting this questionnaire, average your final number.

     12+   Above average

   1-11   Average

Below 1   Need some reconsideration of management style!

Do the thing, and you will be given the power.
                                —Emerson

Kathryn Alesandrini, Ph.D.

MicroConnect
401 Wilshire, Suite 1100
Santa Monica, California 90401
(213) 458-0513

Kathryn Alesandrini:
Although many think of computer graphics as a new field, Dr. Alesandrini has 12 years of experience in designing and creating computer graphics, starting with the PLATO computer system in the early 70's. She credits her Italian ancestry for fostering an interest in visual communication. After completing a Ph.D. at UCLA in 1979, Dr. Alesandrini joined the faculty at the University of Iowa where she taught graphic communication, computer graphics, and computer-based instruction.

Her work has been featured in national publications and national conferences. The design of informational graphics and screen design are two special areas of expertise for Dr. Alesandrini.

Her seminars and workshops always receive top top ratings from participants who appreciate her warmth and enthusiasm.

Dr. Alesandrini is founder and president of the firm MicroConnect based in Santa Monica, California. The new firm is specializing in providing high quality training on graphics and the use of computers in training and instruction. One product is entitled "Graphics in CBT," an audio-visual course being used in training programs across the country by major companies including American Trans Tech, AT&T Communications, Arthur Anderson, GTE, Massachusetts Mutual Life, Tecktronix, TRW, Xerox and others.

2

Get the Picture: Manage Information via Computer Graphics
by Kathryn Alesandrini, Ph.D.

*"Everyone spoke of an information overload,
but what there was in fact was a non-
information overload."*
—Richard Saul Wurman
*What-If, Could Be
(Philadelphia 1976)*

Successful managers will be those who succeed in managing information. The information age is upon us.

Yet, as Naisbitt points out, "We are drowning in information but starved for knowledge."[1] The figures are astounding:

*Between 6,000 and 7,000 scientific articles are written each day.

*Scientific and technical information now increases 13 percent per year, which means it doubles every 5.5 years.

*But the rate will soon jump to perhaps 40 percent per year because of new, more powerful information systems and an increasing population of scientists. That means that data will double every twenty months.

*By 1985 the volume of information will be somewhere between four and seven times what it was only a few years earlier.

To succeed, the manager *must* condense this dearth of information into manageable units. There are two major ways that information can be condensed: 1) it can be "chunked" or combined into patterns of meaningful units and 2) it can be "visualized" or transformed to graphical information. With computer graphics, managers can do both.

Chunking information is something that people do every day although on a limited basis. We need to chunk information because we can process only a limited number of information bits through our short-term memory at any one time, that number ranging from 5 to 9 bits of information.[2] For example, most people can temporarily remember a 7-digit number but probably cannot remember several unfamiliar phone numbers simultaneously without some sort of memory strategy such as rehearsing the numbers. Although short-term memory limits the number of chunks that can be processed simultaneously, the number of information bits contained in those chunks is not restricted to that limit. Information chunks may range in complexity from a single bit of information to many bits. Information processing can be increased by chunking the information—combining separate bits of the information into larger patterns or groups. The new groups or chunks are then easier to perceive and remember than all the separate items. Have you noticed that license plate names are easier to perceive and remember than license plate numbers? As a hypothetical example, the license plate "SPEEDER" is much easier to perceive and remember than "J86L524." Yet both have exactly seven bits of information. Since you automatically chunk the first into a meaningful word, you don't need to perceive or remember each individual letter. You need only glance at the word to identify each bit of information in it.

Chunking can dramatically increase your power to perceive and remember information, as demonstrated by studies comparing the memory of chess experts to novices for locations of chess pieces on a chess board.[3] After briefly viewing the chess pieces arranged as if a game were in progress, chess experts recall the location of many more pieces than do novices. However, after viewing randomly arranged pieces, novices and experts remember about the same number of pieces. When viewing a game, the chess experts are able to chunk chess pieces into meaningful patterns or groups that can be recognized as quickly as the novice recognizes each separate chess piece. When the board is randomly arranged, there are no meaningful patterns, so that the expert must look at each piece separately just as the novice does. The point is that chess masters do not have better memories in general than novice players, but the masters see much more at a glance because they chunk the information into meaningful patterns.

Like the chess masters who need only a glance to see a large amount of information, the manager can deal with ever increasing amounts of information by chunking the information with computer graphics. In the words of a design engineer who uses computer graphics:

> Your eyes can pick up an amazing amount of information in a short amount of time. When I inspect a design on my terminal, I can often spot an obvious problem with a single glance that I might have otherwise completely overlooked.[4]
> —**Rick Lovdahl,** *scientific supervisor*
> *Todd Pacific Shipyards*

Like the productive engineer, today's manager cannot afford to choose anything but computer graphics.

Unloading Information Overload

If you had to choose between studying one page with 20 graphs on it or reading 150 pages of equivalent information, which would you choose to do? An unlikely situation? Not for George B. Blake, the vice president of finance for a major company. He describes his move from information overload to being on top of the situation with computer graphics.

> Of all the frustrations of business life, surely one of the most aggravating and persistent is the flood of paper. Until a year ago, I used to update my mental portrait of my company by wading through a 100-page monthly budget report full of data on the corporation, the divisions, the profit center, and the products. To round out the picture, I also slogged through a series of smaller reports on collections, bank loans, and the like. These added perhaps 50 pages to my pile.
>
> Now I get a better picture from just one sheet of paper. It has 20 small graphs on it . . .[5]

Information overload has come of age. In every field, we are bombarded by new information, usually in the form of a stack of papers or printouts. Computers are spewing out data much faster than humans can interpret and use it. When bombarded with too much information, the human system becomes overloaded. Like any other overloaded system, we may fail to notice important trends, fail to see how the organization is doing compared to the competition, and fail to see new opportunities. Unfortunately, a manager may not recognize these symptoms of information overload until it's too late. Computer graphics can avert information overload and help you as a manager succeed in gaining control over the part of the organization that you are responsible for. Computer graphics can stem the flood of data and raw information by condensing the information to make a terse, visual statement.

Beyond Appearances with Computer Graphics

The computer helped get business into the fix of information overload. Now the computer can help it out by translating data and verbal information into a form that is more friendly to humans—graphics. With user-friendly business graphics software, you don't need to be an artist to create graphics. You don't need artistic skills or knowledge of graphic production methods to produce snappy graphics. All you need is a small computer and some graphics software. Some business graphics software is now as low as $200 and less, making the power of computer graphics available to virtually any organization, large or small. Computers take the tedium out of creating graphics. If you are creating a bar graph, for example, all you do is push some buttons. The computer takes care of calculating how high each bar should be, scaling the graph, plotting the bars, and putting on the finishing touches. The result can be a graph that is camera ready.

But beware! Computer graphics software is a powerful tool, one that must be used appropriately in order to achieve the desired objective. You can use computer graphics to increase revenues, cut costs, save time, and gain managerial control. But the catch is that you have to know how to use computer graphics *well.* Like any other type of information (numerical or verbal), graphics is a two-edged sword. If you misuse computer graphics, they can do you more harm than good!

It is important to realize that there is more to

graphics than meets the eye. Computer graphics should *not* be used merely for the sake of appearances. If you use graphics merely to dress up a presentation, your plan may backfire and the graphics may actually undermine your effectiveness. You should have a definite purpose in mind for including graphics in your reports and other business communications. To really get down to business, you must know something about how to use the powerful tool of computer graphics.

Computer graphics convey a message. The key to using computer graphics well is to make sure that you are making the point you intend to convey. Too often, computer graphics are poorly designed and actually confuse and distract the viewer instead of communicating the intended information. This chapter covers how graphics can be created to convey the intended message. You can learn how to create effective, powerful graphics that really achieve your goals.

Computer Graphics Affect the Bottom Line

Computer graphics look good. But the question you must answer before really getting down to business is "Are computer graphics good for business?" The costs are substantial and must be justified. A few years ago when computer graphics systems were $50,000, not many could afford this new tool regardless of the advantages. But with current price tags as low as $5,000 or less, computer graphics systems are easy to justify. They not only increase productivity and effectiveness but have a direct impact on the bottom line.

Increase revenues. In a recent survey, over 40%

of computer graphics users reported an *increase in revenues* due to the use of computer graphics.[6] Where and how did these increases occur? According to the respondents, computer graphics increased revenues by resulting in:

*Increased client demand
*Better marketing, presentation, and information documents
*Greater productivity by saving staff overtime
*More business
*Increased customer orders
*Increased productivity by using projections to spot trends
*Better data analysis by showing data in several ways
*Increased sales by interpretation of data
*More audiovisual presentations
*Better sales forecasting
*Increased productivity by reducing statistical map production from 2-3 months per map to one a day
*Greater accuracy and creation of designs not possible with manual techniques

Cut Costs. When you compare the cost of computer generated graphics to equivalent graphics done by hand, there will generally be a substantial cost savings due to computerization. A simple bar graph, for example, would probably take an artist an hour to produce at a charge of about $30. An equivalent graph could be produced within a few minutes using computer graphics software. A number of computer graphics users have reported substantial savings.

Allstate Insurance projected a $130,000 savings in determining agent location via computer graphics. That savings has been achieved.[7]

—**Russell Ferris,** *director of office systems*
Allstate Insurance, Northbrook, IL

Beyond the Bottom Line—
Productivity & Quality

There is a growing number of companies and individuals who are reporting a substantial savings due to computer graphics. But the story does not stop with the bottom line. Companies are reporting that in-house graphics are having far-ranging effects from increased security of information to better thinking and productivity by people who use the visual information.

It allows us to explore a lot more alternatives.[8]

—**Mark Cockrill,** *director of product analysis*
Boeing Commerical Airplane Co.

We can show management what's going on without making them go through a truckload of figures.[9]

—**Robert M. Leavens,** *dealer survey manager*
General Motors' Cadillac Motor Car Division

Save Time. Time savings for computer graphics are substantial whether the basis of comparison is verbal information or graphics produced manually. Compared to verbal information and data, computer graphics offer tremendous time savings. Before getting a computer graphics system, one director of office systems at an insurance company sent out market analysis reports that were literally "three feet high" and "went into a bookcase for a year until the new one came out." But this manager discovered that "A picture is worth a thousand printouts" and uses computer graphics to map the same information that had been presented in the voluminous reports. As the director explained, "Boom. Put it on a map and you can see it in 15 seconds."[10]

Reduce Tedium. Repetitive elements can be copied and easily duplicated using computer graphics. The editor of sales publications for a drug company explains how computers helped remove the tedium of designing forms.

> A lot of our forms have to have card-entry formats, with lots of little boxes for individual letters. It takes forever to draw all those little boxes by hand, but with Lisa, you make one little box, and then you duplicate it.[11]
> —**Leslie Mastalarz,** *editor of sales publications*
> *McKesson Drug Co.*

Increase Quality and Accuracy. Graphics created by computer can look better than those done by hand because the computer is consistent, neat, and accurate. Creating graphs such as bar charts, line graphs and so forth is especially suited to computerization. When a graph is created by hand, the artist must compute and scale the visual elements proportional to the data. In contrast, a computer makes the calculations and scales the graph with perfect accuracy. For example, it calculates just how long the bars on a bar chart should be and the size of "slices" in a pie graph. The result is a perfectly scaled graph that can be replicated with consistency and accuracy.

Gain Managerial Control. Managers can maintain better control over their organizations when they know what is happening in the organization. Managers also need to know what is happening within the organization in relation to what is happening in similar organizations, what happened at the same time last year and so forth. Seeing the bigger picture via computer graphics, the manager can monitor progress and spot problem areas immediately.

Exposing the Hidden Cost of Verbiage

Why do you need computer graphics? What's wrong with the old numerical financial reports, verbal business communications, written reports, and verbal sales presentations? Everything! All-verbal presentations and reports are less convincing than graphic presentations and they make the writer appear to be less prepared, less concise, less interesting, and less professional than those who use graphics! That's what a recent study showed about the effect of using graphics in a business meeting.[12] The six-month study was conducted with MBA students at the Wharton Business School under a grant from 3M. The study compared marketing presentations about a hypothetical product ("Crystal" beer) that either included business graphics presented via an overhead projector or included only verbal information. The presenter tried to persuade a marketing group to reach a consensus about whether or not to market the new product. Half of the presentations were in support of the decision to market while half were opposed. Interestingly, the results with 36 groups dramatically supported the use of graphics:

Graphics Are Persuasive. Presenters who used visuals succeeded in persuading the group in their favor 67% of the time while verbal presenters succeeded only 50% of the time. In other words, verbal business meetings resulted in a 50-50 deadlock. So the study indicates that visuals are more effective in persuading a group.

Graphics Shorten Meetings. The meeting time was reduced by 28% when business graphics were used. A representative of 3M noted that the 28% reduction in meeting length could produce savings for executives of up to 42 extra working days per year!

Graphics Aid Decision-making. When business graphics were used in the presentation, 64% of the group said that they made their business decisions "immediately after the visual presentation." When graphics were not shown, the control group delayed decision-making until "sometime after the group discussion following the presentation."

Graphics Promote Group Consensus. Reaching a consensus decision occurred in 79% of the groups seeing graphics compared to a 58% consensus rate for the groups not shown the business graphics.

Graphics Make a Good Impression. The presenters who used graphics as part of their presentations were perceived by the group as being more effective than those not using graphics. Specifically, graphics made them appear more credible, more concise, better prepared, and more professional.

In summary, the study showed business graphics result in:

*presentations that are more persuasive.
*accelerated decision making.
*a greater likelihood of group consensus.
*a 28% reduction in meeting time.
*favorable perception of the presenter to be . . .

 . . . better prepared.
 . . . more credible.
 . . . more interesting.
 . . . more concise.
 . . . clearer.
 . . . more professional

So what's wrong with verbiage and long lists of data? Reading verbiage and numbers results in wasted time and effort.[13] The hidden cost of verbiage comes from:

*boredom during reading.
*longer reading times.
*inferior memory of the information (i.e. the reader forgets).
*additional time needed for review and repetition.
*slower decision making.
*lengthier meetings.
*less favorable attitudes.

Get the Picture: Business Goes Better with Graphics

It's true that graphics are important for appearances. Graphics can make business look good by creating an image of quality and professionalism. But the real power of computer graphics goes beyond mere appearances. The importance of computer graphics for getting down to business cannot be overstated. Studies prove that graphic communication is more effective than verbal communication. Graphics help you maintain control over your organization by staying on top of what's happening. Furthermore, graphics increase revenues, cut costs, and increase productivity. You cannot afford to be without computer graphics in this age of information technology.

> *"I want to reach that state of condensation of sensations which constitutes a picture."*
> **—Henry Matisse**

[1] Naisbitt, J. *Megatrends. Ten New Directions Transforming Our Lives.* New York: Warner, 1984.

[2] Miller, G. A. "The Magical Number Seven, Plus or Minus Two: Some Limits on Our Capacity for Processing Information." *Psychological Review,* 1956, Vol. 63, 81-97.

[3] DeGroot, A. D. "Thought and Choice in Chess." *The Hague: Mouton,* 1965.

[4] "Increasing Shipyard Productivity." *Computer Graphics World,* May 1984, 120-121.

[5] Blake, G. B. "Graphic Shorthand as an Aid to Managers." *Harvard Business Review,* 1978, 6-12.

[6] Cortes, C.C. "Business Computer Graphics Systems & Users: Who, What, Where, Why—How Much?" *Computer Pictures,* Nov./Dec., 1983.

[7] Colby, W. "A Picture Is Worth a Thousand Printouts." *Infosystems,* May 1984, 82.

[8] "The Spurt in Computer Graphics." *Business Week,* June 16, 1980, 104-106.

[9] Ibid.

[10] Colby, W. "A Picture Is Worth a Thousand Printouts." *Infosystems,* 1984, Vol. 31, No. 5, 82.

[11] Rubin, C. "High-Powered Presentation Graphics." *Personal Computing,* April 1984, 65-74.

[12] "Use of Graphics Influences Business Meeting Outcomes." *Computer Graphics News,* March/April 1982.

[13] Peterson, B. K. "Tables and Graphs Improve Reader Performance and Reader Reaction." *Journal of Business Communication,* 1983, Vol. 20, No. 2, 47-55.

To be under pressure is inescapable. Pressure takes place through all the world: war, siege, the worries of state. We all know people who grumble under these pressures, and complain. They are cowards. They lack splendor. But there is another sort of person who is under the same pressure, but does not complain. For it is the friction which polishes us. It is the pressure which refines and makes us noble.
—**St. Augustine**

Ron Wallen, President

Performance Success
1716 Ocean Avenue #62
San Francisco, California 94112
(415) 591-7000

Ron Wallen, Ph.D.

By 1995, Ron Wallen will have spoken to over 50% of the major companies in America. At his present demand rate and schedule he personally exemplifies what he teaches: high productivity and living without limits. Whether he is giving an extended seminar or delivering the keynote address at a convention, Ron's practical, informative, dynamic and humorous style empowers lives and organizations.

Among his clients are Kraft Foods, Inc., Federal Mogul, American Management Systems, University of California School of Medicine at San Francisco, Chevron Corporation, National Association of Executive Secretaries and Pacific Bell.

Ron is President of Farmax Corporation as well as his motivation and consulting firm, Performance Success. While developing his own sales and management skills, he found himself in increasing demand as a speaker. He has been called a "productivity expert" because he shows individuals and companies how to search for, discover and develop hidden strengths, and how to overcome any limitations or barriers to becoming 100 percent performers.

With a doctorate from Boston University, he pulls together his expertise in business administration, psychology, communication skills and positive philosophy of living and working. Little wonder that he is regularly introduced as the "emissary of energy."

3

E = MC²
Formula for Management Success
by Ron Wallen, Ph.D.

"What should be obvious from the outset is that people perform to the standards of their leaders."
—Philip B. Crosby

Leadership is the ability to energize people for results—high energy, high results. Considering the nature of modern corporations and institutions, leadership must be a team responsibility. Corporate complexity necessitates pacesetting cooperation. Therefore, positive interaction among the entire leadership team—

executives and managers—is an essential first step to increased energy and organizational performance. High performance and productivity follow the management team's decision to become an energy releaser, consciously avoiding those things which block corporate energy.

The energy flow of any business or organization is not enhanced or decreased so much by management policies or even management decisions—as ultimately important as these are. It is determined initially by how the management team interacts. To put it more succinctly, "$E = MC^2$". The energy (E) within an organization equals (=) the management corps (MC) multiplying itself (squared) throughout the organization.

What happens among the leadership creates the cultural climate for the entire organization. People are highly sensitive to how their leaders think and act toward one another, as well as toward the rest of the work force. This is true whether you are working with a multi-billion dollar corporation or a start-up company.

If there is mutual respect, positive support, open communication, committed discipline, tolerance, genuine participation in decision making, and dedication to quality among leaders, then these characteristics become valued throughout the company. If there is disrespect, back-stabbing for position, hidden agendas, intolerance of diversity, arbitrariness, and low commitment to quality, then all the organizational restructuring, quality circles, or suggestion boxes in the world cannot change the climate from negative and mediocre to positive and productive.

CEO'S and Dominoes

Albert Einstein, among others, has convinced us that everything is affected by and has an effect on everything else. Every manager needs to be aware of this essential interconnectedness. Structure, whether we are talking about span of control, number of reporting levels, or geographic extension, is no more than the interrelatedness of all the parts of a whole.

Just as the domino theory has its place in international relations, it is equally applicable to the attitudes and actions of leaders as their effects cascade through the organization from one work station to the next. The management team, therefore, must take seriously the direct correlation between how its members energize one another and the level of productive energy throughout the whole company.

Unnatural Acts

Physics teaches us that energy is either expanding or contracting. We know, for example, that overly-contracted energy in an individual is what accounts for tension headaches, stomach ulcers, stiff necks, sore backs and other stress-related diseases. Likewise, tension and negative stress within organizational structures take their toll.

When energy is not allowed to flow naturally it gets contained in a small area where it is exaggerated and becomes self-defeating. The energy that could be used for growth, creativity and productivity is wasted because it is misused or diverted and its natural flow is blocked.

Anything or anyone who blocks the natural flow of energy in individuals or within an organization is therefore guilty of going against what is natural, thus committing an unnatural act!

There are too many leadership teams of companies and organizations committing unnatural acts. This situation points to a serious reason behind much productivity loss in companies and institutions.

Effective management teams in companies such as IBM, Hewlett-Packard, Federal Mogul, Frito-Lay and Proctor & Gamble have developed strategies (formal or informal) for enhancing a positive energy flow among their leadership. In each case there is explicit recognition that what happens among leaders directly affects the entire corporate life.

Doing What Comes Naturally

In working with leaders and managers at every level, I have discovered that a clear feeling of good will is created when the management team members drop their title roles once in a while long enough to ask, "How are *we* doing?"

The Energy Releasing Strategies (ERS) for leadership teams which follow are designed to help answer this question. These strategies have worked successfully for literally hundreds of my clients. Each ERS is designed to make managers effective personal and corporate energy experts. In other words, they are meant to help your team do what comes naturally—to keep one another's energy flowing in such a way that every worker you influence will want what you have.

ERS #1 — It can't happen *through* you until it happens *to* you.

ERS #2 — Quality leadership always leads with quality.

ERS #3 — What you think about human nature determines the nature of your management.

ERS #4 — People produce profits in proportion to participation.

As each Energy Releasing Strategy is discussed, keep in mind the words of my grandfather, Willard Wallen: "If you don't get out of bed to milk the cows, you won't have cream for breakfast." Good management ideas are only as good as the management action taken.

ERS #1 — Secret of Leadership

It can't happen *through* you until it happens *to* you.

The secret of good leadership is getting others to want what you've got, whether that is a vision; a mission; pride in a profitable, high-quality product or service; or knowledge of time and resources. "Getting others to want..." is called motivation; "...what you've got" is ultimately your personal and your team's values. Let's consider motivation first.

It is axiomatic that no one can motivate another person. The fire of motivaton—the desire to do more, be more, have more—has to burn from within. The conditions for kindling that fire, however, can be created. The greatest motivator in the world is the leader who seeks, finds and develops the strengths in other people.

This means becoming a little oblivious to their weaknesses.

When fellow management team members make a habit of emphasizing the strengths in one another, it becomes a training ground for doing the same thing with other workers. If there were only one gift that I could give to your management team which would have the most positive impact on every area of your business, it would be the ability to see the best in one another. My experience has been that there is nothing organizations need more than this mentality at work.

Many managers do themselves and their companies a grave disservice when they allow superficial observations to dictate their conclusions. For example, an aggressive, unseasoned young recruit comes marching into the ranks of management. Perhaps he or she is abrasive, even rude. Instead of the rest of the team understanding (even forgiving the sins of youth!) the newcomer is quickly "put in his/her place." Tolerance and guided acceptance, the things which encourage strengths, such as creativity, innovation and new insights to emerge and weaknesses to recede, are replaced by defensiveness and rejection.

Further, many times I have heard an older individual, one who didn't aspire to, or make it to the chief executive suite, being talked about by other managers as "over the hill" or "past her prime." The truth or falsity of this kind of talk—as with executive washroom gossip—is of little relevance. What it does to the team spirit and mutual support system is dreadful. What it does to secretaries, assistants and other workers in the organization who hear it and feel its effects is counter to productivity and profits.

Golddigger

On my desk sits a little stone figure of a person amid some rocks panning for gold. I keep that figure before me as a constant reminder that my primary job as a leader is to sift and search for the treasure in others, beginning with fellow managers. Whether they fit my private image of "perfection" is of absolutely no consequence. The biggest blind spot a leader can have is to assume that his or her way is the best way.

The greatest lesson Abraham Lincoln taught posterity is that winners use every available positive strength in every available individual. Whether he "liked" them, or even whether they liked him, was no basis for leading a nation out of crisis into productivity. Leaders look for strengths and then use them for all they are worth. Great leaders have no time to waste on petty superficialities and weaknesses.

First Day on the Job

Strength-maximizing influence must reach to every area of the organization. For example, personnel people in charge of initial job interviews should have the direct message that they are highly valued members of the total team. When conducting interviews, some of which will result in adding new "raw material" to the organization, they set a tone which will not soon be forgotten. A friend of mine who does recruitment work for ROLM Corporation told me recently that her enthusiasm for the company and its commitments to people "just naturally spill over when I am speaking with a potential employee." This is as it should be in any company.

In addition, the first months on a new job provide the existing organization prime opportunities to indelibly imprint, "This is who we are, won't you join us?" messages on the new employees. This should be taken as seriously for a new management team recruit as for a new secretary. The domino effect is operable here also. How a newcomer gets received forms the basis for how he or she will, in the future, receive newer employees.

The point I am making is essential. What if the first thing a new employee senses, sees or hears on the job is, "Here, it is one for all and all for one. We conduct ourselves always to reflect well upon one another, our product and customers. We deal with conflict and interpersonal differences as added opportunities to find the best solutions for all concerned."

Contrast that business climate to one where the new person is early pulled aside to be told, "Watch out for Mary, she would sell her grandmother at auction to get a promotion. And incidentally, don't ever get caught in the crossfire between Smith in Development and Jones in Marketing. They are big guns around here and will do whatever is necessary to get their way."

The differences between the two entrance exposures are obvious. What may not be quite so immediately clear is that the management corps sets the climate in both instances.

Big Bad World

The reader may be asking by now, "But aren't you being idealistic? In the big bad world there really are people like Smith and Jones."

Indeed there are, but the team does not have to find such behavior commendable or even acceptable. I make a point in my organization of doing two things in situations such as those exemplified by Mary or Smith and Jones. First, I am open and aboveboard in discussing the problem with the *entire* team—and *never* behind the individual's back. This is always done in a sensitive and uplifting manner for the individuals involved. This way, we save a lot of good people for the company. Secondly, we make a point to never reward, in any way, individuals who attack or subvert the efforts of another team member.

Of course, there will always be conflicts and problems even in the best-managed organizations. Solving problems is one of the management team's primary functions. That is why it is best to have previously agreed upon methods for positive handling of difficulties. What counts is how you solve the problems. Openness, honesty about differences, willingness to respect the fellow teammate's personality and position and above all, a team-group norm which insists on integrity sets a powerful corporate example. It is important to remember that many common problems can be avoided when integrity governs the problem-solvers.

An Old-Fashioned Virtue

Let us now consider leadership in terms of personal and team values. Integrity is an old-fashioned virtue, but it is the backbone of many modern success stories. Its presence can make a management team; its absence can break it. Though the word "integrity" is rarely used these days, people certainly know it when they see it. Likewise, they recognize its absence immediately. Men and women of integrity are the most trusted and valued people in our society.

My good friend, Walt Work, Director of Organizational Planning and Executive Resources for Federal Mogul Corporation in Detroit, said recently, "The issue of trust-building throughout the leadership team is crucial for any company." People of integrity are trust-builders. They draw others to themselves for wisdom, insight, direction and compassion. Why? Because people with integrity inevitably have interwoven into the very fabric of their characters the two most important designs necessary for trust: a sense of self-worth and a deep respect for the worth of others.

My definition of integrity is this: remembering in every instance that your primary business in life is to honestly build persons. After all, what is the main reason for wanting to have success in life? It is to build people— yourself included—with every thought you think, every word you say, every dollar you earn or spend, every act you take. We are ultimately in business for people. To paraphrase Calvin Coolidge, "The business of business is to build persons"—from the all-important company employee to the star of any business show, the customer.

What About Profits?

Some may react to this by asking, "But what about the primacy of profit in business? Isn't that what business is all about?" Indeed, any business that does not maximize profit capabilities is not doing its job. Yet, it has to be asked, "What are profits for?" Profits are made for people, in order to make life better for *all* concerned. Any business or corporation that forgets this and takes the approach that short-term profits can be had at the expense of people or that profits are the means to achieve higher standards of living for only a few at the top, will soon cease to be a viable operation. Where integrity is high and the object of making profits is to build the lives of all concerned, then long-term success is the predictable result.

Why should we work so hard to build a strong economic structure in our nation and in the world? What good is a viable system of supply and demand, goods and services, production and distribution, development and marketing, lending and borrowing, management and labor? The answer is simple: people. We want to create a better environment in which people can live and flourish. A person of integrity insists that this should not be confined only to some of the people, but should extend to everyone concerned.

Integrity is remembering in every instance that your business in life is to honestly build persons. You cannot build persons by dishonesty, manipulation, intimidation, anger, jealousy, resentment, negative thoughts, gossip or back-stabbing. You build persons by honestly, with every thought, word and action, wanting and doing the best for them. Even when they do not deserve it according to your view of things, integrity demands that you expect yourself to do the best for them anyway. It is integrity that will ultimately command people's respect and allegiance, thus allowing you to have positive influence.

Let me say one more thing about this vital subject of integrity among corporate leaders. A person of integrity cannot be pulled apart and fragmented by the vicissitudes and worries that plague most people in this world. "People of integrity," as the saying goes, "have it all together." This applies to your team and yourself, both as a whole entity and in relation to others.

It is relevant to note that integrity has an analogue in arithmetic. It has the same root word as integer, which refers to anything that is "whole or complete within itself." An integer in mathematics is both whole and related to the total scheme of things. So are you when you have integrity. You desire—indeed you insist upon—the best for yourself, yet at the same time you refuse to accept anything less than the best for and from those around you. The entire team benefits when the interaction of all of its separate parts makes it possible for the team to act as a whole unit. Obviously this reasoning gets extended to the integrity of the entire organization.

ERS #2—No Magic Here

Quality leadership always leads with quality.

Quality results are made, not magic. Quality happens by choice, not by chance. Productivity is a by-

product of quality, which means more than manufacturing controls and inspection; quality is a fundamental philosophy. It is a total commitment to doing
things right the first time.

Quality is making sure that *everything* which
happens bears the mark of high standard. It was on an
airplane returning from Colorado Springs recently,
where I had just addressed a national sales and marketing
meeting for Kraft Industrial Foods, that I was reminded
again of the essence of quality: commitment and
attention to details. On the plane I was reflecting upon
why this had been such an exceptionally good meeting.
Then it occurred to me that Jack Maynard, Vice
President of Sales, had left nothing to chance. He made
sure that every presentation, every detail of the gathering,
was top quality—from the displays of Kraft's contributions to the food industry to the breadth of the material
covered in the individual sessions. This is how quality
operates.

A few weeks later I had exactly the same overwhelming sense of quality at the national meeting of the
American Consulting Engineers Council. The reason was
that Tom Wosser, the California President, the planning
committee, and Marion "Sandy" Pearson, the Meeting
Planner and head of the Pearson Group in Washington,
D.C., had worked out every detail. For example, Ms.
Pearson made sure that everyone and everything was in
the right place at the right time—even down to the
delightful split-second timing of dry ice causing "fog" to
completely surround a giant replica of San Francisco's
Golden Gate Bridge. To me, such examples from any

quarter serve to illustrate that quality is an all-out commitment, or it doesn't exist.

I have observed this same attention to the quality of specifics in the ostensibly unwieldy business of management team leadership. A shining example has been my observation of the inner workings of the priority accounts division of Pacific Bell. General Manager of Sales, David Gregory, District Staff Manager, Tony Lloyd and their team are committed to quality in both service and staff interrelationships. This was illustrated recently when we were setting up a weekend management retreat. I was unusually impressed with how their pre-planning conversations continually reflected the desire to draw the management team into ever closer cooperation in improving productivity for the benefit of clients. No possible detail for making this happen went unexplored. This takes a little more time—quality always does at the outset. The time and money saved in the long-run speaks for itself.

The point is obvious; whether it is running a meeting—large or small—or improving marketing productivity, nothing of quality happens by accident.

Quality has to be the watchword for any management team endeavoring to gain the competitive edge. Although most people proclaim that they are in favor of quality, the truth is—as everyone knows—products and services differ greatly in quality. It is one thing to say that "Quality is first in this company;" it is quite another matter for managers to hold themselves and one another responsible for the highest standards.

I heard Tom Peters, of *In Search of Excellence* fame,

say recently at the annual Stanford Conference on Entrepreneurship that businesses which are "turned on" to quality do not do marginally better than their competitors, they do five to ten times as well. One recent study of forty-five successful mid-sized firms showed that forty-three compete primarily on value which means quality of product and service rather than price.

Growing up on a farm in Missouri, my mother gave us a philosophy of quality which any management team could use to competitive advantage: "If it's worth doing, it's worth doing well."

ERS #3—Attitude Alters Everything

What you think about human nature determines the nature of your management.

If the management team members treat one another as trustworthy, generous, worthy of respect and confidence, then their management of others will reflect this mutually agreed upon understanding of human nature.

If, however, the team interacts as though human nature is somehow suspect; if they believe that most of the people with whom they work are basically selfish, need to be manipulated, shoved around, watched out for,then that is exactly the kind of behavior they will engender in the work force around them.

In research conducted at Harvard University (Winter, 1967), a group of MBA students showed that workers exposed to a leadership team which emphasized their strengths were significantly more confident and productive. This approach was contrasted to the lower self-esteem and output of those under the influence of leadership concentrating on weaknesses and faults.

My friend, Jim Hastings, President of New Federal Cold Storage in Pittsburgh, is one of the best team leaders I know. He expects and gets high productivity from his fellow workers. I had occasion to interview some of the people with whom Jim works. I wanted to understand more fully his managerial success. What follows illustrates my point that what a manager thinks of human nature determines the nature of his or her management:

> "We think of ourselves as working with Jim in achievements and not so much for him."

> "He makes sure that everyone knows the important part they play in the overall running of the business, and the interaction of their function on the bottom line. Jim respects us and we know it. He encourages us to respect one another. He emphasizes our strengths and contributions."

> "Jim realizes, and because of him so do the rest of us, that people who feel good about themselves produce good results. Helping people feel good about themselves is one of Jim's best qualities."

> "He always treats each person on his team as a professional. He imparts pride in the team as a group."

To summarize, what you think about human nature determines the success of your management.

ERS #4—The 10,395 lb. Manager

People produce profits in proportion to participation.

I have a friend who tells me that he is a 10,395 lb. manager. His reasoning goes like this: "I have sixty-three people in my department. I guess their average weight to be approximately 165 pounds. If you multiply 63 by 165 you get 10,395. Since we are all in this project together, I figure that, at work, I weigh about 10,395 pounds!"

This man has no illusions as to what management is and what a manager does. The successful manager gets results and those results are a team effort. Why? Because the day of the baby birds ("workers") opening their mouths and swallowing the autocratic directives of the big bird ("boss") is over. Like it or not , a revolution really has taken place in the world of work. There may be plenty of hold-outs, but they do so at their own risk. People, at least in the so-called free world, are demanding respect and a say in what happens to their lives—even at work. They expect to be asked. They want to participate. They are a smart, strong, creative work force when they are given the opportunity. People are at their best when they know that their place on the "team" is respected.

Effective leadership is necessary for the team concept to work in a company. This means that those whose titles and positions mark them as leaders must experience the team approach before they can advocate it. Anything less is asking followers to do what the leaders are unwilling to do. People won't follow that kind of leadership.

In every corporation I know, how the management

corps conducts its business filters into every area of the company. Everyone in the organization knows or senses the open (or closed) flow of management energy. When the current is positive and powerful, the whole organization is charged for profitable action.

Choose a job that you love . . . and you will never have to work a day in your life again.
—Confucius

Merrill E. Douglass

Time Management Center
P.O. Box 5
Grandville, Michigan 49418
(616) 531-1870

Merrill E. Douglass, DBA, CSP

Speaker. Author. Executive. Fortune Magazine *and the*
Wall Street Journal *have called him a top time
management expert. He is also the founder of Time
Management Center and publisher of* Time Talk, *the
international newsletter on time management and
productivity.*

*His interest in effective time management began
almost 30 years ago when his employer suggested he
learn how to get his job done by the end of the day. He
did learn, and since then has studied how thousands of
people manage their time. Today, he conducts
seminars for organizations all over the U.S., teaching
managers and professionals how to use their time
more effectively and achieve greater results.*

*The National Speakers Association has designated
Dr. Douglass a Certified Speaking Professional, a
prestigious honor granted to only 150 people.*

Dr. Douglass is the author of the popular book
Manage Your Time, Manage Your Work, Manage
Yourself *and author of the best-selling cassette tape
album,* The NEW Time Management. *Dozens of his
articles have appeared in many leading magazines and
journals. His contributions have earned him a listing in*
Who's Who in America, Who's Who in Finance and
Industry, *and* American Men and Women of Science.

*Formerly a Professor of Management at Emory
University, Dr. Douglass also has many years
experience as a manager in banking and industry. His
Doctor of Business Administration degree in Management and Organizational Behavior was earned at
Indiana University. He presently resides with his family
in Grandville, Michigan.*

Test Your Assumptions About Time
by Merrill E. Douglass

"Time is man's most precious asset. All men neglect it; all regret the loss of it; nothing can be done without it."
—Voltaire

Time is a uniquely personal concept. Learning to manage time is a personal undertaking. How we spend our time defines our life. To be effective in managing time is to be effective in living. For many of us, this is easier said than done. Part of the difficulty lies in the way we approach our various activities. Our approach is governed by the assumptions we hold about the nature of our jobs, the nature of events around us. Often, we are not even aware of our assumptions. But these assumptions, conscious or unconscious, guide our behavior.

In discussing time management with a variety of executives, we have discovered a number of key assumptions that shape their efforts to gain more control of time. Following is a list of twenty common assumptions. As you read over the list, decide whether you believe they are generally true or false.

Test Your Assumptions

	True	False
1. Most people are overworked because of the nature of their job.	___	___
2. My job is unique and not subject to repetitive time patterns.	___	___
3. No one ever has enough time.	___	___
4. Further delay will probably enable you to improve the quality of your decisions.	___	___
5. Most people can find many ways to save time.	___	___
6. Managing time better is essentially a matter of reducing the time spent in various activities.	___	___
7. My job deals with people, and since all people are important, you can't establish priorities.	___	___
8. Delegating will probably free a great deal of your time and relieve you of some responsibility.	___	___
9. Finding a "quiet time" is usually impossible, especially in small offices.	___	___

10. Most people can solve their time problems by working harder. ___ ___

11. People who concentrate on working efficiently are the most effective performers. ___ ___

12. If you do it yourself, you can get more done in less time. In other words, "If you want it done right, you'd better do it yourself" is still the best advice. ___ ___

13. Most of the ordinary day-to-day activities don't need to be planned, and most people couldn't plan for them anyway. ___ ___

14. It isn't always possible to work on the basis of priorities. ___ ___

15. Most people know how they spend their time and can easily identify their biggest time wasters. ___ ___

16. If you really managed your time well, you'd be working and living like a robot. ___ ___

17. The busy and active people who work the hardest are the ones who get the best results. ___ ___

18. If you really tried to control or manage your time, you would miss out on many unexpected opportunities. ___ ___

19. The problem with time management is that it doesn't allow for spontaneous behavior; it's dull and mechanical rather than dynamic. ___ ___

20. It isn't necessary to write out your objectives. ___ ___

As with many things, there is no absolute "right" or "wrong" response to these statements. However, some responses are generally better than others for managing time effectively. As you read through the discussion of each assumption below, remember that the recommended responses are based on our experiences in working with thousands of managers and executives. In each case, you can probably find an exception to the rule. This only underscores the point that there are no absolutes.

1. Most people are overworked because of the nature of their job. *FALSE.* It isn't the nature of the job, it's the nature of the person. From time to time everyone is overworked. However, if this is a normal occurrence, something is wrong, and the something wrong is usually you. Overwork is often the result of failing to delegate, being unable to say no, failing to establish proper priorities, spending too much time on details and trivia, or having sloppy work habits. The job seldom overworks the person, but people often overwork themselves.

Suggestion: Take an arm's-length look at your job. What are you doing that doesn't need to be done or could be done by someone else? Do you have trouble saying no to people? How important are each of your activities? Do you need additional staff, or do you need new ways to work? Finding answers to these questions will get you moving in the right direction.

2. My job is unique and not subject to repetitive time patterns. *FALSE.* All jobs have patterns. If your job appears to be nonpatterned, you don't know the nature of the pattern. To discover the pattern, you need data—and you need to think about cause-and-effect relationships. An example will help clarify this concept. Many people consider the telephone a major time waster. Yet they seldom know what pattern is involved in their use of the phone. For instance, how many calls do they handle each day—at what time, from whom, about what? How many problems or questions are resolved on the initial call? How many require one or more callbacks? Do particular people call about certain things or call at specific times each week or month? With enough data you can identify the pattern. Once you know the pattern you can predict events, and with prediction you can gain more control. Once you can anticipate, you can schedule.

Suggestion: Realize that every job is patterned. Discover the major patterns in your job and you will take a big step toward managing your time more effectively.

3. No one ever has enough time. *FALSE.* Time is a paradox. No one ever has enough, yet everyone has all the time there is. There simply isn't any more time to go around. The problem is not the amount of time you have but how you spend your time.

The dilemma goes deeper than an apparent shortage of time. It is basically a matter of priorities and values. There isn't enough time to do everything that seems to need doing, but there is always enough time to do the most important things.

The difficulty is knowing what is really important. The answer requires some thoughtful analysis of who you are, where you are going, and how you plan to get there. Most people are too action-oriented to spend much time in thoughtful analysis. They prefer to be doing rather than thinking. Consequently, they seldom discover the right answers.

Suggestion: Think about who you are and what you're trying to accomplish. Write out your objectives and set priorities. Rearrange your schedule so you spend more time on high-priority items and less time on low-priority items. You will be amazed at how much time you really do have.

4. Further delay will probably enable you to improve the quality of your decisions. *FALSE.* Unnecessary delay seldom improves the quality of decisions. It is simply procrastination. You are probably fearful of making a mistake. It is always nice to have complete information before deciding, but in practice that is seldom the case. You should make the decision when you reach the point where additional information is not likely to make a significant improvement in your decision. This point is not always easy to identify. But if you habitually delay decisions until you have every bit of information, you are undoubtedly going too far. Occasionally you can benefit from "sleeping on" a decision, but if you overdo it you will only have nightmares.

Suggestion: For every decision, there is a deciding point. Try shortening the time for some of your decisions. Don't become a hasty decision maker, but don't drag decisions out too long either. A little experimentation will help you learn the proper timing for various decisions.

5. Most people can find many ways to save time. *FALSE.* There is no way to save time. All you can do is spend time. When you say you're saving time, you usually mean that you will spend less time on a particular task. But this "saved" time can't be banked for future spending. All time is current time. It must all be spent now. Too often people will reduce time in one area only to have other things expand to fill the gap. Parkinson's Law—Work expands to fill the time available for its accomplishment—is very real, and hoped-for benefits from saving time are often never realized.

Suggestion: Stop concentrating on how to save time. Instead, focus on how to spend time. The only way to manage your time better is to spend your time better.

6. Managing time better is essentially a matter of reducing the time spent in various activities. *FALSE.* Managing time better involves spending the appropriate amount of time on every activity. For some things it means increasing your time commitment. You will want to reduce the time you spend in low value activities so you can increase the time spent in high value activities. The key is that you must subtract before you can add. Remember, you're spending all your time now.

Suggestion: Look at all your activities. How important is each one in terms of what you're trying to accomplish? Where could you reduce your time commitment? Where should you increase your time commitment? Are there things you're not doing at all that should be added? Your activities should always be consistent with your objectives.

7. My job deals with people, and since all people are important, you can't establish priorities. *FALSE.* All people may be important, but all events people wish to involve you in are not equally important. In fact, in terms of your job, not all people are equally important. Are there some people within your organization that have more influence than others? Do you really treat everyone equally? This is not to dismiss the value of individuals or to deny human dignity. People who hide behind this assumption are usually the ones who don't want to make the hard decisions. All people are important as human beings; however, the activities, demands, pressures, and problems presented by various people are not equally important.

Suggestion: Learn to separate the person from the issue. Be patient but persistent, tactful but direct, diplomatic but firm. Managing your time to accomplish important objectives sometimes requires making hard decisions about how to respond to people.

8. Delegating will probably free a great deal of your time and relieve you of some responsibility. FALSE. In the long run, delegation may provide you with more time, but delegation never relieves you of any responsibility. In fact, delegation creates more total responsibility. After delegating a task, you are still responsible, or accountable, to your superior; but now your subordinate is also responsible to you. If you are not delegating adequately now, learning to do so will take some time. You may have to train subordinates to properly accomplish the delegated tasks. In the short run, this may be more time-consuming than doing the tasks yourself. Failing to delegate, however, is disastrous. Not only do you cheat your subordinates but you wind up buried under a mountain of detail.

There are almost as many reasons for not delegating as there are people not delegating as much as they should. The most frequently mentioned reasons are untrained subordinates; lack of confidence in subordinates; fear of mistakes; occupational paranoia, or a fear that the subordinate will take over one's job; and lack of time. But consider the consequences of not delegating. You become overburdened. Subordinates are not trained and do not develop as they should. Morale declines. In short, the entire organization suffers.

Suggestion: Look at all your activities. Eliminate those that simply don't have to be done. Of the remainder, decide which ones really must be done by you. Then make plans to delegate the balance. This may mean taking the time to train and develop staff people. It may mean learning to think about yourself and your job in new ways. But, ultimately, everyone will benefit—you, your staff, and your organization. Delegation is a case of investing time now to gain time later. Take the time to train subordinates and begin to systematically delegate greater authority to them.

9. Finding a "quiet time" is usually impossible, especially in small offices. *FALSE.* Almost anyone can find a quiet hour—an uninterrupted block of time for concentrating on major projects. Why don't more people utilize the quiet time concept? Many people simply don't believe it will work in their situation. They mistakenly believe they should always be available to their staff or that staff members will resent their quiet time.

Consider the consequences of not finding a quiet time for yourself. Jobs that might be done quickly take much longer with all the interruptions. Your train of thought is broken and your creativity is decreased. Staff members seldom resent quiet time. On the contrary, they will help you eagerly, especially if you help them find their own quiet time.

Suggestion: If your job could benefit from a quiet time now and then, think about how to make it happen. Pick the most appropriate time of day. Discuss with your staff what you are doing and why. Enlist their co-operation and help them find a quiet time, too.

10. Most people can solve their time problems by working harder. *FALSE.* Working smarter always beats working harder. This assumption starts early in life. From childhood you are admonished to keep trying, to try just a little bit harder, to remember that working hard leads to pleasant rewards. "If at first you don't succeed, try, try again." The problem, of course, is not so simple. Sometimes working harder is the best way. However, many people never respond any other way. They do not consider that there might be a way to shorten the task, eliminate some steps, combine some parts, and actually work easier while getting more done. Doing the wrong thing harder doesn't help. The people who believe that the way to get more done is simply to work harder are the ones who work extra-long hours, take work home every night, suffer from stress and tension, punish their bodies needlessly, and still don't obtain results.

Suggestion: Work smarter, not harder. Try finding ways to reduce the number of tasks. Make the job easier or quicker. Analyze the work flow periodically to keep things running smoothly.

11. People who concentrate on working efficiently are the most effective performers. *FALSE.* Efficiency does not necessarily lead to effectiveness. People often equate efficiency with effectiveness, but the two are very different.

Efficiency concerns the cost of doing something, or the resource utilization involved. This is commonly measured in such terms as money, materials consumed, and number of people required. To be efficient is to use the fewest resources for a given task. Effectiveness, on the other hand, refers to goal accomplishment. You either reach your objective, or your don't.

Many people set out to become more efficient in the belief that doing so will make them more effective. The result is that they become quite efficient at doing things that don't need to be done at all or that contribute very little to their main objective. As Peter Drucker once observed, many of us seem to be more concerned about doing things right than we are with doing the right things.

Suggestion: Focus first on effectiveness, then on efficiency. Determine first what you should be doing. Then determine how to do it most efficiently. Do the right things right.

12. If you do it yourself, you can get more done in less time. In other words, "If you want it done right, you'd better do it yourself" is still the best advice. FALSE. Doing it yourself may seem faster and better in the short run, but it is never faster and better in the long run. As long as you believe that only you can do it right, or better, or faster, you will delegate very little. This can be a formidable block. You may end up neglecting the training and development of subordinates, taking on more than you can reasonably handle, getting involved with too much routine detail, and generally winding up with the job on top of you rather than vice versa.

When you begin your career, you are totally

involved with your own task performance. The better you perform, the faster you are promoted. As promotions lead to managerial jobs, the delegation problem begins. Before, promotion and other rewards depended on your performance. Now, more and more, rewards depend on the performance of others. Yet you may continue to rely on personal performance, especially in critical areas, at the expense of training and developing your subordinates.

Suggestion: Recognize that your ability to achieve results is closely tied to the performance of your subordinates. It isn't just your efforts that count, but the collective efforts of your staff. Your talents and time are limited now. If you fail to develop subordinates, your time and talents will be even more limited in the future. Don't be fooled by the apparent truth of this assumption in the short run. The more you are inclined to "do it yourself" the more likely your time is not being well used. You are probably spending too much time on relatively unimportant things and not enough time on the important things that only you can do.

13. Most of the ordinary day-to-day activities don't need to be planned, and most people couldn't plan for them anyway. *FALSE.* The ordinary day-to-day activities are the ones that need planning the most if you want to control your time. Too many people maintain that their situation is unique—"Others can plan their day, but it won't work with me." Too many people accept crises and confusion as part of their job description. Nonsense. Anything can be planned. Those random, hectic days follow some kind of pattern. Some patterns may be harder to discover than others, but they do exist. Discover the pattern and you have the key for anticipating future events—and for scheduling and planning your time. Failing to plan day-to-day activities means settling for random direction. Failing to plan is planning to fail. Whatever happens, take control of your time. To break the haphazard approach, you must plan.

Suggestion: Keep a daily time record to help identify the patterns involved in your job. then use the information in planning and scheduling every day. Remember, though, to leave room in your schedule for the unexpected. In your planning, emphasize early actions. As the morning goes, so goes the day.

14. It isn't always possible to work on the basis of priorities. FALSE. Not only is it possible, it is essential. You will never gain control of your time unless you approach various tasks on the basis of priorities. Managing your time means spending it in the best way possible. Not everything is equally important. When you fail to establish and follow priorities, you literally guarantee that you will be spending some part of your time on less important activities at the expense of important ones. Learning to work on a priority basis requires planning. It also requires constant attention and comparison. When you are tempted to deviate from your plan, stop and ask yourself, "Is what I'm about to do more or less important than what I had planned to do?" If it's more important, go right ahead and deviate from your plan. You'll still be on the right track. If it's less important—and this is very often the case—look for ways to avoid it, postpone it, reschedule it or delegate it.

Suggestion: Make priorities a work habit. Continually ask yourself, "What is the best use of my time? What's more important?" Importance is always based on the objectives you are trying to achieve.

15. Most people know how they spend their time and can easily identify their biggest time wasters. *FALSE.* Few people know how they really spend their time. You don't believe this? Try reconstructing last week accurately. Like most people, you will probably be unable to remember many of the things you did. Why? Simply because so much of your behavior is habitual. Habits are automatic behaviors. When you act out of habit, you are not concentrating on your activities. You follow set routines and patterns. Even if your job consists of unique tasks, you probably approach them in routine ways. When you do not really know your time habits, you can easily spend time poorly. Your time patterns may become inconsistent with what you're trying to accomplish. And, of course, you wind up wasting time.

Suggestion: Keep a time log on yourself. Record your time use for a week or two. Discover your time habits and patterns. Verify where your time is really being wasted. You will probably be surprised at what you find.

16. If you really managed your time well, you'd be working and living like a robot. *FALSE.* It's only when you really manage your time well—doing what is important in all areas of your life—that you achieve the kind of freedom you seek. Psychologists tell us that very few people feel successful, regardless of how success is defined. The reason is that many people have no objectives. It's hard to feel successful without specific accomplishments. Most people shift from one activity to another without any directed purpose, naively assuming that things will take care of themselves or will be taken care of by others.

To manage your time is to control your time, rather than having your time control you. To control time, you must plan. Things don't happen by accident. Things happen because people make them happen. Planning requires objectives. Without objectives, there would be nothing to plan. This is not the dull, routine working of a robot. This is the free, dynamic, exciting operation of a person who has begun to take responsibility for his or her own life. People who plan their time are people who are alive, accomplishing things they value and achieving satisfaction and fulfillment.

Suggestion: Clarify your objectives. What do you really want to accomplish with your life? What are your goals at home, at work, at play? Then match your activities, your use of time, to these objectives. Plan your time better. Your time is your life. Waste your time and you waste your life. Instead, why not live your life?

17. The busy and active people who work the hardest are the ones who get the best results. *FALSE.* Being busy and active doesn't necessarily mean achieving results. This notion was instilled in us early in life by parents and teachers who continually admonished us to "keep busy." It is reinforced at work by supervisors who are constantly looking for ways to keep subordinates busy. Few of us escape this "busyness" trap. Few of us are encouraged to spend more time thinking about what we're doing. Physical activity seems to be far more valued than mental activity. As a consequence, many of us jump right in and start "doing something" without taking the time to think and plan. This kind of activity leads nowhere. It consumes time but returns little in the way of significant accomplishments. Too much time is spent on low-value activities that contribute little or nothing to high-priority objectives.

Suggestion: Spend some time each day thinking about your activities. How much does each activity contribute to your objectives? What activities should you be doing that you are not presently doing? Thinking before you act usually leads to better results.

18. If you really tried to control or manage your time, you would miss out on many unexpected opportunities. *FALSE.* You are far more likely to miss out on opportunities because you haven't managed your time well and thus "don't have the time" to pursue them. Good time management assures that time is spent on the most important activities and that wasted time is minimized. Good time management means decreasing time commitments to marginal activities and increasing time commitments to more important activities. Those people who can effectively control time are in the best position to take advantage of unexpected opportunities.

Suggestion: Take a look at your objectives and the way you use your time. Are your activities consistent with your objectives? How many opportunities have you missed because your time was mismanaged? Get control of your time and you'll find more ways to take advantage of your opportunities.

19. The problem with time management is that it

doesn't allow for spontaneous behavior; it's dull and mechanical rather than dynamic. FALSE. People who manage their time well actually have more time available for pursuing new opportunities and for engaging in spontaneous behavior. Furthermore, they do so without feeling guilty about it. The reason is simple. Manage your time well and you're almost certain to get at least the same results in less time. Hence, you will have more time for other things you'd like to do.

Suggestion: Schedule some fun into your life. A strong motivation for learning to manage your time better is that you get more time to do the things you enjoy. Start on a program of "planned spontaneity." If you are on top of things, schedule time off for yourself. For example, you might take Wednesday morning off. You need not make specific plans for Wednesday morning. Do whatever you feel like, or whatever strikes your fancy.

20. It isn't necessary to write out your objectives. FALSE. Writing out your objectives is important for three reasons. First, it enables you to clarify them. If you only make a mental note of your objectives, they will probably be vague and poorly defined. You may not remember them exactly the same way each time you think about them. Second, putting your goals in writing ensures that you won't forget them. You can keep the goal statement in front of you as a reminder of what you're trying to accomplish. In this way, no matter how hectic your days become, you can keep yourself on track. Third, and perhaps most important, writing out your goals increases your commitment to them. Writing your goals is a valuable motivational technique.

Suggestion: Put your goals in writing, and keep the list in front of you. As you write down your goals, keep the following criteria for good goal statements in mind: Goals should be (1) specific, (2) measurable, (3) realistic, and (4) time-scheduled.

How did you score? Were all your answers in agreement with the general rule, or did you have some disagreements? Score yourself as follows:

20 to 18 correct answers *Excellent.* You are undoubtedly making good use of your time.

17 to 15 correct answers *Good.* You're on your way to becoming a first class time manager, but there are still improvements you could make.

14 to 12 correct answers *Fair.* You need to review your assumptions carefully, as several of them may be hampering your efforts.

Fewer than 12 correct answers *Poor.* You need all the help you can get, as many of your assumptions are getting the best of any attempts to manage time well.

If most of your answers agreed with the general rule, you should have very little difficulty improving your time management skills. If several of your responses disagreed with the general rule, you should objectively and honestly examine your assumptions. It may well be that you're suffering from "assumption allergy." You have some basic blocks to overcome in implementing better time management techniques. You may have to change some of your assumptions before you can manage your time well.

Time is personal. Learning to manage your time better is a personal affair. Only you can do it. Furthermore, you can do it only if you are willing to do it, and if you believe you can. Examine all your assumptions. Are they accurate? Are they reasonable? Your behavior patterns are closely tied to the assumptions you make. Change your assumptions and you will find it much easier to change your behavior. When your behavior is consistent with your objectives, you're managing your time effectively.

There is a tide in our affairs
Which, taken at the flood,
*   leads on to fortune:*
Omitted, all the voyage of our life
Is bound in shallows and in miseries.
We must take the current when it serves,
Or lose our ventures.
                    —William Shakespeare

Jerry E. Smith, F.I.B.A.

Sunshine Makers, Inc.
4791 Lago Street, #201
Huntington Beach, California 92649
(213) 592-5519

Jerry E. Smith, F.I.B.A.

Jerry E. Smith is best known as a sales & marketing consultant in the automotive aftermarket. As President of the consultant firm, Executive Management Office, Smith had worked with many companies on the topic of positioning and image in moving new products through the retail channels of distribution. While working with hundreds of manufacturers representatives, Smith designed and conducted many sales training programs for motivating sales people. The recipient of many awards and honors Smith is now sharing his ideas with sales people throughout the world.

Smith is currently the Senior Vice President of Sunshine Makers, Inc., where the utilization of his sales and marketing skills have introduced the product Simple Green to the national as well as international markets.

Smith is a member of many organizations, including the International Platform Association and the prestigious National Speakers Association.

He is listed in "Who's Who in the West," "International Who's Who of Intellectuals," "International Men of Achievement," "Who's Who in California," "Community Leaders of America" and "Personalities of America." His accomplishments in sales and marketing have recently been recognized by "Who's Who in the World." (Marquis—7th Edition.)

The Motivation and Management of the Manufacturer's Representative
by Jerry E. Smith

*"Service before profits,
work before money."*
—Henry Ford

Congratulations! You have a million dollar idea and you want to take it to the marketplace. How will you go to market with your new products? There is an endless variety of ways to go, so be sure to take the right road.

The Options

With product ready to sell you have two basic choices. First are direct factory salesmen, and second, the manufacturer's representative.

When considering the differences between a direct factory salesman and a manufacturer's representative there are many factors to analyze. The direct salesman will cost from $60,000 to $100,000 each year to maintain. This includes salary, bonus, auto, travel, etc. A *minimum* of ten salesmen are necessary to cover the country, just to call on major retail accounts. This $600,000 to $1,000,000 annual cost is fixed and spread through the year directly affecting cash flow. On the other hand, the commissioned "rep" is paid in direct relation to sales. The commission rates generally average between 5% and 10% and are payable the month following, for shipments in the previous month. Commissions are based on net sales (after discounts, 90 day old past dues and credits) and should be paid by the 15th of the month. As an alternative, commissions may be paid coinciding with collections to help your cash flow. A most important point is to consider the rep's commission as payroll and pay them on time as you have agreed. Another important consideration in the "rep" versus factory sales concept is that with a network of 10 or more rep agencies to cover the country you will have 75 or more salesmen in the field promoting and selling your products. You should expect sales calls not just on the major accounts but on the smaller levels as well.

The Choice

Hiring the correct sales representative for your particular company is not always the easiest of tasks. Just as there are so many various manufacturers and products in the market place, so too are there many varied rep firms servicing the retail market.

It must be recognized that for the most manufacturers, the sales rep is one of the most important links in their program of distribution, so hiring the correct independent sales representative is of fundamental importance. There are a few firms that are large enough in sales volume to warrant and afford factory employed sales organizations. Nevertheless, most of these large firms choose the more flexible and potentially more effective manufacturer's "rep."

Selecting the best reps can only be done by careful investigation of the customers you will be selling to.

Rep agencies work geographic areas which may overlap with another agency you are hiring. Consideration as to which will give your company the best coverage should be based on manpower, how many other lines they carry and who their key customers are.

The fact that the "rep" handles sales for a group of companies can make him more important to the major account. The other lines your "rep" carries do take time away from your line; however, they lend strength to your firm by creating a package for your "rep" to sell, each one complimenting and supporting the others.

Be leary of rep organizations with too many lines. Look for the rep organization that can spend the time for the prompt introduction and marketing of your new product. Always remember that your rep becomes your first line contact with your customers. He takes on a very major responsibility for you, and your working relationship with him is of tremendous importance. This relationship must become a part of your consideration when you hire him, so always put emphasis on your instinctive judgement as how you perceive your ability to work on a day to day basis with him. If you do not feel that your relationship can be reasonably friendly and trusting, then it probably won't be a good relationship for either of you, because although he may technically be an independent contractor, in reality, he should become part of your company family.

The Rep's Responsibility

Your rep really has three major responsibilities for you: 1) to place your line, 2) to keep it in the account through service, 3) to work towards increased sales by that account with the line. The way your particular rep achieves these goals may vary dramatically from one rep to another, from one account to another, and from one factory line to another, but in each case he will ultimately rely on the two commodities that he must have to be successful, and that he must use on your behalf; his *time* and his *reputation*. The reputation he has with customers is not just based on friendhsip, but also performance. Years of building a relationship with his customers is invaluable. If anyone should know the "ins" and "outs" of a customer it should be the rep. He knows what your customer needs, and what is of significant importance to that account. In short, he should know what turns that particular customer on, and what turns him off. Your rep's past performance in that account will determine the trust the buyer puts upon the rep's statements and suggestions.

The amount of *time* your rep dedicates to your line is his other key tool to success, and the effectiveness of his time is something you must work to improve. You can do this in a number of ways, such as education. Education begins with supplying current market data, such as customer lists, annual volume comparisons, product mix by territory and customer, competitive price analysis, recommended orders and last but not least, a simple but complete product education. Product knowledge for the rep need not be as technical or complete as in factory sales people, rather it should be more general and sales oriented. Telephone communication and simple sales bulletins are effective.

Traveling with the reps within a thirty day period of hiring them is the most effective way of educating and motivating them. (You also may learn a few things about your market!)

When you travel with reps remember they have other lines and responsibilities. It is also necessary for them to have advance notice and for you or your sales manager to work within their travel routine. Don't let your rep spend his time entertaining you and visiting favorite customers. Make him take you where the problems are. Get started early and have as many appointments prearranged as possible. Make your travel effective.

In the area of *support* for your rep make sure they have a supply of catalogs, price sheets, merchandising and selling aids, and all other sale material. Back them up with customers. Don't allow them to be your scapegoat. Remember they are the ones that must go back and get more orders. Always notify the reps in advance of changes in policy, price, delivery or product. Never let them find out about a change from the customer. This will strengthen them and get you more business.

Again, whether it be education or traveling with the rep personally, you are in both cases attempting to gain more effective use of your rep's time, and as we have begun to indicate, getting a more effective piece of his rep's time is really the manufacturers responsibilities.

The Motivation

To most manufacturers a monthly sales commission of from 5% to 10% of the company's gross sales should seem sufficient motivation for any rep, but the fact is, that the rep's commission alone is often not enough of an incentive to keep him continually *working* a line month after month and year after year. If the average sales organization represents ten manufacturer's lines, theoretically a manufacturer can expect that no more than a tenth of the salesmen's time will be spent pushing that company's products. If we assume that the commission rate is similar on all the rep's lines, then initially there is no motivation for that rep to spend more time with one line than another, and it is here that a manufacturer has a responsibility to himself to create sufficient motivation for that rep to want to devote an extra 5% or 10% of his time on your line, at the expense of the rep's other lines. It is only then that a manufacturer is truly benefiting from his rep organization, and thereby increasing his firm's sales.

The additional motivation that I refer to may take many forms, but in each and every case they are designed to make the rep either consciously or unconsciously spend more time with your line. The most fundamental additional form of motivation for a rep beyond his commission rate is an overall coordinated marketing program that makes a line easier to sell. Effective trade and consumer advertising help to make a product better known and better accepted in a market place, and therefore a less resistant sale for the rep. This is where repetition in advertising is so important, creating product and company identity. Good, clear, self explanatory catalogs and price sheets are another important part of that coordinated market approach reps need for an easier sell. If a rep or his customer can not clearly and easily work from your catalog, then he will never really be comfortable working with parts of the line he does not totally comprehend.

Another incredibly important part of a manufacturer's overall market program is his terms, policies and freight program. If these policies are not reasonable, simple and conforming to general industry standards your rep will almost immediately find himself on the defensive with his customer, rather than on the offensive, extolling the benefits and ease of doing business with your firm. It stands to reason that if a rep feels defensive about your program his human nature will tend to lead him to spend time on those lines in his briefcase that do not leave him uncomfortable.

Additional sales tools such as in-store demonstrators, sampling, signs, shelf talkers or posters all help to reinforce a rep's ability to convince his customers that your company is out to increase consumer sales for him, and when a rep has this kind of support behind him, he is far more likely to devote that precious time to your line.

Beyond a well coordinated marketing approach one of the most important ingredients to motivate a rep into building sales for your company is through temporary promotional programs. These short term promotions do not necessarily mean additional percentage points directly to the rep, his commission from sales should be sufficient, but rather, they can be incentives for the warehouse or retailer that boost sales, and indirectly boost the rep's overall commission check.

A few years back a major product manufacturer offered a direct promotion to his reps that was based on a percentage of gross sales increase in a territory. This formula allowed any one of his territory organizations to win, and each rep thought he had an excellent chance to spend two delightful weeks in Acapulco. The results were fantastic. Business for the factory increased overall in that 90 day period by almost a third and that meant that every rep around the country, including those that did not win the trip profited by a healthy commission check. The rep that won the two free weeks in Acapulco, by the way, also had an increased commission check that period that could have sent him to Mexico for a few weeks on the increase alone. How did the factory president feel about the promotion? Well, his investment of $3,000 in a vacation trip meant nearly ten times in profits for his company.

You can bet in the case of each of these factory stimulated promotions, that the rep spent extra time with the promoted line at the expense of all his other lines. If the promotion is properly structured all promotional costs for the factory will be easily offset by the increased sales volume, while at the same time the rep will enjoy a bigger commission check. In short, everyone profits. Perhaps the most important profit for both manufacturer and rep is not so easily recognized. That is the long term spin off of such a promotion. The spin off may come in the form of a closer relationship between factory and rep, or a greater understanding by the rep of what he needs to do to sell the product line, or it may mean a greater commitment over the long haul by the warehouse and retailers, but in each case it will result in a higher motivation on the part of the manufacturer's sales representatives.

The Role of the Rep

Looking at the role of the rep from the retailer's eyes will further support this theory, for there is no other person in the distribution chain who is more required to be an expert on product lines than the busy retailer. He is bombarded with literally thousands of products every day, and each manufacturer promises a better deal for him than the next. It is up to every store owner or manager to know why brand A is a better deal for him than brand B, and what makes brand X better than brand

Y. Not only must he determine which products are best for him in terms of a purely business standpoint, but he must also learn every detail of a product as to how it relates on a consumer level. So who does he look to, to serve as his fountain of knowledge and education . . . the sales rep of course. The retailer looks to the rep to explain to him everything he needs to know about this myriad of products, and especially why he should buy that rep's product rather than his competitor's. It is this same basic field work that we find to be the most important service rendered in the minds of so many.

All in all, retailers and warehouses are both looking for the sales rep organizations to supply them with that all important factory service and product education that will help make the companies they represent a little more competitive in the market place. It is when the sales rep organization successfully fills this service to his customers that he is then fulfilling his valuable role for both his customers and his factories.

The Relationship

The business relationship between manufacturer and rep is usually based on a contract. This contract should specify commission rate, the method of calculating commissions, time of payment, territory covered, termination specifics, return of or charge for samples, and any agreements as to special accounts or programs. The term of contract should be one year with an automatic renewal. Termination through a 30 day notice from either party should be incorporated. On termination, commissions should be paid for all orders shipped through the date of termination.

Let's face it: everybody is in business to make money. Show your rep how to be successful with your product and make him feel part of your corporate team. Share your corporate goals with your sales force, so that you can reach these goals together.

Marketing your new product means spending money on advertising and promotions. Your sales reps have years of experience, ask them for their ideas and recognize those who contribute to your program. After all, your success is their success.

"Before you can score, you must first have a goal."—*Greek*

When searching for promotable people, Management looks for those who achieve expected results, have consistency, and think of those who work under them as "Their People." Managers are performance orientated.

—Dottie Walters, C.S.P.
Publisher

James F. Hennig, Ph.D.

J.F. Hennig Associates, Inc.
Box 10855
1548 Western Avenue
Green Bay, Wisconsin 54307-0855
(414) 499-5550

James F. Hennig, Ph.D.

People who have heard Jim Hennig speak come away with a renewed sense of vitality. His sense of humor and enthusiasm is contagious. He speaks from experience, having been president and major stockholder of four corporations in four divergent fields. With a Doctorate from Purdue University, where he also taught for several years, Dr. Hennig is a frequent guest on TV and radio shows and has hosted his own weekly television show, "Pathways."

As an author, he has written a popular and effective time management cassette learning system entitled, "It's About Time!" He has also recorded a speed reading cassette learning system entitled, "Rapid Reading."

As a consultant, he works with small and large companies to increase productivity and profits using the newest and most innovative techniques.

As an athlete, he was a member of the 1962 Big Ten Championship team—the last University of Wisconsin Rose Bowl team.

As President of the Wisconsin Professional Speaker's Association, Dr. Hennig keynotes conventions throughout the country and provides training seminars on time management, negotiations, interpersonal effectiveness, and increasing productivity.

With more than 25 years of research, analysis and practical application, Dr. Hennig has condensed his findings into dramatically effective presentations designed not only to entertain and inform, but also to help change lives. Additionally, Jim's entire family, including professional speaking wife, Susan, and five children, often combine to provide creatively different spouse, family, and childrens' programs throughout the country.

15 Techniques to Overcome Procrastination
by James F. Hennig, Ph.D.

"Successful people have formed the habit of doing those things unsuccessful people dislike doing and will not do."
—Author Unknown

Procrastination plagues almost all managers. If you're a manager who has overcome procrastination yourself, chances are it's greatly effecting the performance of one or more of your subordinates. It is estimated more plans go astray, more dreams go unfulfilled, more time is wasted by procrastination than any other single factor. As a manager, it can ruin your career, destroy your happiness, and even shorten your life. It's not only a thief of time, but more importantly, a thief of self-respect.

But it can be overcome! By identifying the cause of procrastination, by following the simple four-step procedure to overcome procrastination, and by applying one or more of the fifteen steps to overcoming procrastination, it can be a thing of the past for you and your subordinates.

Most procrastination can be traced to five causes. We tend to procrastinate:
1. Things that are unpleasant.
2. Things that are difficult or overwhelming.
3. Things that involve tough decisions.
4. Things that require the risk or fear of failure.
5. Things that involve major change.

These are the very things that contribute most to our effectiveness and to our success, and yet these five things—the unpleasant, the difficult, the tough decisions, the risk of failure, and the major change—are the things that we most often tend to procrastinate.

There are four major steps to overcoming procrastination:

1. ADMIT IT. Until we recognize the fact that we are indeed procrastinating, little progress can be made.

2. IDENTIFY THE REASON FOR YOUR PRO-CRASTINATION. Why are you procrastinating? This will usually involve one or more of the five major reasons listed above.

3. CONSIDER THE CONSEQUENCES OF THE PROCRASTINATION. This is an *extremely* important step. There is a paradox in postponing unpleasant tasks. On the one hand, it is an attempt to make life easier for one's self, to avoid the unpleasantness. On the other hand, procrastinating the task usually increases the total unpleasantness. If it is a task that must eventually be done, the actual work may expand with waiting. Waiting until the last possible moment forces you to work under increased pressure.

4. SELECT ONE OR MORE OF THE 15 METHODS TO OVERCOME PROCRASTINATION THAT FOLLOW. Remember you're a unique individual. Although everyone suffers from procrastination your solution may require a different combination of techniques than anyone else. To make the best use of the concepts presented here, you will need to select the specific techniques that work best for you and your situation.

Technique #1: DO IT FIRST

Some people find that the best way to handle unpleasant, difficult tasks is to do them first. Try scheduling your most unpleasant tasks, the ones you tend to procrastinate most often, at the very beginning of your day. Do the distasteful first and get it behind you, rather than dreading it and continually putting it off. You'll replace that feeling of guilt with a feeling of pride and accomplishment.

Do something significant the first hour of the day and you'll find the whole day goes well. Take a lesson from the child who eats his spinach first to get it out of the way, so he can enjoy the rest of the meal.

Technique #2: TAKE IT IN SMALL BITES

Sometimes it helps to tackle unpleasant tasks in small pieces. You can endure anything for a few minutes at a time. Try tackling that unpleasant task in short time blocks. You may find that it is not as unpleasant as you had expected and even if you do quit before finishing, you are gaining on the task. An added benefit of this approach is that the short task can be fitted into many odd moments during the day that would otherwise be wasted.

(Special thanks to Dr. Merrill E. Douglass, and Donna W. Douglass for ideas contained in this technique and several others from their excellent book, *Manage Your Time, Manage Your Work, Manage Yourself.*)

Technique #3: SET A DEADLINE

The pressure of a deadline, even a self-imposed one, can be significant to create action. Make sure your deadline is realistic and put it in writing. Post the written deadline, set it on your desk or put it wherever you will see it frequently.

Technique #4: MAKE A COMMITMENT TO OTHERS

Setting your own deadline is a good idea but an even better idea is to let others know your deadline. While we frequently break commitments to ourselves, we are not so likely to break commitments that we make to others. It's painful and embarrassing to admit we haven't done it. So make a commitment to your spouse, or secretary, or boss, or friend.

Schedule appointments with them to discuss results, set deadlines, promise action, and see if you don't find it much harder to fall behind and risk losing face with the other person. A public commitment usually gets honored much quicker than a private one.

Technique #5: PROMISE YOURSELF A REWARD

Another way to get yourself started and keep going is to promise yourself a reward for completing the task. For instance, you might reward yourself with an extra special lunch for finishing that project you've been putting off, or a weekend vacation for painting the house, or maybe take Friday afternoon off if you finish all your assignments by noon. A reward can be anything that appeals to you— large or small. Two main points to remember though. If you don't earn the reward, don't give it to yourself. If you do earn it, be sure to take it. Rewards now and then can make life more interesting while helping you conquer procrastination.

Technique #6: DELEGATE

Some unpleasant tasks will get done much quicker if you can get someone else to do them. Consider buying a reprieve! For instance, you won't have to continue dreading the thought of conducting that market research if you hire a well qualified research firm to do it. Many times the cost of hiring it done can make good sense economically as well as psychologically. Frequently a subordinate would consider the task you're procrastinating a real challenge—it would help him or her grow and give them increased prestige and greater job satisfaction. How many of your procrastinated tasks could be done by someone else?

Technique #7: CHANGE YOUR ATTITUDE— GENERATE ENTHUSIASM

Now I know many of you are saying, "You've got to be kidding! Get enthusiastic about doing the thing that I have been dreading for weeks!" A friend once wisely said, "I don't sing because I am happy, I am happy because I sing."

As you do an unpleasant task, you have a choice. You can do it grudgingly and feel miserable, or you can make up your mind to do it cheerfully. Why make things any worse than they are? Begin to generate some enthusiasm to counterbalance the unpleasantness. As Abraham Lincoln said, "Most of us are about as happy as we make up our minds to be."

Technique #8: SIMPLIFY THE COMPLEX

Quite often we avoid difficult tasks because we simply don't know where to start. The task may be so complex it simply overwhelms us. This approach requires finding some way to reduce the apparent complexity so the task no longer appears difficult.

You start with the desired results of the finished task, and then work backwards. Keep asking, "What has to happen for this result to come about?" This way you can break even the most complex tasks into very simple units, ones that are not so overwhelming to undertake.

For example, you've been putting off doing a feasibility study for a new process that might help your company. No one has ever applied this process in your industry. There are no guidelines to follow. How do you break it down into simpler parts? You might start by outlining the finished report. What should the key topic areas be? Then look at each topic area and determine what needs to be covered in each area. What steps are necessary to find the information you need? Who will you need to talk with? Continue in this fashion until you've broken the task into its various elements. The smaller and simpler elements never look as difficult as the entire task.

Once you've got the simpler elements remember this important principle: *focus on only one element at a time.* Use the power of laser vision, completing each element before thinking about the next one. You'll find a feeling of *great* accomplishment as you complete each element. And it won't be long before that insurmountable task is completed.

Technique #9: START SOME PHYSICAL ACTION— INSIGNIFICANT AS IT MAY BE—THAT WILL CAUSE YOU TO BEGIN

This is especially good for those times when you're procrastinating because you just don't feel up to doing a task. Let's consider that report you haven't started yet. One obvious way to start would be to make notes on the points you need to cover. But if even this seems like too much to tackle, you might try sharpening your pencil and getting some note paper ready.

A beginning action should be extremely easy, quick,

and require no planning. It should require very little conscious effort on your part. Rolling a sheet of paper into the typewriter can lead to typing that letter. Picking up the telephone can lead to calling a new customer. Buying a paint brush can lead to resuming your art lesson. You certainly can't finish a task until you first get started.

Paul Tournier, author of *Adventure of Living,* describes the importance of beginning, "There is an astonishing contrast between the heavy perplexity that inhibits us before the adventure has begun and the excitement that grips us the moment that it begins. As soon as a man makes up his mind to take the plunge into adventure he's aware of a new strength that he did not think he had, which rescues him from all his perplexities."

Sometimes the difficult task you keep postponing calls for creative thought. You keep saying that you are *waiting* for inspiration, or you're *waiting* for the *right mood* to strike you. Someone once said that inspiration is 90% perspiration. If you wait for inspiration, it seldom appears.

Sir Arthur Sullivan, the great composer said, "One day work is hard and another day it is easy, but if I had waited for inspiration, I should have nothing."

WEAK PEOPLE LET THOUGHTS CONTROL THEIR ACTIONS. STRONG PEOPLE MAKE ACTIONS CONTROL THEIR THOUGHTS. There is real wisdom in *that* saying. You can control your *thoughts and moods* with your own action.

One additional variation of this thought: If you don't feel in the mood for a particular important project you have been procrastinating, ask yourself, "Is there a task, no matter how small, I am willing to do on this project?" You may not feel like papering the kitchen today but you *might* be willing to at least select the wallpaper. You may not be willing to write the report, but you might be willing to gather the data. Once you find something you are willing *to do and do it,* you are beginning to make your moods work for you instead of against you.

Technique #10: GIVE YOURSELF A PEP TALK— USE THE POWER OF POSITIVE AFFIRMATIONS

You may say, "that's kid's stuff." It's not. It's psychologically sound. Consider this. Pep talks or affirmations work according to the law of displacement. According to Paul J. Meyer, president of Success Motivation Institute, Inc., "The conscious mind can concentrate on only one thought at a time. The subconscious mind, however, is filled with many memories and impressions we have gathered over the years." We never really forget anything, at least not completely; it's stored somewhere in our subconscious. Many of these stored thoughts are negative. As we deliberately feed our conscious mind with a positive thought, a positive affirmation, it displaces a negative thought from the past. Because thought precedes action the more positive thoughts we have in our mind, the more positive actions we get. There is another advantage to giving yourself a pep talk and using positive affirmations—you create more positive impressions in the subconscious. Each positive thought displaces a negative one, just as each stone placed in a full pail displaces an equal amount of water. When the pail is completely full of stones, very little water remains. So it is with our subconscious mind. The more positive thoughts we create in our conscious mind, the more positive thoughts our subconscious mind stores up and the more positive thoughts it has to draw from for positive actions.

Technique #11: GET MORE INFORMATION

Things often seem difficult because we don't know enough about them. Non-familiarity often leads to confusion and lack of interest. The more we know, the more likely we are to get involved and excited. So get more information. Attend a class, read a book, talk with an expert. A short course in speed reading may help you stop postponing the needed goal to read one book a month. Finding a photo of your great-grandmother may get you started on developing your family tree. Learning about linear programming may make you excited about using it to solve an inventory control problem you've been putting off.

Technique #12: FORCE YOURSELF TO MAKE DECISIONS

Indecision is one of the greatest causes of pro-crastination. Indecision usually comes from a strong desire to be right, or a strong desire to avoid being wrong, or a desire for perfection.

There is a time to deliberate and a time to act. The time to act is when further information will probably add very little to the quality of the decision. Delay beyond that point seldom improves the decision.

No one is right all the time. More often than not, there simply is not "right" or "wrong" involved. Make a sincere effort to obtain the best information possible within the time you have available. Then make the decision and move on. Above all, don't keep fretting and fussing over the decision, and don't keep rehashing it. Frequently the action we take after the decision has been made is more important to the decision's success or failure than the actual decision itself. Example:

You have to make the decision as to whether or not you should increase the price of the product you manufacture because of increased raw materials cost. After gathering all the facts the decision is a toss-up—and a difficult one.

Which decision you choose may actually be less important to the eventual outcome than how you implement that decision.

For instance, you decide to increase the price, but combine that with an advertising campaign pointing out the many advantages your product has over its competitors. Net results—stable sales at higher prices produces increased profitability.

Or perhaps you decide the reverse, not to increase the price and use that fact as a sales point with your salespeople—plus providing a bonus for increased sales. Net results—increased sales at slightly lower profits per sale producing increased profitability.

In each case the decision was different but the new result the same. The correctness of those decisions may be more effected by your actions after the decision than by the decision itself.

Technique #13: DON'T ALWAYS BE A PERFECTIONIST

Authors who keep rewriting Chapter 1, striving for just the right words, seldom publish books. Managers trying to prepare that perfect report for the boss, don't have time to do the important job of supervising production. Perfectionism frequently causes you to take twice as long to get the job done with only a marginal increase in the work accomplished. Remember, it's not how long you work or what you do that's important, it's the results as they relate to your objectives. Often we need to learn to do our best the first time around, and call it good enough.

When always tempted to reach for perfection remember the perfectionist principle: If the task normally takes you an hour, next time you try the task do it to the best of your ability in a half hour. You'll probably be surprised to find that you have accomplished 90% of what you wanted to accomplish in 50% of the time. Keep in mind Parkinson's Law: Work generally expands to the amount of time alloted for it's completion.

Technique #14: CREATE A WORRY LIST

Write down all the things you worry about and all the things you think might go wrong. Keep the list. From time to time read it over and note what has actually happened in each case. You will probably find that most of the things you worry about never happen. A worry list will help you learn to worry less.

Much indecisiveness can be traced to vague worries

and fears that something will go wrong. Interestingly enough, people don't naturally set long range goals without training in goal setting. It's amazing, however, the time almost everyone will spend on long range worries.

Don't borrow trouble, and don't procrastinate over vague worries. Instead, focus on what you want to accomplish. Write out all the possible obstacles or problems you can think of which could prevent you from achieving your desired results. Look over each one of the problems and think of the various ways you might solve them. Write down all the possible solutions and pick the ones most likely to work for you. You now have the basis for some positive planning and action which will take you beyond your procrastination.

Technique #15: PROCRASTINATE POSITIVELY

This is the final technique—the one to use when all else fails. It's shared by Alan Lakein in his book, *How to Get Control of Your Time and Your Life.* Sit in a chair and do nothing. That's right—absolutely nothing. Don't watch TV, don't read the paper, don't plan, don't pick up a book, don't write a letter. Just sit completely still.

After 10 to 15 minutes of doing absolutely nothing, you should start to get uneasy. Lakein says this is the technique he uses, and after a few minutes he is uneasy enough to tackle even that tough job he's been pro-crastinating.

Procrastination is a pyschological problem and the ultimate victory is essentially a psychological one.

Like any habit, procrastination is not easy to

overcome—but it can be done! One of the world's most powerful locomotive engines can be prevented from moving by placing a one-inch block of wood in front of each of the drive wheels before it begins to move. However, that same engine moving at full power can crash through a steel-reinforced, five-foot-thick wall of concrete! So it is with us and those we manage. If we can overcome the inertia of procrastination which has held us motionless, we too can release the tremendous power within us and accomplish the great tasks that lie ahead.

Fred Siegel

Prudential-Bache Securities
P.O. Box 56337
New Orleans, Louisiana 70156-6337
(504) 581-1404
(800) 562-9025 Louisiana
(800) 535-9747 National

Fred Siegel

Fred Siegel's reputation as a gifted financial professional comes from his clear insight into the investment world as well as his unique ability to translate the complexities of that world into understandable concepts for his clients and the general public. His two hour tax investment seminar, The Government's Gift, *has been deemed one of the most practical in the industry. His daily Stock Market and economic comments on* WSMB *Radio have been widely acclaimed.*

Fred is Vice President and Tax Investment Coordinator in the New Orleans, Louisiana, office of Prudential-Bache Securities. He participates in the firm's Partnership Council.

Fred is presently serving on the local board of directors of The International Association for Financial Planning and The National Speakers Association. He is a member of the Institute of Certified Financial Planners, The Financial Professional Advisory Panel, The American Mensa Society and Intertel (The International Legion of Intelligence).

Fred operates his investment business as part of a team that consists of his partner, Stu Barnes, and Municipal Bond Specialist, Brenda Brocato. "Because of the constant explosion of information in the investment field," Fred explains, "the team approach makes sense. Our clients really get three heads instead of one, thus helping to assure that they're being presented with the best opportunities at any given time." Their practice includes clients in 22 States and several foreign countries.

Fred is in great demand as a seminar leader and speaker. He will accept invitations to any area where he has a client base.

Fiscal Fitness—Money Management for Financial Health
by Fred Siegel

"Take care of what is difficult while it is easy, and deal with what will become big while it is yet small."
—Lao Tsu

In my financial planning practice I have observed that most successful business owners and professionals know more about the financial state of their business than their own personal situation. They have spent time to formulate comprehensive business plans in order to reach future goals while their personal financial strategy proves to be of a "hit and miss" variety.

This chapter will help you to understand why personal total financial planning is essential for the age we live in. Just as we have learned in recent years how important physical fitness is for a happy and productive future, we must also employ certain basic principles to develop "fiscal fitness" and thus insure a healthy *financial* future. I will give you the exercises necessary to achieve this.

Twenty years ago financial planning was simple. You worked, saved, invested a little, educated your children, and then they moved out of the house and got jobs. That left you free to plan for your retirement and live happily ever after. Well those days are over. Because simplicity—when it comes to financial matters—passed with the sixties.

There are at least three reasons why simple planning is no longer possible:

Economic Uncertainty

First, there's the issue of economic uncertainty. There are many things that would illustrate this. Let's look at one index—inflation rates. In the early sixties, you really didn't have to worry about inflation very much when planning for your financial future. From 1960 until 1967, the annual inflation rate stayed between one percent and three percent. Then, between 1968 and 1973, it went up, averaging around five percent. Look at what's happened since 1973. Double-digit inflation figures hit an all time high of 13.6 percent in 1980. While the rate has dropped since then, there is no one who can predict with certainty that we'll never see double-digit inflation again. That's one reason why planning for the future is no longer a simple task.

New Financial Products

Point two: There are so many new products available today for investors, they make planning complex. Twenty years ago, you bought stocks or bonds and some life insurance, or maybe a CD at the bank.

But today you can choose from literally hundreds of different investment vehicles. The financial services industry has greatly expanded its array of alternatives. Prudential-Bache, and most of the large financial service firms, have approximately 100 investment products available.

Because of this kind of diversity, I recommend developing a total financial plan with the help of a professional in the investment field.

Changing Regulations

As if economic uncertainty and unfamiliar products weren't enough to contend with, we are also living in an era of changing rules and regulations.

Let's take just one area affected by government rules and regulations—your taxes. In the past eighty years, we've had four major tax law changes. One important aspect of Total Financial Planning is tax planning. And you need expert advice to take advantage of these constantly changing tax laws.

Total Financial Planning

C.S. Lewis once said, "The future is something which everyone reaches at the rate of sixty minutes an hour, whatever he does, whoever he is."

No matter what we do or do not do we are plunging inexorably into the future, with or without a financial plan. John Galsworthy observed, "If you do not think about the future, you cannot have one." Those words ring true if you want to enjoy *a healthy financial future:* You must think and plan NOW.

If you're like most people, you invest a little here and there without any overall guiding philosophy to direct your investments. It's time to stop this hodge-podge approach to buying financial products and start developing a carefully thought out strategy for the future.

What is planning? Planning is a problem-solving process that charts a course to meet your present and future goals. If you enlist the assistance of a financial planning professional you will find that Total Financial Planning is actually a five-part process. I'll comment on these points in the rest of the chapter as if you were my client and we were going through the process together. This is generally the method all financial planners use.

Analyzing

Let me sit down with you. Let's make a plan especially for you.

First, I need to analyze your *current* financial situation. We begin with understanding you, your financial goals, your investments, your tax situation, and your financial temperament. I take a detailed look at your current investment portfolio and together we determine how well it fits your goals.

There are many ways to analyze your current situation. One concept you may be familiar with uses the investment pyramid. This pyramid is a fairly simple way of deciding the amount of risk you should be taking with your investment dollars.

The base of the pyramid should consist of safe foundation dollars. You should not take many risks with this part of your portfolio. It represents your home, your insurance, bank and solid conservative investments such as government and municipal bonds or annuities. Foundation dollars represent your long-term security.

Growth Level

The middle level represents growth. As we move up your pyramid we move from conservative growth instruments— such as blue-chip stocks or convertible bonds—into more aggressive growth instruments. In the aggressive growth area we might be talking about such products as high growth mutual funds, some tax shelters, or investment real estate.

Finally, at the top, we have your risk money—the

dollars you can afford to speculate with. With this money, you might purchase speculative stocks, buy call or put options, invest in commodities and collectibles, purchase low-quality bonds—those rated C or under—or become a limited partner in a tax shelter that offers high write-offs.

The key point to remember when analyzing your portfolio in terms of the investment pyramid is that each person's situation is unique. There is no one pyramid that is right for everyone.

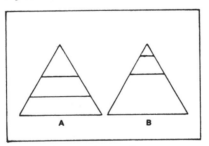

For example, let's look at these two pyramids that were developed for two different clients. Pyramid A met the needs of a forty-year old client who could afford to take more risks. Pyramid B suited a sixty-year old client who concentrates his investment strategies on building foundation dollars and conservative growth instruments.

We are each unique. I can't say that if you are forty your portfolio should look like pyramid A, or if you are sixty you must strive for Pyramid B. As a general rule, the older we get the less able we are to speculate. But before we start trying to pigeonhole you into some "general rule," we need to analyze your situation.

Total Financial Planning begins by gathering a lot of information about you and your investment needs.

Prioritizing

The second step in your financial plan is to prioritize your goals. I find as I work with clients that most people haven't done a very good job of deciding what they want to do with their money. "Making money" is really not a goal. It is the consequence of achieving goals.

The real question is, what do you want to do with your money? How much risk can you afford to take in pursuit of your goals? In the planning process, I ask questions to help you prioritize your objectives. Ask yourself what you want in terms of such things as:

- retirement planning
- educating your children
- reducing taxes
- adding to current income
- estate planning
- or even those more "fun" goals such as a trip that begins with a dinner in Paris and ends with a nightcap in Monte Carlo.

Goal setting is not something you can do once and be "set for life." Our goals change as we move through the financial life cycles. As we mature, most of us go through three important periods of investment personality change:

    A. The building phase when we are younger

    B. The preserving phase of our middle years

    C. The retirement phase

If we're planning well, our investment pyramid should change dramatically as we pass through each life cycle.

Phase A

In the *building phase,* we have rising incomes yet never seem to have enough cash. Think of a two-career couple in their thirties, for example. They are buying things—houses, cars, furniture, boats, children's clothes—to name just a few expenditures.

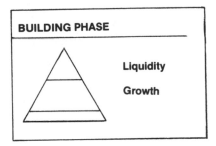

They need liquidity—access to their assets. They can afford to take risks. Losing money hurts, but when you are younger with a long working career ahead of you, you have time to accumulate more money. So, a key concept for people in the building phase is *growth* of assets through planned investment strategies.

Their financial pyramid might look something like this one. A smaller foundation, some growth, and more speculation.

Phase B

In the second phase, we think about *preserving* our assets.   By this time, we are nearing fifty and are at the peak of our career. Because our income is high, reducing taxes has become a major concern. Also, the need to plan for a comfortable retirement is increasingly compelling. So, we need to reduce risks in our portfolio. Our

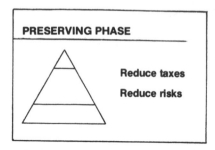

investment pyramid might look more like this one—with its stress on conservative growth and preserving the foundation dollars.

Phase C

Finally, we enter the third life cycle—*retirement.* By this time, we should reassess our entire investment portfolio. A common fear is that we might outlive our money. What we need to do is use the assets we have so carefully built and preserved to maintain our lifestyle. Additionally, we want to protect our assets for our own use and for our heirs. Our investment pyramid might resemble this one—

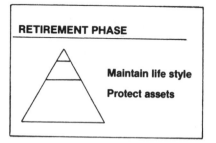

with its heavy emphasis on foundation dollars and conservative income-producing investments. Total Financial Planning involves prioritizing your goals and, even more important, changing your priorities as you move through the financial life cycles.

Developing

Analyzing your current situation and prioritizing your goals are the first two key decisions you must make when planning. The next decision is your financial planner's responsibility—a good planner works with you and a team of financial specialists to develop strategies that will work correctly for you.

There are five strategic areas that may be a part of your financial planning goals:

A. Risk management
B. Financial independence
C. Reducing taxes
D. Education funding
E. Estate planning

A. Risk management means protecting your assets. One major way we can protect our assets is by buying insurance. We thus transfer the risks to the insurance company. You may say, "I have enough insurance." But do you? For example, how much disability insurance do you have right now? Will it be adequate to maintain your standard of living if you develop a long-term disability? Statistics show this type of protection should not be overlooked.

As part of your total financial strategy, you need a review of all your insurance—disability, life, and property—to make certain you are adequately covered in this important area of risk management.

You should also protect yourself from loss of income due to business conditions. Although there is no precise rule, many people feel they should have about three months' living expenses set aside in a liquid investment for such emergencies. Without such a fund or access to a line of credit, you might have to sell an asset at a time when conditions are less than favorable.

A third important aspect of risk management is monitoring your investment portfolio. Every investment portfolio needs continuous monitoring. It's usually a good idea for busy business and professional people to leave that in the hands of a trusted investment professional.

B. Financial planning strategy involves striving for *financial independence* during retirement. Sadly, only ten percent of Americans will achieve financial independence by age 65. Is your plan to be among the wise 10% who set financial goals?

Given the uncertainty of inflation, do any of us know how much income it will take to maintain our standard of living when we retire?

The key is to develop a strategy that is right for you. Make certain your biggest worry upon retirement is your golf score!

C. Many people focus on reducing the amount paid to the IRS in *income taxes.*

For many of my clients, reducing taxes becomes a top priority. There are a number of legitimate, practical ways in which you can make a real reduction—not just a cosmetic one—in your tax burden. The four basic strategies you might use are: conversion, deferral, deflection, and deduction.

Simply put, *conversion* means taking assets that are taxed as short-term gains—or ordinary income—and converting those assets into tax-free or tax-favored income, i.e. municipal bonds or income real estate or income oil and gas partnerships.

A second strategy is called *deferral*. This means deferring current tax liability to some future time when, we hope, your tax situation will be more favorable, such as at retirement. IRA and Keogh plans and annuities are among the investments that fit the bill here.

Deferral of taxes, using any or all of these methods, means that your money will grow at a much faster rate.

A third strategy for reducing the tax bite is called *deflection* or *income shifting*. This means repositioning assets, shifting the tax liability to someone in a much lower tax bracket, or none at all. This is a common strategy for people who are faced with both high taxes and children to educate. Funding a custodial account, according to the Uniform Gifts to Minors Act, can make a lot of sense in this case.

There are other methods of deflection. Space doesn't permit me to discuss other techniques such as the Clifford trust or the charitable remainder trust. If drawn up properly by a qualified attorney, these instruments could save you tax dollars.

The fourth and final strategy for reducing taxes is called *deduction*. This strategy involves selecting investments that produce actual deductions from your taxable income. This generally involves investments in real estate, oil and gas, equipment leasing and research and development limited partnerships.

In addition to deductions, you should anticipate receiving cash as well as the potential for capital appreciation from a well-managed limited partnership.

I strongly believe you should not invest in limited partnerships only for tax deductions. I only recommend partnerships that offer the potential for solid economic benefits to you.

E. The final strategy I would like to suggest to you is *estate planning*. This is a complex area that deserves a book of its own. At the very minimum, estate planning requires that you have a current will. Three-quarters of American adults do not have a will that is in keeping with current tax and estate regulations. That's really tragic. Whether you are in the building life cycle, preserving phase, or already retired, you need to plan for how you will dispose of your estate upon your death. This is an important area to discuss with your financial planner and your attorney.

Implementing

No matter how thoughtfully we analyze your current situation, prioritize your goals, and develop strategies to meet those goals—all will be meaningless unless you take the next two steps. You need to *implement* your strategies and then *monitor* your investments to make certain they continue to work for you.

It's your financial planner's job to help you select investment alternatives that match your goals and to encourage you to act on these recommendations. However, in the final analysis, YOU must decide to implement them.

Whether your plan involves setting aside $100 a month in a mutual fund, or repositioning your entire portfolio to reduce the tax bite—you must be willing to *act now* when time is on your side.

Monitoring

Once you've implemented your strategies, it is the mutual responsibility of you and your financial planner *to continue to monitor your investments as well as to make changes in your financial strategies.* A new job, a bonus, a spouse returning to work, an inheritance all may require reevaluating your strategies.

What To Do Now

I am confident that you can now see the value of having a financial professional to help you get on the road to financial independence. In order to truly evaluate your position consider what we've already discussed and ask yourself the following questions:

A. Where are you in terms of the financial life cycle?

B. What are your *goals?* Which ones are truly important now, and which are you willing to set aside until you are in a better financial situation?

C. How much risk are you *willing* to take? How much risk can you *afford* to take to realize your goals?

D. What is your *tax situation?* Should you be converting some assets, deferring or deflecting the tax burden on others, and seeking deductions?

E. How much *liquidity* do you need? *Are you paying a liquidity penalty by having too many of your investments in lower-yielding liquid assets?* Remember, each investment involves trade-offs in terms of its liquidity, risks, and tax ramifications. Make sure you understand each investment in this light as well as how it fits in your personal strategy.

In the book *The Richest Man In Babylon,* by Ben Sweetland, I found this insightful comment, "Opportunity is a haughty goddess who wastes no time with those who are unprepared." By arranging your affairs in the manner we have discussed, you will be better prepared to take advantage of opportunities to improve your financial position in the future. You will also have greater peace of mind in that you are adequately caring for your personal investment affairs. With this feeling of assurance, many of my clients have been able to concentrate more fully on their own business and profession, thus earning even more money as a result.

Please remember that time is one of the necessary elements in building wealth. So start now, lay out your blueprint. Plan your labor and materials. And build a sound financial future.

When you see admirable people, emulate them. When you see someone who is not, turn and examine yourself. Virtue is to love people. Wisdom is to understand them.

—Confucius

Robert B. Moore, President

Effectiveness, Inc.
P.O. Box 23403
5010 West Kennedy Blvd.
Tampa, Florida 33623
(813) 870-3628

Bob Moore

Bob Moore is a performance improvement specialist and conducts workshops on high performance leadership and management. His clients include businesses and industries, and health care, educational, financial, and nonprofit organizations and ministries. He is often the featured speaker for professional associations and societies, and civic organizations.

Bob is founder of Effectiveness Ministries, a nonprofit ministry dedicated to increasing organization and leadership effectiveness for churches and Christian organizations. His programs use Biblically based concepts that have received "outstanding" ratings from over 20,000 pastors and Christian executives.

A graduate of North Carolina State University, Bob has also done graduate work and extensive research in management and organizational behavior. He is an active member of the American Society for Training and Development, the Organization Development Network, the National Speakers Association, and is a past chairman of the Education Council of the Greater Tampa Chamber of Commerce for whom he frequently conducts seminars and workshops.

Bob works extensively with management problem-solving teams to improve organization effectiveness. He also conducts organizational and individual assessments to identify opportunities for performance improvement.

Achieving Excellence Through Team Management
Building a High Performance Organization
by Robert B. Moore

"You can employ men and hire hands to work for you, but you must win their hearts to have them work with you."

—Tiorio

Management Crisis

The United States is facing a crisis in the world market. Many contemporary American organizations are in trouble. American productivity and quality are not what they should be. The problem is defined by many of today's top thinkers, writers, leaders, and executives as outdated leadership practices, and not so much by obsolete equipment, or lazy workers. Organizations of all types are facing the most extensive change with more far-reaching implications than anything since the start of the modern industrial revolution. We are in a period in history that deserves the label of a "transforming era." Circumstances are changing to such an extent that a thorough examination of our management practices is critical.

The main thrust of industrialization was to de-humanize work. Workers were required to conform to rigid schedules and production practices. The technology of the industrial revolution called for a large and relatively unskilled labor force, willing to work hard at difficult jobs with few intrinsic rewards. In 1910 most people had only a grade school education. By 1970, the average worker had two years of college. Modern workers have grown up in a more affluent society. They have not felt the deprivation known by many of the previous generations and are no longer satisfied with survival. The old motivators are not working, and a new work ethic is revolutionizing America today. Workers today still want money and security, but they also want more. Supporters of humanistic or participative approaches to management are convinced that further progress, technological and economic, will depend upon making fuller use of human resources.

New Values

Daniel Yankelovich and John Immerwahr, in *Work in the 21st Century,* state that is is important to look at the evolving relationship between the values and expectations that people will bring to their jobs, and the qualities that the jobs will demand from the work force: "Our thesis is that the economic health of the nation (and of specific organizations) will be a function of how well these factors can be integrated."

Yankelovich and Immerwahr foresee the growth of two trends. The first concerns the increase in the amount of control and discretion that jobholders have over their work; the second concerns the emergence of a new set of work place values which they call "the philosophy of expressivism." These trends already have transformed the American work place and can be expected to have an even more significant impact as we enter the twenty-first century. They believe that "barring major catastrophes such as nuclear war, there is a strong probability that a high-discretion/high-expressivism work place will emerge . . .".

The authors further state that "the determination of whether the country is able to forge a successful integration of this new combination of hard and soft factors will largely be in the hands of managers and administrators. Specifically, managers and administrators must find ways of structuring work so that it appeals to the needs of expressivist jobholders for autonomy, creativity, community, and entrepreneurship. Managers will need to re-evaluate the rigid hierarchies and sharp status differences that characterize the low-discretion work place."

Research indicates that high-discretion workers respond poorly to rigid hierarchial structures. Changes will also be needed in the sharp status division that inhibits the sense of teamwork and community that is so vital to obtaining commitment from expressivist job-holders. Expressivist jobholders are willing to give a great deal to their jobs if their expressivist needs can be met in the work place.

Megashifts

Evidence of these shifts has already been documented by John Naisbitt in his best-seller *Megatrends*. Naisbitt details America's shift from industrial production to providing services and information. He states that we are moving in the dual directions of high tech/high touch, matching each new technology with a compensatory human response. He cites that the trend of giving up our dependence on hierarchial structures in favor of informal networks (teams) will be especially important to the business community.

Naisbitt believes that the failure of hierarchies to solve society's problems forced people to talk to one another—and that was the beginning of networks. Net-works are simply people sharing information, ideas, and resources. One of the attractions of networks is that they are an easy way to get information. However, networks can go beyond the mere transfer of information to the creation and exchange of knowledge. It is possible to generate new ideas from the synthesis that occurs as each person takes in new information.

Naisbitt further notes that there are a number of trends pushing for the creation of a new management style based on the network. There is increasing pressure from younger, well-educated, rights-conscious workers to participate in management decisions. The shift from a representative to a participatory democracy translates on the job front into a networking approach—a participatory or team approach to management.

A Look at Management

Several recent best-selling books have addressed the need to examine our management practices. William Ouchi in his book *Theory Z,* compares traditional American practices with those of Japanese companies. He believes that team management can help solve the productivity and quality problems we face. Pascale and Athos in *The Art of Japanese Management* showed how the "soft" people management skills have tended to be overlooked. Peters and Waterman in their best-seller, *In Search of Excellence,* further identified those management practices and other characteristics that produce corporate excellence found among America's best run companies.

Peters and Waterman cite the Dana Corporation as one of the most impressive success stories in people and productivity. Dana is a $3 billion corporation with 18,000 employees manufacturing primarily axles, clutches, and universal joints for cars and trucks. In the 1970s Dana became the number two *Fortune* 500 company in total return to investors.

Dana is characterized by the key ingredient, productivity through people and a creative and innovative management system. Under the leadership of Rene McPherson, the corporate staff was reduced to one-fifth, and the layers of management from eleven to five. McPherson is quoted as saying, "I am opposed to the idea that less government, few regulations, capital formation incentives, and renewed research in development activity are what we need most to improve productivity. My suggestion: let our people get the job done."

The Best Companies

Dana Corporation is also included in *The 100 Best Companies to Work for in America,* written by Robert Levering, Milton Moskowitz, and Michael Katz. The authors comment that Dana is rewriting the book on American management. Many trappings of traditional management—organization charts, policy manuals, a large corporate staff, written reports and memos—have fallen by the wayside. When McPherson took over in 1973, he literally dumped a 22½ inch stack of policy manuals in the trash can and replaced it with a one-page policy statement. Some of the key points include: "We discourage conformity, uniformity, and centralization. We believe people should be involved in setting their own goals and judging their own performance. The people who know best how the job should be done are the ones doing it . . .".

It is interesting to note that there were some significant, common characteristics among the companies found in *The 100 Best Companies to Work for in America.* The authors state that each company is unique but that there were certain themes they heard over and over again. In addition to good pay and strong benefits, these companies made people feel that they are part of a team or, in some cases, a family. They encouraged open communication, informing their employees of new developments and encouraging them to offer suggestions and complaints. They stressed quality, enabling employees to feel pride in the products or services they were providing. They reduced the distinctions of rank between top management and entry-level jobs.

The Importance of People

Dr. Rosabeth Moss Kanter, Professor of Organization and Management at Yale University, and much sought after advisor by major organizations, states in her book, *The Change Masters,* "In every sector, old and new, I hear a renewed recognition of the importance of people, and of the talents and contributions of individuals, to a company's success." She continues, " . . . companies must rely on more and more of their people to make decisions on matters for which a routine response may not exist." It is the people who generate the ideas and can make the big difference in whether change becomes an opportunity or a crisis.

In 1981, Dr. Kanter asked an expert panel of sixty-five vice-presidents of human resources in major companies to identify those corporations which had been the most progressive and forward-thinking in their systems and practices with respect to people. Forty-seven "most progressive" companies were identified. These companies were "matched" with a non-nominated company in the same industry and as close as possible in assets, sales, and number of employees in 1980. The twenty-five year financial performance of the progressive companies was compared with that of the non-nominated "matches." The research indicated that the companies with reputations for progressive human-resource practices were significantly higher in long-term profitability and financial growth than their counterparts.

The progressive companies are effective managers of change and the use of innovation. Dr. Kanter calls such companies or people Change Masters—those people and organizations are adept at the art of anticipating the need for and leading productive change. Change Masters are also masters in the use of participation and team work.

What About Participation!

Perry Pascarella, Executive Editor of *Industry Week* magazine, says in his book *The New Achievers,* "Companies that are not pressured by competitive conditions may get by without participative management, but even they may eventually feel the impact of the movement. They could become vulnerable to a flow of workers to companies that have more positive corporate cultures and invest in the development of their human resources. Even in the weak job market of the early 1980s, more than one young job-seeker said he or she was looking for a 'good company' to work for. The ones they had in mind were those that offer challenging work, a chance for continuing education, and room to grow."

Abraham Zaleznik, professor of Leadership at Harvard Business School, states that "participatory methods are so fundamentally rational as to make one wonder why they have not been universally accepted." Elton Mayo wrote about participation in the 1920s and

1930s. Kurt Lewin urged their adoption during the 1940s when he wrote about his experiments with autocratic, democratic, and laissez-faire styles of leadership. Douglas MacGregor also advocated participation during the 1950s when he discussed Theory X and Y types of management. Rensis Likert, Chris Argyris and many others writing in the 1960s and 1970s also presented a case for more expressive, democratic, and participatory methods.

Dr. Marshall Sashkin, professor of industrial and organizational pyschology at the University of Maryland, believes that participative management has positive effects on performance, productivity, and employee satisfaction because it fulfills the basic human work needs: increased autonomy, increased meaningfulness, and decreased isolation.

Managing Participation

Team Management is a complex management approach, requiring considerable support and effort if it is to be implemented and operated effectively. Prior to publishing *Change Masters,* Dr. Kanter wrote an article which appeared in *Organizational Dynamics* entitled *The Dilemma of Managing Participation.* She examined some of the problems involved in implementing and managing a participative-management program and commented that participative-management failures often occur because of too much emphasis on "participative" and too little on "management." The key here is balance and patience. It takes more time to build a team than just to give orders. If there is pressure for quick results, there is not likely to be strong support for participation or the use of a team management approach or style.

After considering fifty years of research, Dr. Sashkin contends that the differences in the effectiveness of participative management are primarily how well certain contingency factors were taken into account and managed. Other factors are how skillfully participative-management approaches are implemented and the support structure provided.

Richard Boyle, vice president and group executive for Honeywell Defense and Marine Systems Group, in an article for *Harvard Business Review,* said that the absence of clear guidelines, policies, and support structures made becoming a participative manager like "wrestling with jellyfish." Honeywell managers and employees encountered many frustrations and explored several blind alleys before discovering some central truths: that means are as important as ends and that participative management must be managed. Mr. Boyle states, "The realization that we needed more structure was a real turning point for us."

He cites numerous examples of returns on their investment in team management and believes that participative management is yielding such significant benefits that he is able to work on other management concerns. While he spends more time managing parti-cipation, he spends less time refereeing internal squabbles or soothing irate customers. His employees are solving little problems before they become big problems. Many decisions are made at lower levels of the organization. He feels that anything they want to keep out of his office is fine with him. Concluding his article he states, "Participative management does require a greater commitment of time compared with traditional management intervention, at least in the short term. But the long-term rewards of *managed* participative management are abundant. Not the least of them is the fun I'm having doing my job."

Action planning is essential for the success of any team development effort. Action planning assures that needs have been identified, that the right time scale has been adopted, and that the basis for measuring results is determined and agreed upon by those involved. It is also important to use practical and appropriate methods and resources. In most cases, assistance from a consultant or someone external to the team is needed since it is difficult for the leader or a member of the group to fulfill the role of trainer and facilitator.

Management Teams—the Place to Begin

From my experience and research, I am convinced that to provide adequate structure and support, team management must be a top-down process. Top management must set the pace, provide the example, and shape the values and climate of the organization. The members of top management must be willing to share their commitment, ingenuity, and energy with each other before the rest of the organization will do so.

Management teams, designed primarily for top and middle management, are useful in introducing the team management concept or providing further development for existing management teams. As members of management serve on teams, they learn team concepts and team-building skills. These skills can be applied in their everyday activities which soon lead to full-scale team management. Management teams also provide a vehicle to become more proactive in dealing with decision-making, problem-solving, planning, preventive practices, and improvement projects.

Proactive Management is what Guy Hale and Lorne Plunkett describe in *The Proactive Manager* as skills used to resolve the uncertainties facing managers. There are specific skills called Process Management Skills used for each different form of uncertainty. Process Management is to the management function what the manufacturing process is to the manufacturing function. In order to obtain a result or finished product, raw materials must be put through some type of process. The raw materials that managers use to obtain results are data, information, advice, education, and experience. The process is a mental process—they think.

Managers are involved with issues that deal with the past, the present, the future, and past, present, and future all together. When the question is "Why did something happen?" or "What caused the situation?" we are dealing with the past and need to use a process called cause analysis. We are in the present and use a decision-making process, if the question is "Where do we go from here?" or when something needs to be done. The future is concerned with "What will happen as we progress toward our objective?" and "How can we ensure the success of our plan?" The ability to implement a plan successfully is generally more important than the development of the plan and is addressed in the process known as plan analysis.

Sometimes many of our concerns are results of "scrambled" events. This requires that managers assess the situation to know how and where to begin resolution. This process is called situation review. The situation review helps the manager to determine which specific Process Management Skill to use to deal with the concern.

It is essential that the management team develop these proactive, Process Management Skills in order to function effectively. Of course, these skills are utilized by individual managers on a daily basis in their particular area or department as well. Proactive team members become proactive managers.

Organization and Structure

I recommend that management teams be organized into task teams, project teams, permanent teams, and functional teams as described by Don Butler in *Management Problem Solving Teams*. This assures that the necessary structure is provided and guards against the problems Richard Boyle described in *Wrestling With Jelly Fish.*

Management Task Teams are ad hoc or special teams created for the moment to solve a problem. They include peer groups who represent the many disciplines throughout the organization. Usually, the team completes the task and is disbanded.

Management Project Teams can be assembled to study a project in-depth, and to make recommendations based on the knowledge, experience, and skills of the team. Permanent Teams can be assigned to study multi-discipline problems such as career development, salary review, or safety issues.

Functional Teams can also be formed for specific areas within the organization. These can include Personnel, Marketing, Sales, Research, Engineering, and others. They can review new product development, customer service, and a host of other subjects. Some can become permanent teams, and others may be temporary and disband when the goals have been reached.

Culture and Style

Team management means that managers must learn to share power rather than to accumulate it. This concept confronts many managers with the need for fundamental changes in philosophy. A beginning place is to examine the culture of the organization. Culture reflects your value system, your philosophies, and why you do what you do. What assumptions, practices, and concepts are presently operating in your organization?

Before the team management concept can spread throughout the organization and on down to supervisory and work teams, some key issues need to be considered. For example, a new definition of work and working relationships may be required for both the manager and the worker. Do you really believe that productivity and quality answers can come from the workers? Are you willing to utilize their full potential in problem-solving and decision-making? Is top management practicing team management effectively?

Another consideration is management style—the

manner employed in getting things done. Team management requires a style of management that promotes group action instead of individual action. A manager's style must reflect a sharing and caring attitude for team management to be effective.People are looking for ways to become more involved in the decisions that affect their work and most are willing to become more participative. However, managers and supervisors must allow it to happen by becoming a team leader rather than the boss.

Building Effective Worker Teams

Achieving organizational excellence demands the development of high performance worker teams. Will you as a manager or supervisor accept the challenge to build and lead an effective team? Ask yourself these questions: Are you comfortable sharing power and authority? Can you recognize the power of employee participation? Will you encourage participation and not dominate the thinking of your team? Will you practice systematic process management skills that will guard against autocractic decision making? Will you make use of group dynamics such as brainstorming? Will you provide regular feedback to the team regarding recommendations that have been generated? Will you commit to improve interpersonal relations?

High performance teams are the result of a trust relationship among the members of the team. Whenever a group must work closely together to achieve a task, they will form judgements about each other's "style of work behavior" and their underlying patterns of motivation. The extent to which people understand, trust, support, respect, and feel comfortable with one another determines their effectiveness as a team. In the team building programs I conduct, team members and the leader examine their individual behavioral tendencies by completing a self-report behavioral style profile. This results in a greater appreciation for the differences that exist among the members of the team.

I also have the team check and if necessary attend to its mission at the beginning of the Team Development Program. It is essential that the mission and purpose of the team be understood and accepted by all team members.

An effective team will utilize the full range of its resources by practicing the Process Management Skills described for use by Management Teams. Logical and systematic cause analysis, decision-making, planning and situation review methods must be utilized for teams to be a useful tool to improve quality and productivity. As the leader you will need to demonstrate that a team can accomplish results more effectively than an individual.

To work effectively together, the expectations of team members must always be clear. It is important that a procedure be developed to deal with role clarity. Role clarity is the clear understanding of what each member of the team and team leader expect or want the others to do. Role conflict may occur as a result of conflicting expectations between team members. The frustration that results can drain valuable creative energy from the team.

The effective team also manages its time together in meetings in order to maximize work output and carry out necessary team maintenance (how well the team is working together). Finally, an effective team will recognize task-related conflict as an opportunity for learning and growth rather than an unfortunate hindrance and will have procedures for managing conflict.

Continued Development

The continued performance of effective teams is not automatic. High performance is based on the team's response to the following elements:

1. Evaluating Results—where have we been?
2. Analyzing Needs—where are we now?
3. Setting Objectives—what should we do; how will progress be measured; what indicators will be used?
4. Determining Accountability—who will do what by when?
5. Measuring Progress—how are we doing?
6. Appraising Performance—how did we do?
7. Recognizing Improvement—how will we be rewarded?
8. Projecting the Future—what must we continue to do; what should we stop doing; what should be changed?

The late Paul "Bear" Bryant, legendary coach of Alabama and the winningest coach in college football, offered some advice for those who aspire to be leaders of winning teams. Bryant says there are five things that winning team members need to know,

1. "Tell me what you expect from me."

2. "Give me an opportunity to perform."
3. "Let me know how I'm getting along."
4. "Give me guidance where I need it."
5. "Reward me according to my contribution."

This is a competitive world. But it is a world that responds positively to effective leadership. That is what you can do. Be the leader; take the initiative in team management, and you will get results. It begins with your attitude. Your enthusiastic example can be the catalyst for innovation and growth by everyone in your organization and when the "Who's Who" of a decade ago is rewritten, you can assure that your organization will be among the "Who's Left."

Jim Pence

James M. Pence and Associates
P.O. Box 968
Marion, Indiana 46952
(317) 664-4996

James M. Pence

*Jim Pence is a successful, small-business entre-
preneur. After graduating from Earlham College with a
degree in Economics Jim entered his family's retail
lumber and building material business. In partnership
with his brother, Jim expanded the business to include
branch operations in five different cities. With over 20
years of experience in the day-to-day management of
his own successful businesses, Jim has earned the
right to share ideas with other businessmen and
women.*

*For the past ten years Jim has been sharing his
exciting ideas in workshops, seminars and convention
programs for over 150 different client organizations.
His speaking-training career includes over 600
presentations and has taken him from Alaska to Puerto
Rico—and from Hawaii to Newfoundland. Jim is
regarded as one of the finest small business trainers in
North America. His clients range from small trade
associations to major, international corporations such
as Beatrice Foods Co., Owens-Corning Fiberglas
Corp., and Triad Computer Systems.*

*Jim specializes in small business financial
management, personnel development, sales and
marketing training and compensation/incentive
programs. He is in great demand as a convention
speaker, making over 90 appearances each year across
the United States, Canada and the West Indies. Jim
also shares ideas with thousands of small businesses
through his monthly "Good Idea! Newsletter" and his
audio and video cassette albums.*

*Jim has been active in the Jaycee organization and
has been honored as the "Outstanding Young Man" for
the state of Indiana. He is married and the father of two
daughters.*

Help Stamp Out T.N.M.J.
by James M. Pence

"We must learn to balance the material wonders of technology with the spiritual demands of our human nature."
—John Naisbitt

I need your help. I want you to join with me in a campaign to fight a very serious disease that is running rampant throughout our free enterprise system. This is a disease that has destroyed thousands of businesses, organizations and institutions, large and small, over the past several years.

No organization is immune. Every employee, every manager, every owner is a potential carrier of this vicious disease. I call this disease T.N.M.J.—"That's Not My Job!" Like many dreaded diseases T.N.M.J. strikes most often at people and organizations that are enjoying a period of growth and success. Tragically, top management rarely knows the organization has been fatally infected until it's too late.

You have experienced T.N.M.J. You know just how frustrating and infuriating it can be. In fact, we all encounter T.N.M.J. so often that we are growing used to it. We take it for granted. We do nothing to overcome it.

It Can Infect the Best of Them

A few months ago I was a speaker at a large, national convention in a major U.S. city. My client had arranged a very nice room at the convention's headquarters hotel—one of the newest showplaces of a primary, international hotel group. It was considered to be the finest hotel in town. And, I must admit, the physical plant, the decor and the appointments left nothing to be desired. Untold millions of dollars had obviously been spent building this magnificent monument to a decent night's sleep. The meeting facilities, the quality of the sleeping rooms, the built-in conveniences were most impressive. They had thought of everything! Yet, I had the feeling that the most important element of business success might be missing.

I noted my misgivings on several minor occasions but there was no doubt the morning I was ready to check out and be on my way. Like many larger hotels this one had a single huge front desk divided into well-

identified service areas of activity: Registration—Information—Keys and Mail—Cashier. Everything was
computerized for utmost speed and efficiency. Each of
the activity areas had terminals and work stations for
several employees.

As I entered the lobby early in the morning to check
out I noticed each area of the massive front desk was
staffed by only one person. There was a total of four neatly
uniformed people behind the desk—one at each area of
activity. They all wore a large "smile" button instructing
me to "have a nice day." I hoped I would.

I also saw a line of eleven guests (yes, I counted
them) waiting patiently and not-so-patiently to check
out. Although there were several computers and work
stations in the "Cashier" area there was only one staff
member slowly processing the departing guests. I could
see it would be at least thirty minutes before it would be
my turn—and I had to catch an airplane!

I glanced down the length of the front desk and saw
that none of the other three hotel employees seemed busy.
There were no guests requiring service in their area of
activity. My entrepreneurial instincts got the better of me
and I decided to do the hotel a favor and help them solve
this potentially explosive customer-relations problem.

I walked over to the lady positioned underneath a
sign that read "Registration." She was busy filing her
fingernails but I was able to get her attention by saying,
"Excuse me. Would it be possible for you to help
check out some of us? We all have airplanes to catch,
schedules to meet, and some of your customer guests are
becoming irate at this unreasonable delay." Without

looking up from her immaculate fingernails she replied, "That's not my job." T.N.M.J.—the death rattle for a magnificent business.

I politely asked her if any of the other people of the hotel staff were trained in the checkout process and could possibly help the one employee who was trying to handle the heavy crunch of guests waiting to leave. She remarked, "Oh yeah, we all know how to do it, but . . . that's not my job."

Maintaining a calm attitude I asked her, "Just what *is* your job?" She informed me that her job was to register new, incoming guests. I observed, "It's 7:30 in the morning! There is no one in sight wanting to check *in*. There are twelve, no now there are fourteen, of us wanting to check *out!* Couldn't you possibly move down ten feet and help the cashier during this brief overload?"

She said, "I could—but that's not my job." The real tragedy was that she was doing *exactly* what someone (management) had told her to do. Nothing less, and nothing more. When I asked to see the manager or person-in-charge I was told that he was "on a break" and was not to be disturbed. I might have known.

People Make the Difference

In *Megatrends,* John Naisbitt's excellent best-seller, the point is stressed that all businesses today must recognize the need for "high touch." Naisbitt contends that "whenever new technology is introduced into society, there must be a counter-balancing human response—that is, high touch—or the technology is rejected. The more high tech, the more high touch."

The point is clear. The more we refine our systems with computers and other technological devices the more we need people. Virtually all machines are alike, people make the difference in a competitive system. And too many organizations have lost sight of that fact in their enthusiasm for crunching numbers at the speed of light. Customers cannot always be crunched. People need people. Those organizations that understand this phenomenon will surely succeed, grow and prosper in the coming years.

In every organization—manufacturing, wholesale, retail, public service, government agency, banking, insurance, distribution, transportation, communication— the basic reason for its existence comes down to being of service to people (customers). And these services to human beings must be rendered by other human beings.

The UPC price scanner at the supermarket is not nearly as important as a smiling, friendly checker. The computer controlled machines that produce the suits I wear are not as important as the salesman that helps me put it on and tells me, "You look great!" The robots that built my car are nowhere near as valuable as the car dealer that helped me buy it—and helps me when something isn't right. Tons of computer-generated, personalized "junk" mail is ignored at the sight of a small, light pink, hand-addressed envelope.

Success in every business is basically a people-to-people proposition. People make the difference. But here's the rub—people in organizations that can make the difference between success and failure, prosperity and bankruptcy, growth and stagnation, don't just happen.

As Timothy S. and Michael H. Mescon observe, "They are carefully selected, trained, motivated and rewarded by organizations who are committed to excellence and recognize that the attainment of excellence is a never-ending process". We must begin our fight today against T.N.M.J. We must help build people in our organizations who can make the difference.

Some of the Causes of T.N.M.J.

SPECIALIZATION. In our search for productivity and quality we have discovered a vital technique; the division of labor towards a high degree of specialization (expertise). This has resulted in some of the most on-target innovations and specific developments in all of mankind's progress towards achievement. Unfortunately, this specialization has also created the negative by-products of tunnel vision, misunderstanding of overall objectives and a keyhole view of life.

As T.S. and M.H. Mescon state it, "All too often we expect complex people to perform routine tasks resulting in situations where 'work' is viewed as an unpleasant interruption between week-ends." The more specialized a person becomes in his or her job function the more likely they will say, "That's not my job." Too many people have lost sight of the big picture, the "real" job, if in fact they ever saw it at all.

JOB TRAINING. The popularity of written job descriptions and the high degree of specific (often technical) job training has caused us to forget to teach the most important, the most basic of all jobs in every organization. The basic job must be attention and service to the needs of customers!

Perhaps we have put too much emphasis on written job descriptions and not enough on written company policy—a policy that states firmly that direct, responsive, people-to-people customer service takes precedence over *all* other job functions and responsibilities.

ISOLATION. Many people do not have any personal contact or involvement with the customer of their product or service. Because of technological advancements in communications, marketing and manufacturing most goods and services reach the consumer with very little person-to-person contact.

An example of this can be found in the banking industry. People on the inside (bank employees) often have little or no contact with people on the outside (bank customers). Virtually all banking services can and are being conducted through the mail, with checks and drafts, with direct deposits, over telephone computer lines, and with drive-up, automated teller machines that recognize only your magnetic card and can electronically flash it's instruction to "have a nice day." When a bank customer requires person-to-person help or information it is often difficult to find a bank employee that does not say, "That's not my job."—because it usually isn't. All too often the only time you will get "high touch" treatment from the bank is if you are overdrawn or overdue.

Job isolation is causing us to lose the important factor of neighborliness. Our increasingly transient population is here today—gone tomorrow. We don't take time to get to know each other. It's easier to treat customers as numbers rather than as people. I'm not proposing a return to the "good-old-days," but I'm just a little partial to the insurance agent that knows me and my family as real people; the butcher that knows how thick I like my steaks, the stewardess that genuinely asks if I'm on my way home and where home is. I appreciate and support businesses and organizations that are able to relate to me personally through their employees. All organizations must remember that their success is built upon hundreds or thousands of people customers—out there, somewhere—living, breathing human beings. These people need high touch, and they will reward people and organizations that provide it.

PERSONAL INDIFFERENCE. Somehow, during the past generation we have lost the willingness to go the extra mile, to do *more* than is expected, to bend-over-backward, to arrive early and stay late, to be worth more than we are paid. Exceptional job performance and superior achievement are out of fashion. Because of nation-wide peer pressure, it requires a great deal of courage to "bust the quota" or exceed the goal. A high percentage of our work force believes that only the rich get richer, profits are inherently "bad," and only a fool works hard.

Too many people feel that their personal success and reward is strictly a matter of "luck." This is especially prevalent among those who work in organizations that treat their employees as a lump of non-individuals. People that feel lost in the shuffle, or inconsequential in the direction of things, tend to feel the same way about themselves. Personal pride is destroyed. Professional golfer, Gary Player, summed it up by remarking, "it's funny—the harder you work, the luckier you get."

America's most successful companies, large and small, usually have been able to overcome T.N.M.J. and personal indifference, by making sure they understand and treat each employee as an individual. They have demonstrated the power of making sure all employees understand the truth. And the truth is, "the biggest mistake you can make is to think you are working for someone else."

A great deal of the blame can be leveled at the mass media and public education. But you and I must also accept responsibility for not working harder to overcome these factors. Unfortunately, the rigor mortis attitudes are becoming more the rule than the exception in organizational life today. Our contentment or complacency, our commitment to sameness, permeates our everyday lives.

LACK OF LEADERSHIP BY EXAMPLE. There is a well-known concept in business known as the reflective phenomenon of management. This concept points out that almost all employees will consistently and invariably reflect the attitudes and behavior exhibited by their upper management (bosses).

Too many people in supervisory management positions have adopted the attitude of "do as I say—not as I do." For some reason, as people are promoted to ever higher levels of responsibility and leadership they often demonstrate a decreasing willingness to service the customer. They feel they have more important things to do. This sets the tone for the whole organization. If the boss ever says, "That's not my job." it's a good bet his or her employees will parrot this attitude in their attempt to follow-the-leader.

Effective leadership (management) must be by example. Top management must demonstrate the importance of customer service. Invariably, if you experience T.N.M.J. from front-line employees, chances are they are merely reflecting the behavior they witness at the "top" of the organization. In too many organizations the mirror is cracked!

PROTECTING ONE'S TURF. Business politics have devastated organizations large and small. We have learned to irrationally defend our job functions and job talents in the mistaken viewpoint of short-term security. We have also learned not to step on toes, don't rock the boat, go with the flow, don't make waves, and similar attitudes of personal job protection and isolation. This has caused thousands of organizations to be ruined because they totally lost the concept of "team," if they ever had it at all. For too many years we have stressed short-term results and economic protection. The result has often been long-term destruction.

We have encouraged and rewarded those who have justified their paychecks all the way to retirement rather than encouraging and rewarding people for thinking, questioning, innovating, changing, designing and planning toward personal and organizational excellence. One of the causes of T.N.M.J. is an over-zealous attempt to narrow the answer to the question, "Just what *is* your job?"

The smaller the definition of a job, the easier the job is to protect. Likewise, the more a person can continue to maintain the status quo and justify their existence, the less they feel threatened by innovation and change. All of us are in a race between obsolescence and retirement. And we are all hoping for a tie!

For all too many the lifetime career is not to get laid-off, and to qualify for retirement pensions. The perpetuation of "That's not my job" is one of the best ways to protect your turf and accomplish this short-term security—providing your business or organization doesn't go belly-up before you do!

O.K. So What's the Cure for T.N.M.J.?

First, if you agree that this disease can devastate our businesses and organizations, and silently cripple the competitive, free enterprise system, I ask you to join with me in the fight. Send no money! I only solicit your enrollment in the campaign to overcome this basic malady. I ask you to pledge your willingness to stand up (often times alone) and confront T.N.M.J.

I ask you not to tolerate it in business, in government, in organizations of all sizes and types—especially in our own organizations! I ask you to have the courage to point it out and not ignore it for convenience sake. I ask you to take the time and trouble to state your case, even when you may appear as foolish as Don Quixote.

Mind you, the most frustrating and difficult of all confrontations will be when you encounter T.N.M.J. coupled with I.C.C.L. (I couldn't care less). This is most common in larger organizations where your observation, constructive suggestions and attempts to reverse the trend will fall only on deaf ears. You must make your point as high as possible in the organization. Surely there will be someone, somewhere, who will respond and act—before their walls come tumbling down.

The Prescription

The basic cure to "That's not my job" must be in the correct definition of just exactly what *everybody's* job really is. There is only one answer in a competitive, free enterprise system: *Everybody's job is service to the customer!* Without customers there are no jobs—period.

Peter Drucker, the guru of modern management principles states it very succinctly when he states that the primary function of management is to create customers. Service to the customer must be the primary function of every member of an organization, from top to bottom. This function must take precedence over *all other* job definitions, descriptions and training. If it has to do with service to a customer, it is most definitely your job—and mine!

Service to the customer must receive demonstrable priority over all other phases of a career. It supersedes the boss' instructions and priorities, it supersedes specific job training, it supersedes personal comfort, it supersedes short-term profits, it supersedes everything short of calling the fire department because the place is burning down!

Service to the customer must be taught to all employees—especially if you think you can take it for granted that they will always do it anyway. Employees must be taught how to ask questions, how to listen to the answers, how to take action towards serving the needs of every customer, and therefore the long-term needs of the organization.

Service to the customer is more important than starting time, quitting time and lunchtime. It's more important than getting dirty, sweating, and doing things you're not supposed to have to do. Service to the customer is more important than your paycheck—or the boss' paycheck!

Service to the customer is a twenty-four hour a day priority. Service to the customer must be applied even to those customers you don't like very much. It's more important than "who did it?" It's more important than what someone else told you to do. It's more important than every job description ever written!

Top management must lead by example. They must practice "management by walking around," keeping their ear to the ground for employee and customer feedback that relates to overall customer service. They must also take action. They must personally become involved with customer relations and they must take responsibility for the shortcomings as well as share credit for the successes. They must polish the mirror. As someone once said, "There is no limit to what can be accomplished if it matters little who gets the credit."

The next time you hear or sense T.N.M.J. in your experiences with other organizations it's time to take action and help cure the disease. If you hear it or sense it in *your* organization—it's time to panic!

Work is the great cure for all the maladies of mankind. Honest work that you intend getting done.

—Thomas Carlisle

Burt Dubin, Implementation Specialist

Management Achievement Institute
P.O. Box 1542
Santa Monica, California 90406
(213) 393-3230

Burt Dubin

"Five Star Rating! Excellent, outstanding, far superior in quality to any other seminar I've ever attended."

Burt Dubin, quintessential product of the American Dream, philosopher, successful businessman, seminar designer, implementation specialist, is a powerful and gifted educator.

Co-author of the Achievement Handbook, he is authentic—possessing rare insights and understanding. The creator of several educational cassette programs that are snapped up in his workshops, he shatters illusions so that people and organizations may face the reality they create.

He serves as trainer or consultant for many of the largest companies and institutions in the world, and for dozens of government agencies and universities. He provides organizations with keys, tools, techniques that empower and inspire. His methods create commitment to company goals, to greater productivity, plus enhanced well-being and fulfillment for individuals.

As an implementation specialist he presents information-packed, laughter-punctuated trainings, both in-house and public, all over the United States. His seminars are recognized as models of excellence and inspiration.

Slim, youthful, health-conscious, (and single), he runs 5K most mornings, loves dancing, listening to fine music and attending plays.

These Burt Dubin-designed trainings are available in 45 minute to two day versions:

The Triple Play: Intentions→Actions→Results

Ease Away Stress	*Create Better Relationships*
Melt-down Conflicts	*Make Masterful Decisions*
Up Your Career	*Train Groups Right*
Strategic Selling Skills	*Achieve Personal Excellence*
Communicate Better Now	

Implement Management Excellence
by Burt Dubin

"It must be considered that there is nothing more difficult to carry out, nor more doubtful of success, nor more dangerous to handle, than to initiate a new order of things. For the reformer has enemies in all those who profit by the old order and only lukewarm defenders in all those who profit by the new..."
—Machiavelli, "The Prince"

Creating your management team today is more complex, more challenging. There is a new breed of executives and managers who simply do not respond to the old stimuli. "The Man In The Gray Flannel Suit"and "The Organization Man"(or woman) don't live here any more.

In this chapter I propose to first share insights from several recognized sources. You'll find dozens of ideas and strategies you can start to use at once. I'll then share some conclusions including more keys, tools and techniques that I teach in my management seminars. Take them. Make them your own—as you create *your* management team.

I

Let's start with John Ingalls. In "Human Energy, the Critical Factor for Individuals and Organizations"(1979, Learning Concepts, 8517 Production Avenue, San Diego CA), he wrote of the waste of human energy in organizations today, particularly among managers. He advocates a new approach that recognizes and facilitates the personal growth needs of individuals.

Alvin Toffler in "The Third Wave" (1980, William Morrow & Co., New York) wrote that an American Management Association survey revealed 40% of middle managers unhappy in their jobs. He urges more bonding between individuals and their company. He wants people to feel more emotional satisfaction as a consequence of their daily work.

Daniel Yankelovich in "New Rules"(1981, Random House, New York) wrote:

"The new rules associated with the search for self-fulfillment can help America respond to its new economic challenge . . . to build a more productive economy in which the cravings of the spirit as well as material well-being can be satisfied."

"By the late seventies, my firm's studies showed more than seven out of ten Americans spending a great deal of time thinking about themselves and their inner lives. Their life experiments engage what we might call the 'getting/giving compact.' They now engage new demands for intangibles, seeking to satisfy both the body and the spirit. They express a longing for connectedness, commitment, and creative expression."

"People speak of 'becoming conscious' as if it were a single memorable event, a moment of blinding insight. Acting with great vigor, (they) recreate their life, virtually reversing all former beliefs, identifications and values."

(There is a new) "ethic of commitment . . . toward connectedness with the world. What is required of Americans in the eighties . . . is to . . . make industrial society a fit place for human life."

Michael Maccoby in "The Leader" (1981, Simon and Schuster, New York) writes of "the leadership revolution of the 80's":

"The old models of leadership no longer work. The ideal leader must bring out the best in people. Young managers are less motivated by career advancement. The new managers are less driven by the promise of promotion and status. They are not attracted to power nor do they defer to it. They want interesting work and satisfying emotional relationships, characterized by kindness, sympathy, understanding and generosity. Even successful managers no longer automatically sacrifice personal life for advancement. The new social character is more oriented to self than to craft, enterprise or career. The new character is not loyal in the traditional sense of submission and self-sacrifice to the organization. There is a strong need for meaningful relationships at work. There is a willingness to give one's best."

"All this demands competent and caring leadership. A new model of leadership that expresses an ethic of self-development is needed, not just at the top, but at all levels of large business."

Kenneth Blanchard and Spencer Johnson in "The One Minute Manager" (1982, William Morrow & Co., New York) with recognition of the emerging need for psychological gratification and for personal growth among today's employees, wrote of the need people have to feel good about themselves, and that we should "catch them doing something right."

Tom Peters and Bob Waterman, in their runaway best-seller "In Search of Excellence" (1982, Harper & Row, New York), continue the theme. They emphasize caring and commitment as essential ingredients on the management team. Their "eight basics of management excellence," detailed in the book, are simple, direct and true.

In "Megatrends" (1982, Warner Books, New York) John Naisbitt refers to the need for "high touch" to complement "high tech."

The conclusions of these authors support and validate my own research. Years ago I recognized this new breed of executives, managers and workers. I realized that it was essential to accept their feelings and their needs. I developed ways to engage those feelings and needs, as well as the emerging quest for inner fulfillment on the job—and connect them to organizational and departmental goals. As an Implementation Specialist, concerned with converting objectives into results, I've made this the central theme of the management trainings I create and present.

It is definitely possible for your middle managers, your first-line managers, your staff and technical people, all of your people—to be inspired to have the attitudes, think the thoughts, and take the actions that cause departmental and organizational achievement. To experience less stress, more clarity and purpose. To possess a clearer insight into their relationships with others. To enter a new world of effectiveness, eagerly dedicating themselves to the achievement of their assigned goals. Now, in the second half of this chapter, I plan to share some of the techniques, ideas and strategies that I teach. Feel free to use this material to create a superior management team, to implement management excellence.

II

Do you really want to implement management excellence? Is your true intention to manage those on your team so that you deliver more productivity and higher profits to your organization? Then please accept this truth: There's a new breed of employee out there today. These people—your subordinates—are brighter, more aware. It's appropriate to handle them differently, in accord with new rules.

If you know the new rules, the new ways of

understanding and addressing these subordinates of yours, you have a chance to get more yield out of them. For your own survival, your own growth, your own prosperity, you need that chance.

To implement excellence on your management team, in the light of the new realities of this age, several new insights are called for. I propose to share these insights with you. Insights you can use at once to get more of what you want from your people. Let's look into the hearts of this new breed. Let's understand their psyche. Let's find the hot buttons that release their brakes, that get them in gear on your behalf.

Here are the lucky 13 insights my research revealed:

1. Your people are now more inner-directed. They are more interested in their own well-being than in the well-being of your company.

2. Your people are more concerned with their own personal growth than they are with the growth of your organization. And—they want their personal growth accelerated through their work in your department.

3. Your people are more attached to their own fulfill- ment than to the fulfillment of your objectives.

4. Your people have a longing to make a difference in the world. They really want to know that they matter.

5. Your people yearn for connectedness and closeness, instead of separation and distance, within their work environment. They want their work relationships to be emotionally satisfying.

6. Your people need to be involved in making key decisions affecting their work, including what to do, how best to do it, and why.
7. Your people seek more meaning and purpose in their lives. They want what they do to produce more than just a paycheck.
8. Your people want to be valued as human beings first, and as units of production second.
9. They desire to take risks, to be creatively daring, to express their own autonomy, their own sovereignty.
10. They crave acceptance as "OK" exactly as they are.
11. They are hungry for commitment—to give it and to receive it—and they want that commitment to be linked to something higher and more noble than just being paid for their work.
12. Your people ache for a chance to stand out, to receive recognition for their contributions and accomplishments.
13. Your people would so like to have a little fun while getting the job done!

Here are seven benefits you may enjoy by accepting these insights:

1. You may forge a union between your organization and your people—a union in which you are united, aligned and focused on one prime purpose.
2. You may inspire peak performance and effectiveness from your people.
3. You may create a positive bond—cause your people to feel a part *of* your company instead of apart *from* your company.

4. You may connect each employee's natural need for a sense of personal well-being with your company purpose.
5. You may provide your people with a better sense of who they are and how they relate to their tasks.
6. You may motivate your people to work harder and smarter because they now enjoy co-creating results with you.
7. You may get outstanding results from your people because you, in return, provide them with the new psychological gratifications for which they thirst.

It's obvious, of course, that in this one chapter I cannot share all the in-depth insights and understandings that I set forth in my seminars and workshops, or even in my one-hour talks. However, I'll share all that I can in our available space.

In return for these golden nuggets of management wisdom, I want something back from you. I want your passionate commitment. I want action. I want your positive, enthusiastic involvement for the next 17 weeks. You'll discover that it's easy, fun and safe. You'll get the amazing results you want. Your environment will come alive with vibrant excitement. You'll have more energy, you'll look and feel great and your people will love you for this living proof of your competence and caring.

Here's what to do: Take one each of the following 17 Golden Nuggets of Management Wisdom and integrate it into your operation during each of the next 17 weeks. One a week. That's all. It's simple. Act as if this stuff really works. Get behind it all the way. Commit yourself to create a team of champions. Commit yourself to achieve management excellence.

At the end of the 17 weeks a new cohesiveness, a new power, a new spirit will infuse your environment. Don't stop there. That's only the first plateau. Now, start again, reinforcing each enhancement. Go on—onward and upward—you'll feel so great about who you are and what you're doing. And so will your management team. Shining stars, every one, you and your people may now rise to your highest aspirations. Excelsior! You have found the golden fleece, the keys to heaven and the end of the rainbow, all rolled into one.

The 17 Golden Nuggets of Management Wisdom:

1. **Create shared mission:** This causes the assigned work to become like a game, to become play. It releases otherwise untapped energy. Think of yourself as the coach of your team. (You are, you know.) Tell your players of the true consequences of what they are doing, of the benefits generated, of how your team's work fits into the whole picture. Let your people be aware of the higher value and the service to others that what you do produces.

2. **Remember that people will do what you want only when it's for their own reasons, not yours:** So tell them what's in it for them when you accomplish your team tasks. Everyone wants to know, "What's in it for me? For *me!* For ME!!!" Give your people reasons, powerful and compelling reasons to deliver championship performance—and they will not let you down.

3. **Be sure that people know that you care:** That

you care about the well-being of each of your subordinates, about your department, your organization, about the impact of your work upon your entire management team. That you care about what you do. That you care about excellence in all that you undertake. That you care about the effect of your work and your departmental output on the reputation and the competitive position of your organization. These words bear repeating: "People don't care how much you know—until they know how much you care."

4. **Bring out the best in your management team:** Expect and demand extraordinary performance. Believe in each of your team members and let each of them know it! Here are eight magic words. "I know you can do a great job." These words cause people to do their utmost to live up to your high expectations. You must mean what you say. The words must be spoken with total sincerity. Look your subordinate directly in the eyes as you speak. Include emotional content in your voice as you say "I know you can do a great job." The power of your belief—of your positive expectancy—is incredible. The other person will not want to disappoint you, and will act to prove that you are right.

5. **Allow members of your management team to set their own team goals and to set their own individual goals:** Then let them have reasonably free rein in acting to achieve those goals. It's a fact of human nature—people will set more difficult objectives for themselves than they will accept from you.

Be sure that their goals are in writing, that they are specific, measurable, and that there is a definite target date for their attainment. Request a signed and dated copy of each goal statement for your current files. Be there as a counselor, a resource, a coach. Without visible pressure observe your team members' actions to achieve their target on time. You may be surprised at the team spirit and the ardent effort to meet or beat the intended objective.

6. **Have total, absolute integrity:** This goes well beyond simple honesty. Be consistent and predictable relative to your word. Be a model of impeccable faithfulness relative to your word, with no exceptions, ever. This will contribute to peace of mind among your team members. You will be setting a priceless example, inspiring your people by your utter reliability.

7. **Use these seven keys to create team spirit:**
   a. Do not ask subordinates to do anything you wouldn't do.
   b. Keep your door open. Be available to your people.
   c. Answer your own telephone.
   d. Praise fine work generously and publicly.
   e. Have backup people trained for every key job.
   f. Play no favorites, don't gossip, and don't mess in internal politics.
   g. Have no interest in the private life of your people unless your advice is requested.

8. **When in doubt about what to do, be guided by the Golden Rule.**

9. **Use this simple decision-making strategy:** Ask

yourself, "Does an action being considered serve my organization's primary interest (usually *profit* and *growth)* and not harm anyone?" If so, it's a good decision. Go for it. If not, don't do it. Period.

10. **Do not be a personal friend to any subordinate:** This never works. There's fundamental incompatibility between friendship and the superior-subordinate relationship. Be a professional friend, yes. Care about each of your people. Care a lot. Yet, it's essential that you be able to evaluate performance dispassionately. That you treat people with even-handed fairness. There is no way to do this with a personal friend.

11. **Always treat your people with consideration and respect:** There are no exceptions to this.

12. **Create meaningful work for each of your team members:** Infuse every assignment with positive, upbeat excitement. Be sure there's a personal growth opportunity for the individual assigned to each job, and that each of your people clearly knows of what s/he has to gain by performing with excellence. Never, ever, allow any of your people to be assigned to a dead-end situation. Build your people. Encourage them to experiment and to take risks. Help them stretch and grow.

13. **Create a "happy ship" and persist in keeping it happy:** Nobody's perfect. In spite of your careful screening and your patient willingness to show people the way, a few won't cut it. They cannot or will not be happy in the heady, exciting, excellence-oriented, high achieving team environment you have

engendered. Get them out. Get them reassigned, fast, firmly, remorselessly. It's really the kindest act for all concerned.

14. **Focus on results, not methods:** There are times when you do ask someone to do what you want. Do it like this. Use mission-type instructions. You tell the person what you want and when you want it—but not how to do it. Let the individual decide the how to. (Always have oral instructions repeated back to you, and ask questions to assure that you are understood clearly.)

15. **Set high standards—your personal high standards—for your management team output:** Expect your people to be dedicated champions. Nothing less will do. Whatever your group may convert, design, improve, process or produce, accept excellence as your minimum standard. Then proceed to measurably higher levels of excellence as your team standard. Devise measuring instruments that fit your tasks. Post huge, colorful charts on a prominent wall so that everyone knows how the team is doing. Get every member involved in a team approach to surpassing the "possible" and creating new, higher standards. Finally, celebrate your wins!

16. **Bring a spirit of fun to your team and your environment.** It's OK to lighten up. The world of work doesn't have to be a grim and heavy trip. Laughter lightens the spirit and relaxes people. Celebrate the wins of your people and your team. Create spontaneous joy at the drop of a birthdate or an anniversary. (This includes the anniversary of

people starting to work in your department.)
Recognize these events with lunch hour or after-
work festivities that fit your corporate culture.

17. **Establish a dream or a mission for your
    management team:** Make it something trans-
    cendent, something that will make a difference. Let it
    be a mission that unites minds, hearts and spirits.
    Yes, lead your people to go beyond themselves. Let
    your personal vision propel your team to higher
    levels—up, up, up—to a new dimension, a higher
    orbit of implementing management excellence.

*"Destiny is not a matter of chance, it is a matter of
choice. It is not a thing to be waited for, it is a thing
to be achieved."* **—William Jennings Bryan**

Lawrence F. Lottier, Jr.
5515 Southwyck Blvd., Suite 205
Toledo, Ohio 43614
(419) 865-8954

Lawrence F. Lottier, Jr.

Larry Lottier has been a part of the Human Resource Development world since 1963 when he began training for United Airlines. He not only has an extensive education and training background but he also has a variety of industrial experience. He has also worked for railroads, hospitals, restaurants and, since 1974, with Dana Corporation.

In addition he has also developed and conducted seminars and workshops for such clients as Hilton Hotels, Champion Spark Plug Company, Hotel Sales Management Association, Bowling Green State University, The University of Toledo, Hillsdale College, and many other varied organizations.

He is an active member of the American Society for Training and Development serving at both the local and national level. He was president of the Greater Toledo Chapter, National Chairman of the Professional Development Workshop Committee, and is currently National Chairman of the Society's Ethics Committee. In 1982 he was presented the Society's Torch Award for his contribution to ASTD and the Training Profession.

When not conducting workshops or consulting to management on training and development matters, Larry is a consultant for Junior Achievement Project Business. He is a member of the Woodlands Group, a well respected organization of training professionals. A frequent speaker and seminar leader, he is active in the National Speakers Association and the Ohio Speakers Forum.

Managing A Productive Environment
Culture = Values + Philosophy
by Lawrence F. Lottier, Jr.

*"Pit a good performer against a bad system
(culture) and the system will win every time."*
—**Geary A. Rummler**

*"Whether good or bad, the culture will
quickly whip you back into line."*
—**Martin Broadwell**

Whatmakes a good system? A good culture? And how
can you, the manager, build such a system?
Let's look at two different managers and see how

they act out their organization's values which in turn develop their organization's culture. That's what a "culture" really is, the acting out of values and philosophies. As you read this chapter think about your values, philosophies and the way you manage your business.

It's what you think about the people in your organization that causes you to feel the way you do about them. And how you feel determines your behavior on the job. For you are the model, the one people look to. You set the culture.

Is it easy? No. But then we know that nothing ever worth having is easy. A very successful fast food restaurant chain in Florida has as one of their operating values, "'Soft' things are numbers, percentages, reports. 'Hard' things to do are the values, the beliefs." A culture develops one way or another, so let's work at it and develop a good one.

And now to our two managers and the contrasting cultures they developed.

The Railroad

It was a muggy July afternoon. Four of us were taking another "break" from sorting diesel parts and cleaning up the scrap yard. It was getting toward the end of our day, I had finished up my job and all I wanted to do was get out of the heat. Since none of the buildings were air-conditioned I found a cool place in the shade of the roundhouse. The sweet smell of diesel fuel and creosote hung heavy.

This break was to take us up to the 3:25 quitting

whistle. I heard a whistle—but not the one I was waiting for.

It was Hank, whistling.

Hank was our boss and whenever he came out to the yard he always whistled his warning—"The Yellow Submarine." It wasn't that Hank was always happy, but he knew people and as a result was a good manager. You see what Hank was saying everytime he came out of the office and started to whistle was, "I know you're sitting down. But, I also know you do your work so I'm not concerned. However, railroad rules and regulations say if I catch you sitting down on the job I can or, in some cases must, discipline you. So stand up and look like you're working and we'll all be OK."

Hank crossed the loading dock, gave us a wink, and walked out into the yard. We sat down and waited for the other whistle. I liked Hank and respected him. I would work hard for him. He respected us and treated each of us as a manager. That was the culture Hank helped create in Markham yard that summer.

The Hospital

The dietary department is like any food operation with the notable exception of special diets. Our job was to prepare the patients' meals and hope to deliver them to their bedside hot—but without the Jello running into the mashed potatoes.

About six months into my career, as an Assistant Food Services Director, we were preparing for lunch. I didn't realize at the time that all manner of chaos was about to break loose. John, the manager, was on his usual rampage and the food service people were trying hard to please him. Today success was to elude them.

During the height of our "rush" I was helping out on the line. As the ladies chatted with me while setting up and passing trays, their feelings came through loud and clear. "Why can't he leave us alone?", "Why doesn't he understand us?", "Why does he always have to shout at us?" They were truly upset and frustrated. I soon found out in this department you were told—not asked—what to do, when and how to do it.

With no real answers for them, I listened.

Then out he came. He asked me to go to my desk while he proceeded to throw the lunch line up for grabs. It's a small wonder any of our patients got their meals that day.

Well . . . It seemed my "rush hour visits" were more than John could stand.

I sat at my desk trying to think of what I would say. Nothing much came to me except thoughts of self-preservation and wonder as to why my style of management of walking and talking was such a problem.

Later, as the last meal was sent upstairs, he called me into his office and shouted, "What were you doing out there and what were they talking about? What did they say and what did you say to them? We have enough problems around here without you disrupting the line— and they have work to do. We have a job to do around here and visiting isn't a part of it." With that he stopped to take a breath—and so did I. Convinced I was going to get fired, I was scared and angry. Here I thought I was doing the right thing since I cared for those people and they needed someone to talk to. After all, the job was getting done . . . John treated each of us as a child that had to be managed.

The upshot of that scene gave our department a new rule—"No talking to people when they are working." And yes, my job was eliminated a short time later.

Contrasting Cultures

These two contrasting situations taught me my first lessons on the importance of personal values and how they translate to work behavior and which determines the environment or culture of the work group. At the time I didn't know what to call it but I know what I felt.

Both of these managers were contributing to the culture of their organizations. The railroad foreman developed trust with his people—they would and did perform for him. In the dietary department a different culture developed—hostility, distrust, and anxiety. Production fell and quality suffered.

A lot of things go into making up the culture of an organization, many of which are under the direct control of the manager. We'll look at a few approaches successful managers have taken to develop positive, energizing environments.

Beliefs and Behaviors

T.J. Watson's philosophy in building IBM was that an effective organization must have beliefs and must adhere faithfully to those beliefs. Today, we look at successful businesses and see how their beliefs and values are congruent with their behaviors. These companies are building cultures—productive environments in which people are committed.

Why is it important to be concerned with culture or climate in an organization? Because every organization, irrespective of its size or mission, has a culture that is either a benefit or a detriment to the group. So, as managers, we should want our cultures to be both positive and productive. But why doesn't it happen? In my opinion it's because we are not aware of what a culture is and how it develops.

Culture Defined

Webster defines culture as "a complex of typical behavior or standardized social characteristics peculiar to a specific group." From this we see that any group has a culture—whether it is a department, plant or the total organization.

What follows are parts of a successful philosophy which makes up the typical behavior of some of our major corporations.

Make Every Employee A Manager

Think, as you read this chapter, on how you manage the many aspects of your life. You are able to get to work, keep your home running, balance your checkbook, have money to buy food, see that your children are educated, and pay your bills. You manage groups such as Little League, church committees, the PTA. In general you do a pretty good job of managing your life.

And then you go to work. Are you still a manager? No, I don't necessarily mean by title. Do you manage yourself on the job? Or are you managed? You're still that same person who yesterday was managing your life successfully aren't you? But what happens when you walk through the door at work? Does the culture "quickly whip you back into line"?

It's amazing that in so many of our organizations we are told "what to do," "how to do it," "when to do it" and generally treated as though we were children. What a waste! Companies with their rules and regulations, policies and procedures ignore the tremendous potential each person brings to the job. Employers often view them as merely being "an extension of the machine." In other words, many firms today still feel people have to be managed.

How can we grow and be competitive in a world market if our greatest resource is not being used? We must begin to create the working climate which allows our people to grow and develop—to use those God-given resources we have all been blessed with.

Help Your People Grow

A friend once told me, "You can't expect a man to respond to something he hasn't been taught." As managers we have a responsibility to both our employers and our people to instill a "thirst for knowledge" and a system to help quench that thirst. The future of our organizations depends on how we develop our people both personally and professionally. I don't believe we can separate the two and still survive. As Ed Foreman (Executive Development Systems, Dallas, Texas) says in his executive seminars, "We build people . . . people build companies."

Before anything can happen in educating your people you, the manager, must first believe education and training is an investment—not just an expense. As the saying goes, "If you think training and development is expensive—try ignorance." You are making an investment in your people just as you would in a piece of equipment or a building. And you should demand a return on that investment. People don't go to training just to "get away." They are there to learn and to apply that learning when they return.

Start small. Begin with one or two short classes to meet the immediate needs of your people. Demonstrate to them you are interested in their development—for them as well as for the organization. If you have had no training programs in the past your people will be wondering what you are up to. So, get their inputs at the beginning to show you are truly interested in meeting their needs.

One major corporation began training with one supervisory workshop while at the same time providing "non-work" related courses such as woodworking, photography and auto repair. These courses were attended by both management and non-management people. This gave them a flavor of the "classroom" and let them know going back to school was "OK." As a matter of fact many of those non-work courses were taught by the employees. It worked so well, both types of programs expanded. Education became the norm and people actually looked forward to going to class.

Your Future Managers

Where will your future managers come from? If your company doesn't have a way to provide training for all your people you run the risk of having too small a pool from which to draw for promotions. If you promote from within, I believe you have a responsibility to develop people so they can be promoted. Too many people learn how to manage and supervise by watching their boss. This is probably the least effective way of learning unless you are lucky and have a good leader and coach.

Again, Tom Watson. "We have learned that a company must be prepared to make a commitment to internal education and retraining which increases in geometric proportion to the technological change the company is going through."

Getting The Most Out of A Training Program.

When you're sending people to a program:
- tell them the purpose and content
- tell them why they were selected
- let them know what's in it for them
- indicate what you expect them to get from the program and that you'll meet with them on their return to discuss the application of what they learned.

While at the program let them know you expect them to:
- get involved and participate
- be open to new ideas and concepts
- not to worry about the "back home" job while they are learning
- take full advantage of this opportunity.

When they return from a training program:
- let them know they've been missed (small but important point)
- have them share the ideas they learned and how they can be applied to the job
- tell them you'll work with them to help implement new ideas and approaches
- get their inputs on how to enhance your return on investment.

Let Your People Know First

I recall when working for the airlines I always found it frustrating to hear about the schedule and fare changes from the passengers—who read it in the papers. Sometimes there were valid marketing reasons for having to hold information back. But many times there was no excuse. I guess some managers feel secure if they have more information than their people.

To be an effective and successful manager, meet with your people regularly. Keep them informed of customer reactions, cost figures, the profit picture and generally what's new that they should know about. When it comes from you, rather than the grapevine, it builds your credibility. After all, your people are the ones who make the product, provide the service and keep your enterprise going. So why shouldn't they know what's going on?

There are many ways to communicate with your people. You can use newsletters, letters from the president, memos and personal notes. These are all fine and will get your message across. But by far the best method is face to face. You should do this on a regular basis through plant wide meetings, team meetings and, when appropriate, on a one-to-one basis.

As part of a recent management development workshop for a savings and loan group, the president and his controller spent an hour and a half with the class in an open question and answer exchange. This was a part of their operating philosophy—"keeping people informed." It's the way you build your credibility.

Involve All Your People

Your best managers know that management doesn't have all the answers. I tell my management students "all people come—free of extra charge—with a God-given brain." It works in our own best interest and the organization's interest if we tap into that valuable resource.

Peter Drucker, in *Managing In Turbulent Times,* says, ". . . even in routine work—the only 'expert' is the person who does the job." No supervisor or manager can know all there is about every job in the department. How can you improve your operation? Ask your people— they'll tell you."

Let Your People Set Their Goals and Judge Their Performance

Research has shown us that when people in a work situation are involved in setting their department and individual goals the goals tend to be high—and are frequently higher than the manager would dare to impose. These same studies also show us that these team developed goals are also highly realistic.

When you set a climate of trust and openness these

same people will judge their performance fairly and honestly. When they know you won't be punishing them for mistakes but letting them learn from them, then their judgement will be accurate. You'll also find these people will tend to be harder on themselves than you would be.

I conduct a number of management development workshops around the country. When setting my client schedule, I am much harder on myself than my manager would be. Why, if he gave me the schedule I give myself I'd wring his neck. But when I do it to me—that's different. Also, I am more committed because it was my decision.

We, as managers, need to recognize the importance of involving our people. The majority of employees in today's organizations want to contribute, want to be involved. They are a valuable resource waiting to be tapped.

Discourage Conformity

I believe it was Thomas Edison who said, "There's a better way to do it. Find it." All too often as managers we set a climate of not changing and of adhering to company "standards," "rules," "policies" and other constraints. We need to set people free so they can use their creative energy toward the growth and development of our organizations. An old saying goes like this:

> *"The reasonable man adapts himself to the world.*
> *The unreasonable man adapts the world to himself.*

*Therefore, all progress comes from unreason-
able men."*

In meeting with a manufacturing manager in Chicago recently, I came across an interesting example of non-conformity. While touring the plant I noticed a group of bright orange machines amid the dull gray and blue ones. I asked why. He told me those orange machines made products for one special customer. Those machines were once scattered all over the plant. The people came up with the idea of having them all in one place. This way all raw materials, processing and quality checks would be at one location. Then, to set themselves apart they wanted the machines painted a different color. They chose orange and called their section "Operation Orange."

The bottom line of Operation Orange is that the customer is getting excellent service, production is up, quality is up, morale is up. Without a positive environment this plant would not have achieved these results for that customer. Does the customer come first in your organization?

The Florida restaurant chain I mentioned earlier has a value which says, "Suggest a small shake for a child when a mother orders a large." "Suggest a courtesy cup for a child to share a drink." That sure is a deviation from the traditional "sell up" business philosophy we encounter in most fast food places.

We need to ask ourself, "Am I sacrificing a quality operation so as to conform with some long outdated concept as to how things should be?

It's Your Decision

All the things you have been reading in this chapter center around the values and philosophies of an organization. Those values come from management. And those values tell you a great deal about the culture or environment you live in. Yet, as managers we each influence our own domains—our department, our office, our facility.

Take a look at your environment. Ask, "Does this reflect my value system?" "How does it affect the people who work here?" "What can I do to make it even better?"

Belief systems are stated in many different ways. Here is how Borg-Warner, a major multi-national corporation, presents their belief system:

"WE BELIEVE IN THE DIGNITY OF THE INDIVIDUAL.

However large or complex a business may be, its work is still done by people dealing with people. Each person involved is a unique human being, with pride, needs, values, and innate personal worth. For us to succeed we must operate in a climate of openness and trust, in which each of us freely grants others the same respect, cooperation and decency we seek for ourselves."

As managers we can't really motivate people. All we can do is to create an environment or a culture where people can motivate themselves. What we think determines what we feel and what we feel determines our behavior. And that behavior will determine the environment in our organizations. Will that be a positive environment? Manager, it's your decision.

Let's pit our people against a good system and make it a win-win.

*What lies behind us and what lies before us
are tiny matters compared to what lies
within us.*

—Emerson

There are two types of people in the world: those who come into a room and say, "Here I am!" and those who come in and say, "Ah, there you are!"

Shall Sinha, Ph.D.
7 Medhurst Crescent
Sherwood Park, Alberta
Canada T8A 3T5
(403) 427-8178

Shall Sinha, Ph.D.

Shall Sinha was brought up in the Oriental culture where he learned yoga and mind control.

He earned a Ph.D. degree in Engineering from McGill University in 1972 and specialized in Stress Analysis of aircraft components.

In 1980 he developed "Essential Hypertension" and complicated vision problems. His doctor put him on "pills for the rest of his life." He then got more interested in the stress of the human body than that of aircraft components. He decided to take control of his body. Within three weeks he stopped taking pills. Six months later he got the restriction of wearing glasses removed from his driver's license. Since that time he has not taken any medication except occasional doses of vitamin C. He believes that our body is capable of maintaining perfect health if we provide it with the right environment.

Besides yoga, Shall practices annual "7-day fast," living on water only. He says that fasting provides an opportunity for the vital organs to do their house cleaning. Once, during a 25 day span, he undertook 2 fasts—one for 7 days, the other for 11 days. After that he felt at least 5 years younger.

Shall Sinha is an Able Toastmaster, a graduate of the Dale Carnegie Course, a member of Lion's International and National Speakers Association. His favourite talks are, "It's Your Right To Live Better" and, "You Can Laugh Your Way To Success".

He is married to Pramila Sinha who is also a Toastmaster and a graduate of the Dale Carnegie Course.

Manage Your Life by Managing Your Breathing
by Shall Sinha, Ph.D

"He lives most life whoever breathes most air."
—Elizabeth Barrett Browning

Breath Is Life

Since air is the cheapest commodity on earth, we do not seem to realize its importance. It is the vital fuel of life. By using good quality and quantity of this fuel, we can run the machinery (our body) for the longest duration and with least problems. Nature has provided us with abundance. Fortunately no government has rationed or taxed it so far. If we are not making full use of this facility, it is entirely our fault.

When someone dies and energy and vitality leaves we say that he/she has expired. When someone feels more mental energy and creativity, we say that he/she has become inspired.

You can survive without food and water for several days but you can not survive without oxygen even for a few minutes. You can not store oxygen in your body. Every one of the billions of cells in the body requires fresh oxygen every minute. Our brain cells require 3 times more oxygen than the cells of other parts. It is estimated that we breathe in about 35 pounds of air every day— several times more than the consumption of food and water. If the carotid arteries on either side of your neck were to be pressed only for a matter of seconds, blocking the passage of oxygen carrying blood to your head, there is a good chance that you would black out. If the pressure is sustained for a few minutes, you could suffer brain damage and possibly death.

Breathing and Mental Performance

The yogis discovered centuries ago that breathing was the elixir of life. They found that mental performance could be stepped up through a brisk supply of oxygen to the brain cells.

When I was in high school, I remember that whenever I felt exhausted of studying for the exams, my mother would say, "Go out and take a walk in the fresh air." I would follow her advice and find new energy to continue my studies. Neither my mother nor I knew the reason behind it. We simply knew that it worked.

An interesting experiment was made in 1969 by clinical psychologists at Veterans Administration Hospital in Buffalo, New York. Thirteen patients were placed in a pressurized chamber and exposed inter-mittently to 100% oxygen. After two treatments daily for 15 days, the patients showed a 25% increase on the standard memory test. If this brief exposure to increased oxygen can make such a remarkable difference, think what benefits you could get if you developed a better breathing habit. And it won't cost you a penny.

Breathing and the Autonomous Systems

Our physiological systems may be classified into two types, autonomous and voluntary. The autonomous systems work automatically, day and night, even while we are sleeping. They are not really within our control. Examples are the pumping of the heart, functioning of the liver, etc. The voluntary systems, on the other hand, are mostly under our control. One example is our muscular system; we sit down when we want to sit; we walk when we want to walk and so on.

Breathing is the only system which is partly voluntary and partly autonomous. We can control our breathing—to a great extent—when we so desire. But when we let the control go, the autonomous system takes over. For example we breathe during our sleep and even when we become unconscious.

An interesting fact is that by consciously controlling

our breathing we can control—to some extent—our autonomous systems. For example, by deliberately increasing our breathing rate, we can increase our heart beat. And by slowing it down, we can slow down the heart beat. It is a well known fact that all systems slow down during meditation. The key here is slowed and rhythmic breathing.

Breathing and Concentration

Breathing has a direct influence on our ability to concentrate. The slower the rate of breathing, the greater the concentration. You can verify this by doing the following experiment.

Place an alarm clock (the mechanical type that ticks) approximately 12 to 15 feet away from you. Then gradually concentrate on the ticks. Try to keep all other thoughts out of your mind. You may find it difficult to do so but if you persist, you will succeed. Continue this until you are able to concentrate for a few seconds without distraction. You will notice that unconsciously you may have completely suspended your breathing—or at least you had slowed down your breathing rate.

You may try yet another experiment.

Try opening the lid of a jar which is closed very tightly. As you concentrate to gather your energy, you will notice that you held your breath for a few seconds. Holding the breath slows down all systems and redirects the energy for the execution of the task in hand.

Breathing and Personality

There is a growing evidence of a correspondence

between personality types and breathing patterns. It appears that the relationship between the breath and the mind is reciprocal.

This means that if a certain state of mind results in a certain mode of breathing then, by consciously adopting that mode of breathing, we can evoke the corresponding state of mind. In other words, a person can change his/her mood by changing his/her breathing pattern. This is the fundamental principle of meditation.

Our Breathing Efficiency

Most of us use only the top third of our lungs during breathing. This part has a poor supply of blood, firstly because of the difference in the distribution of the blood vessels and secondly due to the influence of gravity. This means that in normal breathing we achieve a very inefficient gas exchange (about 10% efficiency). Some experts say that the average person today is not breathing but merely avoiding suffocation and by a smaller margin than most of us realize.

Consequences of Poor Breathing

While the sudden or total deprivation of oxygen can be fatal, gradual deprivation also has significant effects. Lack of oxygen is a prime cause of tiredness, of brain fatigue and headaches. Stiff joints, muscular pains, backaches and the pains associated with rheumatism and neuritis are all considered to stem from years of improper breathing. Yawning is your body's attempt to obtain more oxygen.

The rate, rhythm and depth of breathing determines

how the body is energized and how well it can cope with its physiological needs.

Types of Breathing

There are 3 basic types of breathing.

1. Shallow Breathing which uses the chest only;
2. Diaphragmatic Breathing which uses the diaphragm only; and
3. Complete Breathing which uses the chest, the diaphragm, the neck and the shoulders.

The last two are generally called "Deep Breathing".

Shallow Breathing is the most common type of breathing. Air is inhaled in small amounts through small expansion of the chest and it is exhaled almost immediately. The lower lobes of the lungs virtually remain undisturbed. Hence the name Shallow Breathing.

Diaphragmatic Breathing supplies fresh oxygen to the lower lobes which receive most of the blood. This enables better oxygenation of the blood. It can be done either lying flat or sitting in a comfortable position. Be sure to loosen your tight clothes. If you are sitting in a chair, place your hands loosely on your thighs. Keep your spine straight but not rigid. If you are lying on your back, bend your knees and keep arms to your sides. It will help if you place one hand on your abdomen. This way you can make sure the emphasis of breathing is on the diaphragm. The chest should remain relaxed.

To practice Diaphragmatic Breathing, inhale deeply through the nostrils and expand the abdomen. Exhale slowly through the nostrils while pulling in the abdomen towards the spine. Be as relaxed as you can. When you are able to control your breathing in this way, concentrate on maintaining a steady rhythmic pattern:

inhale to the count of 5:

exhale to the count of 10.

Repeat this pattern 10 to 15 times a day. You will begin to feel that the breath is taking control of your body.

Complete Breathing is an extension of the Diaphragmatic Breathing. Inhale slowly through the nostrils expanding the abdomen. When the air enters the lower lobes of the lungs, continue to inhale, pulling the air up to fully inflate your lungs. Try not to be tense. Let your shoulders rise freely. Hold your breath for a while. Now exhale through the nostrils, drawing in your abdomen. Allow the air to be released very quietly and smoothly while your rib-cage closes in, reducing your chest cavity. Repeat this pattern with your eyes closed and follow this ratio:

inhale to the count of 5;

hold your breath for a count of 20;

exhale to the count of 10.

You can do this exercise lying on your back, sitting or standing. This is an exhilarating way to perk up the brain cells in the morning or to pick up your energy as it lags behind during the course of the day.

Benefits of Deep Breathing

If you practice deep rhythmic breathing 3 times a day—10 minutes each time—for 2 months, with gradual and equal prolongation of the inhalation and exhalation, your body will experience a sense of deep relaxation and rest—even more rest than that of the deepest sleep. You will remain free from the stress and strain which is the source of many physical and psychosomatic illnesses. Your nerves will be calm and your voice will become sweeter, and the harsh lines of the face will be replaced by a soft glow.

It's Ours to Manage

Yogis believe that at birth everyone is given a certain number of breaths which will last for his/her life time. It is up to us how we manage this limited resource.

By managing your breathing you can revitalize the cells in your body. You can create a reservoir of energy and later direct it where extra energy is needed. You can build recuperative powers to calm your nerves, induce restful sleep and slow down the aging process.

Most of us breathe shallowly because of ignorance and poor habit. Deep breathing can be easily learned. Within a matter of weeks it can become habitual. It will improve not only your ability to concentrate and relax but, more importantly, your overall health. It will rejuvenate you in a short time.

I know you are going to say that you don't have the time to practice deep breathing. It does not really take any extra time. You breathe deeply in the same time that you breathe shallowly. Of course in the beginning it may take half an hour a day of your time to form the habit. Remember that an hour spent in planning saves many hours in the implementation of the plan. Moreover, the results are better, since it makes provisions for potential problems. The same is true in the practice of deep breathing.

Once a reporter asked George Burns, "What's your secret of living so long?" George replied, "Keep on breathing."

You, too, can live long if you keep on breathing properly.

Let me conclude this with a short story which, I think, has a deep message.

Some years ago a huge reserve of oil was discovered in an Oklahoma field. The oil company bought the land from the farmer who moved to the neighbouring town. For a while the farmer felt depressed but then he decided to enjoy the rest of his life with the money that he had received. He ordered the most expensive car. When the car arrived, he hitched it to two horses. The horses pulled the car and he rode it everywhere. He was really amazed at the power of the two horses attached to the outside of the car. He did not know that inside the car lay hidden the power of hundreds of such horses.

We are all looking for some help from external sources. But we are not aware that within us lies tremendous latent power. You can develop this awareness and generate the necessary inspiration by managing your breathing.

God has given you control on your breathing system. You can manage it the way you like. Nature takes over the control only when you abdicate this right. By managing your breathing you can add not only many additional years to your life but also a great deal of new life in each remaining year.

After all YOU DESERVE TO LIVE BETTER.

A friendship founded on good business is better than a business founded on friendship.
—John D. Rockefeller, Jr.

Dr. Larry D. Baker, President

 Time Management of St. Louis, Inc.
3855 Lucas and Hunt Road, Suite 223
St. Louis, Missouri 63121
(314) 385-1230

Larry D. Baker, D.B.A.

Dr. Larry D. Baker is President of Time Management Center of St. Louis, Inc. As an author, he has published many articles in leading journals. He presents over 100 seminars and speeches each year.

Since 1978, Dr. Baker has been one of the most sought-after time management seminar leaders in America. He has a special ability for helping managers use basic time management and delegation concepts.

Dr. Baker has helped develop and present the highly successful Time Management Seminars sponsored by American Management Associations. He also conducts seminars for leading firms such as ARCO, American Cyanamid, Pioneer Electronics, Monsanto Company, Great Northern Paper, Cabot Corporation, General Motors, U.S. Chamber of Commerce and others.

Prior to assuming the presidency of Time Management Center, Dr. Baker was a management professor at University of Missouri-St. Louis. He is a member of American Management Associations, Academy of Management, American Psychological Association, American Society for Training and Development, and the National Speakers Association. Dr. Baker earned his Doctor of Business Administration degree in Personnel and Organizational Behavior from Indiana University.

Dr. Baker is also the recipient of many scholastic, civic and professional awards including a special achievement award presented at the White House by the President of the United States.

13

Delegating Effectively for Better Results
by Dr. Larry D. Baker

"Confidence placed in another often compels confidence in return."

—Livy

Managerial success depends on the ability to get results through effective delegation. Understanding a few basic concepts makes it easier.

Let's start with a quick quiz: **HOW WELL DO YOU DELEGATE?**

	Yes	No
1. Are you afraid your people will make mistakes?	□	□
2. Do you frequently take work home or work late at the office?	□	□
3. Does your operation function smoothly when you're absent?	□	□
4. Do you spend more time working on details than you do on planning and supervising?	□	□
5. Is your follow-up procedure adequate?	□	□
6. Do you over-rule or reverse decisions made by your subordinates?	□	□
7. Do you by-pass subordinates by making decisions which are part of their jobs?	□	□
8. Do you do several things which your subordinate could, and should, be doing?	□	□
9. If you were incapacitated for six months, is there someone who could readily take your place?	□	□
10. Will there be a big pile of paper requiring your action when you return from a trip or absence?	□	□

SCORING KEY: Give yourself one point for each "yes" answer to Nos. 3, 5, 9, and one point for each "no" answer to Nos. 1, 2, 4, 6, 7, 8, 10.

A good score is 8 or above. How did you do? If your score is in the high range, good for you. If it's not, well, don't despair. This chapter will show you how to improve quickly.

Basic Elements

Delegation is "sharing responsibility and authority with subordinates and holding them accountable for performance." We often talk about "giving" an assignment. To many managers this means giving up responsibility and authority. Delegating effectively requires only that you share. You give up nothing . . . unless you abdicate. If you abdicate, you forfeit control and accountability; that never works well.

Responsibility. Your responsibilities relate to the specific results you are expected to achieve. Responsibilities are assigned to a position. Some responsibilities must be performed by the person in that position, while others may be delegated to subordinates. You must decide what to do and what to delegate. Responsibilities of all subordinates are ultimately the responsibilities of the manager. If a subordinate does not do the work, the manager must do it, or find someone else to do it.

Authority. Authority is formal power. When delegating, managers share their authority with subordinates. Collectively, managers and their subordinates should have the authority to carry out those functions and activities necessary to get the results expected of them. Authority should be delegated within defined limits. They should not restrict performance, but must provide for reasonable control.

Authority may be delegated at different levels. Understanding the various levels of authority will help you determine the level appropriate for a given assignment.

Levels of Authority

Level 1: Look into the problem, report all, I'll decide what to do.

Level 2: Look into the problem, let me know alternative actions including pros and cons of each, and recommend one for my approval.

Level 3: Look into the problem, let me know what you intend to do, don't take action until I approve.

Level 4: Look into the problem, let me know what you intend to do, do it unless I say no.

Level 5: Take action, let me know what you did.

Level 6: Take action, no further contact with me is required.

The level of authority you grant to a subordinate will depend on many factors: the complexity or importance of the assignment, the subordinate's expertise, time constraints, and your confidence and trust in the subordinate. Each level of authority has a purpose. Lower levels are used in early training, while higher levels are granted to more experienced subordinates.

Accountability. Accountability is the key to control. In delegation, control should never be an afterthought. As responsibilities are being identified and authority determined, follow-up guidelines should also be set to assure successful performance.

You don't want to impede your subordinate's ability to learn and grow, but you must know that the assignment is under control. Control may be varied by how the assignment is structured, how involved you are with the details and how much feedback and follow-up you require.

Structuring may range from light to heavy. With light structure, subordinates are told what is expected. The rest is up to the subordinate: when, where, and how the assignment is carried out; plus when and how feedback is given to the manager.

With heavy structuring, the manager thoroughly defines the task and how, when and where the work will be completed. The manager may perform some critical tasks and coordinate them with those of subordinates. There may be more frequent feedback on progress and problems.

Obviously, there are many ways a manager can directly, or indirectly, gain information on the progress of an assignment. Reporting can vary from extensively written reports, to filling out a simple form, to a brief oral report. You may choose to have tables, charts or other graphs as part of the report. Milestones or critical events can be identified.

Two questions are basic to all reporting. First, has expected progress been made toward the intended results? Second, have the resources been adequate and their use kept within limits? Effective delegation means you not only get the right result, you get it efficiently, with the least amount of resources necessary.

Subordinates' Commitment

Understanding and commitment are vital. Subordinates should not be expected to commit to an assignment they don't understand, don't have the skill to accomplish or don't have the authority to assure success. The manager must know the specific results desired and communicate them effectively. A subordinate's commitment will also depend upon the trust and confidence the manager has created by delegating successfully.

What to Do and What to Delegate

Deciding what to do and what to delegate are continual decisions; the more rapid the change in your responsibilities the more frequent the decision. Managers who periodically analyze how time is spent and what results are achieved, usually make better decisions.

The following short quiz will help determine if you need to analyze your job. Mark all statements which best describe your situation.

- ☐ I'm not always sure what results are expected of me.
- ☐ I'm not sure how I spend my time.
- ☐ My boss and I don't agree on the importance of many things.
- ☐ My boss does not actually know how I spend my time.
- ☐ I listen to my boss, then do it my way.
- ☐ I'm not always sure what results to expect from subordinates.
- ☐ I'm not sure what my subordinates actually do with their time.
- ☐ My job description is out of date—it doesn't relate to what I do.
- ☐ Discussions about expected results with my boss or subordinates usually end in frustration.
- ☐ Things often seem out of control.

The more statements marked, the greater the need to analyze how time is spent. What can be done? First, don't wait on someone else to initiate improvements. Second, believe that you can make a difference; commit yourself to do so. Third, follow the plan described below and benefit from the results.

Start with your job. Keep daily time logs to find out how you spend your time. Consider the results generated from your activities. After collecting this information for 5-10 working days, prepare a summary of your findings. It should be organized to provide information about the specific results you are achieving. Identify major and minor functions and activities in which you are involved to achieve these results. Determine the percentage of work time spent on each function or activity.

Before deciding what to do and what to delegate, clarify any uncertainties you have about the scope of your responsibilities. Make an appointment with your boss to discuss your desire to make a positive contribution. Discuss any concerns about your work and describe the results of your job analysis. Ask for clarification and recommendations. This initiates a process that will lead to additional discussions and should ultimately clarify your job responsibilities.

Have a meeting with your subordinates. Share your work analysis with them. Discuss the benefits gained from talking with your boss. Let them know how it's helping you focus on the most important things and how it will help you delegate more effectively.

Delegation Profile

The Delegation Profile will aid in your job analysis. The more accurate the information used in completing it, the greater the benefit. Use information gained from your time logs and discussions with your boss and subordinates.

my delegation profile

Things I Have Already Delegated	Things I Could Delegate	Things I Am Uncertain About Delegating	Things I Cannot Delegate
Identify and Solve problems (see p. 19) data collection tabulate data	data analysis decisions for minor problems implementation schedules	decisions on bigger prob. implementation schedules that require coordination with other departments	reporting to superior accountability for solutions

In the first column, write all the functions and activities subordinates are now performing. In the second column, write those functions and activities you're performing that could be delegated. The third column is for listing activities you have questions about. You may not be sure your boss would want you to delegate the work to a subordinate, or maybe you're not sure your subordinates have the time to do the work. In the fourth column, write those functions and activities that must be done by you; these cannot be delegated.

Analyze your Delegation Profile. How do you like the balance of the workload between your subordinates and yourself? They're doing the things in the first column; you're doing everything in the last three. Is the workload balanced, or do you see why you're working excessive hours, never seem to get everything done and jump from one task to another?

Determine which subordinate can best handle the items in column two, and then delegate them. Seek answers for all questions associated with items in column three. Once you have the answers, you're ready to move the item to column one, if delegating it, or to column four if continuing to do it yourself. Your objective should be to clear columns two and three. Be careful; don't overload any of your subordinates. To balance the workload, you may need to do some training and development.

How often should a Delegation Profile be completed? Anytime you feel uncomfortable about the balance of work. The more susceptible your job is to change, the more frequently the profile will be beneficial.

Matching Responsibility and Authority

Managers must give considerable attention to developing the abilities and experiences of subordinates. Both are determinants of present performance and create opportunities for further development.

What levels of authority (1-6) do you tend to delegate most often on tasks having different levels of importance? Work up a chart for each of your subordinates. For each item delegated to your subordinate, identify the level of authority delegated and the importance of each task. Discuss the chart with your subordinate. They may perceive a different level than you intended. Analyze the charts to help spot areas where you can improve your delegation efforts. Do you tend to delegate more to the people you trust most? Is the pattern of authority levels due to subordinate's tested and proven capabilities, your perception of their capabilities, or "hit and miss" delegation? Why is the subordinate working at designated authority levels, and are you comfortable with the subordinate at these levels? Is there too much or too little authority delegated on some functions? What additional functions and activities could the subordinate assume immediately? Can the subordinate be trained to handle functions and activities of greater importance or authority? Exactly how will you know when subordinates are ready for greater things?

RESPONSIBILITY-AUTHORITY CHART

(see following page)

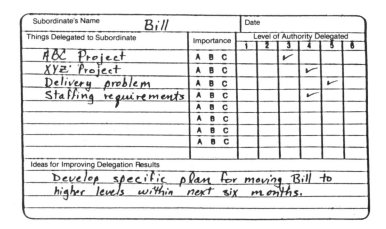

Subordinate's Name	Bill		Date						
Things Delegated to Subordinate		Importance	Level of Authority Delegated						
			1	2	3	4	5	6	
ABC Project	A B C				✓				
XYZ Project	A B C					✓			
Delivery problem	A B C						✓		
Staffing requirements	A B C					✓			
	A B C								
	A B C								
	A B C								
	A B C								

Ideas for Improving Delegation Results

Develop specific plan for moving Bill to higher levels within next six months.

Keep Responsibility-Authority charts up-to-date. When assigning new work or balancing workloads, you'll be in a stronger position to make rational decisions. You can also use these charts to discuss future opportunities for personal development with each subordinate. Both of you will be more aware of present strengths, future opportunities and how to gain the best of each.

Here's another exercise that might lead to better results. Make a list of the major responsibilities for each subordinate. For each area of responsibility, define outputs or hoped-for results. Then, ask the subordinate independently to do the same things for the job as he or she sees it: "What are your major areas of responsibility, and in each area of reponsibility what results or outputs do you think the boss expects?" Then compare your list and the subordinate's list. Discuss differences calmly and seek ways to improve.

Delegation Assignment Sheet

The Delegation Assignment Sheet is a powerful tool in preparing an assignment. It encourages a systematic approach to delegation.

delegation assignment sheet

Describe responsibility in terms of results to be achieved:
Purchase new typewriter within 90 days

Level of Authority						Level of Importance		
1	2	3	4	5	6	A	B	C

Authority-Parameters	Controls—What and When:
1. *$2000 limit*	1. *Monthly progress reviews*
2. *Tan or blue color*	2. *Review comparison features and suppliers*
3. *Variable spacing*	3. *Review contract before signing*
4. *Good servicing*	4.
5. *Try before deciding*	5.
6.	6.
7.	7.
8.	8.
9.	9.
10.	10.

Write down the specific results you want the subordinate to achieve. Read it. Have you been clear and concise? Will the subordinate understand it the same way you understand it? You may need to write the statement of responsibility more than once to remove troublesome ambiguity.

Think about authority for the assignment. Choose a level. In making this decision, consider the level of importance of the job (A, B, or C) and the person(s) to be assigned the work. If one of several subordinates might be given the assignment, consider a range between 1-6 which you are willing to delegate. For example, you might bracket 3 to 5. You are simply indicating you do not wish to delegate below level 3 or above level 5. The specific level can be decided as you complete the planning process and select the subordinate.

What resources and operations must the subordinate have authority over to get the results expected? What are the limits or boundaries within which the subordinate must function? Will there be a budget; what is the limit; within the limit is there room for the subordinate to use discretion? What materials, equipment and human resources are needed? To what extent may the subordinate determine the nature of the final results? How long will the subordinate have the authority to work on the assignment; is there a target date; is it flexible?

What information or feedback is necessary to hold your subordinate accountable? Your controls should be neither too tight nor too loose. Are there milestones and/or critical events in obtaining the desired results and in using resources that need your attention? Do you want oral reports or written reports with tables, charts or graphs? How frequently do you want them?

Start early. Write out the assignment, and think about it for awhile. Make necessary changes. Remember, this analysis and planning activity is to help you become a more effective delegator. As you gain experience, you're more likely to get it right the first time. You'll automatically ask the right questions and do things better.

Making the Assignment

After planning an assignment, you're ready to share it. If well prepared, you'll be comfortable, and so will your subordinate.

Relate the assignment to longer range objectives. You may wish to discuss your reasons for selecting the subordinate, and how the work can relate to the subordinate's personal achievement and development.

An outline for both you and the subordinate is advisable for highly critical and complex assignments. Major, long term assignments and projects may require considerable documentation. Be methodical, but don't overload the subordinate with information and create confusion.

Invite questions. Ask the subordinate for opinions. Don't act as if any questions or ideas are trite. What appears to be a poorly conceived question or idea may result from confusion, or even anxiety. Get to the root of the uncertainty so that you can resolve it.

If there's a difference of opinion and you believe you're in a better position to understand and decide, stick to your decision. Help subordinates feel comfortable expressing their ideas, even when they differ from yours. Respect their opinions, and thank them for being candid. You may be surprised how much openness and trust you can generate when subordinates, and their ideas, are treated with respect.

Summary of Guidelines for Better Delegation

1. Analyse Your Job
   a. What are your objectives? What results are expected of you?
   b. What can you actually do? Where is your time spent?
   c. Can anyone else do it for you?
   d. Can anyone be trained to do it?
   e. Discuss job analysis with your superiors to obtain ideas and agreement.

2. Decide What to Delegate
   a. What decisions do you make most often?
   b. Is your staff better qualified in some areas?
   c. Are these areas you dislike? But, remember to delegate both the good and the bad.
   d. In which areas do subordinates need development?
   e. What things would add variety to subordinates' jobs?

3. Plan the Delegation
   a. Strive for "whole job" unity.
   b. Review all essential details and decisions.
   c. Clarify appropriate limits of authority. Try to

make authority equal to responsibility.

d. Establish performance standards.

e. Determine appropriate feedback controls, including what information is needed, how often, and in what form.

f. Provide for training, coaching, or back-up people.

g. Remember, if you can't control it, don't delegate it.

4. Select the Right Person

a. Consider subordinate's interests and abilities.

b. What degrees of challenges can they handle?

c. Which person needs it most?

d. What training or coaching will be involved?

e. Try to balance and rotate tasks.

5. Make the Delegation

a. Clarify the results intended and the priorities involved.

b. Clarify level of authority and other operating limits.

c. Clarify the importance of the job.

d. Take time to communicate effectively. Encourage questions.

e. Clarify feedback and reporting requirements.

6. Follow-Up

a. Insist on results, but not perfection.

b. Insist on timely performance and reports

c. Act promptly and appropriately.

d. Encourage independence.

e. Learn to live with differences.

f. Don't short-circuit or take assignments back.

g. Reward good performance.

Receiving Assignments

Most managers are also subordinates. Long before we were managers, we started learning how to receive assignments. Usually, we followed a "hit or miss" approach. Sometimes we don't learn how to receive an assignment until we learn how to make one. They key to success lies in the basic elements of delegation and in the Delegation Assignment Sheet.

Many managers have walked away from the boss's office with two things, a new assignment and an uncomfortable feeling. What does the boss really want me to accomplish? Do I have what is necessary to get the job done? How and when am I supposed to let the boss know how things are going?

To solve this problem, make sure the desired results are specified. Seek clarification of authority and limits. Confirm feedback and control procedures. How do you get this information? Ask the boss the questions which enable you to fill in the Delegation Assignment Sheet. Your boss may not understand delegation the way you do. It's up to you to resolve uncertainties.

Don't be surprised if the boss is a little startled by your new approach. Be tactful to avoid being offensive or threatening. It may take several assignments before the boss can anticipate your questions. In time your boss will realize you have had a positive impact on his/her delegating effectively. Meanwhile both of you will be enjoying greater success.

Togetherness

Management is not a "do-it-yourself" job. It takes all of us, working together, to produce top results. Effective delegation will help everyone achieve more and feel better, too. Why not start today, right now, to improve the way you delegate? You'll be glad you did.

Common Reasons for Delegation Failure

1. Lack of agreement on specifics of delegation
2. Lack of performance standards and guidelines
3. Lack of proper training
4. Poor understanding of performance objectives
5. Lack of confidence in subordinate's capabilities
6. Lack of confidence in self, unwilling to take risks
7. Fear that subordinate will perform better
8. Fear of punitive action by superiors
9. Interference by superior's superior
10. Interference by superior
11. Failure to understand advantages of successful delegation
12. Superiors liking to do a particular job themselves
13. Belief that you can do it faster yourself
14. Desire for perfection, belief that you can do it better yourself
15. Belief that things are going well enough as they are
16. Ambiguous understanding of own job responsibilities
17. Failure to establish adequate follow-up procedures
18. Fear of criticism
19. Unwillingness to allow mistakes
20. Desire to be "liked" by subordinates.

Woody Young

10893 San Paco Circle
Fountain Valley, California 92708
(714) 962-8611

Woody Young

Woody Young is a graduate of the Ohio State University where he majored in business administration and ornamental horticulture. He is currently the owner of the California Clock Company which is known the world over for its Kit-Cat Klocks. Having acquired and sold companies successfully in a variety of industries as well as starting some new business ventures, Mr. Young has had extensive experience in the operation of small businesses. He has worked for the smallest of companies to the largest of corporations, IBM, and his experiences run the spectrum from working as a truck driver to an investment banker, account executive, regional manager and now owner of his own companies.

Mr. Young resides in California with his wife, Beth, and two daughters. He is a ruling elder in the church he attends.

A member of the National Speakers Association, Woody Young is known as a motivator who speaks and consults on all aspects of business. He has been recognized and awarded these outstanding honors: Jaycees (JCI Senatorship), Toastmasters (DTM), California Association of Nurserymen (O.C. Nurseryman of the Year), and the City of Fountain Valley Distinguished Service Award presented by the Jaycees.

As evidenced by his activities, Mr. Young enjoys helping and inspiring others not only by word, but also by deed.

Managing Life With A Vision
by Woody Young

"If it is to be, it is up to me."
—Mary Crowley
President, Home Interiors

PART A: EXPERIMENT WITH LIFE

How is life like a wheelbarrow? Both stand still unless someone takes the initiative and gives a push!

What will you do with your life? Will you let it sit, or will you be willing to experiment, to venture out of the pattern you are in, to give it a push? Don't be so afraid something will happen that you can't control, that you end up keeping yourself from enjoying life. Venture out and see how you can expand your horizons. See how you can make things happen!

Someone has said that the view from the valley is limited. But as you proceed up the hill you get a larger and larger view. Finally, when you get to the top, you find that your view is limitless.

It is exactly the same with you. When you are at the bottom of the valley you have a sharply limited view of what life can offer you. What you must do is try, step by step, to climb up that hill. You will be amazed at the beautiful horizons that will come into view as you attain the plateaus in life. As you proceed higher and higher up the hill, many views will open up to you that you never imagined possible. But first you must be willing to experiment.

Start Small

Your first few experiments should be minor. In your mind, envision a goal that you would like to obtain. But be careful. Don't be like a bald friend of mine who, when asked if any of his boyhood hopes had been realized, replied, "Yes, one. When my mother used to comb my hair I would wish I didn't have any!"

Make your goal a positive one. Whatever it is, try to experiment by going a little bit farther and doing a little bit more than you otherwise would.

Are you beginning to see what I mean when I advise that you experiment with your life? When you get part way up that hill, you'll start to see so many different avenues you never knew existed! A brand-new dimension of the world will open up to you. You'll become aware of so many new ideas, that you'll get a whole new feeling of how great it is to be alive.

But before you can reach those vistas, you have to start experimenting. When you're in the valley it looks limited and limiting, but remember, you do not yet see what can be. You can't imagine the potential that lies ahead. Until you start your climb up that hill, you cannot begin to envision that better life.

Don't Be Afraid

Believe in yourself! Imagine better things! Go for it! Expand your life and live it! If you're not willing to experience anything new, you can never accomplish anything new. You will end up simply reliving the same experiences over and over, day after day. You may ask, "What's so bad about that?" But I ask you, how can you be sure that there are not many other, much better experiences that you are missing?

Had our forbears been afraid to expand their horizons, had they been willing to settle for things the way they were, our society would not be what it is today. To illustrate this point, let's consider something as commonplace and mundane as a refrigerator. Can you imagine what it would be like to try to store food without that modern-day convenience we take so much for granted? Someone had to experiment and expand his horizons or there would be no refrigeration today. We are the ones who enjoy the fruits of the labors of the inventors and experimentors who preceeded us.

You can think of many things that are just as simple as the everyday refrigerator, and yet make our way of life what it is today. We have gas and electric heating systems to keep us comfortable You need only take a long hike into the wilderness to see what it would be like to live with no shelter, with only a blanket and a fire to keep you warm.

But that isn't the way we live, is it? We relax in our heated and cooled homes without so much as a second thought. Yet someone had to experiment—to actively use his own mind and imagination—to come up with such everyday things that have become ingrained into our lives.

Make Your Life Count

It's not only for yourself that you must be willing to experiment; it is also for the generations that will follow. Will you simply come, live your life, and then depart, leaving the world no better off than you found it? Will anybody in the future benefit because of something you have created or done? Whether it's a work of art, a written thought, a vocal piece, a musical score, or perhaps something no one has yet imagined, you should leave some legacy for future generations.

I was traveling through Hannibal, Missouri, where the great humorist, Mark Twain, spent his childhood days. "Did you know Mark Twain?" I asked a white-bearded proprietor of a roadside stand. "Sure I knew him," was his prompt and indignant reply. "And I know just as many stories as he did, too. Only difference is, he writ 'em down!"

This is my challenge to you: find a missing link that will help make life better. Whatever it might be, reach out for that unique experience, extend your perception and, experiment with life. Try something different. Something new. Something creative. Climb to the top of that hill. Seek out those vistas you have been missing all these years! Sense how fresh the air feels as you view your new horizons.

I'll promise you this: as you climb higher, each step will get easier. This is because your excitement level will also be climbing, urging you on to the top to see the glorious visions that you are yet to behold. Remember, the valley is the pit. It's the top where the visions are. So start your climb. Experiment and enjoy life! Never let it be said of you:

> *He was a very cautious man,*
> *Who never romped or played.*
> *He never smoked, he never drank,*
> *Nor even kissed a maid.*
> *And when he up and passed away*
> *Insurance was denied.*
> *For since he hadn't ever lived,*
> *They claimed he never died.*

PART B: PRACTICE THE ART OF LIVING

The trouble with life is that you're halfway through it before you realize it's one of those do-it-yourself deals. I talked earlier about envisioning your goals. Learning and practicing the art of living is the next step.

You might say, "I already know how to live. I breathe, I eat, I sleep, I bathe my body, I go to bed at night and I get up in the morning. I live just like everyone else does." But I ask, do you really? Stop and think about it. Have you actually been receiving all the joys life affords? Have you honestly envisioned what life could be for you? Have you learned how you can create happiness for yourself?

What is it that would make you happy? Stop and look back at some of the things you have done in the past that have brought you joy. When I think of joy, I remember Christmas morning and the pleasure I received from watching my children open their Christmas presents. They were wildly excited! They rushed up to me and gave me the biggest hug and kiss imaginable. Now that's what I call pleasure! That's joy! That's the art of living!

Position Yourself for Happiness

If it's hard for you to enjoy happiness, maybe it's because you can't envision what happiness is. Maybe you haven't positioned yourself in such a manner that you are able to be happy and enjoy life. The key to the art of living is knowing how to maneuver your own body and mind in such a way as to allow you to be receptive to the joys of living. Unless you place yourself into that type of situation, you can't possibly enjoy life to its fullest.

You may ask, "How do I place myself in such a position?" The answer is that you use all the principles of goal setting. You envision what makes you happy. You start to put your mind to work, thinking of what you can do to ensure your own happiness. You write down your goals. Then you analyze what might keep you from reaching those goals.

Let's look at a specific example of how this works. You may decide that being around your family, sharing their joys, is what would make you happy. Now think of ways to spend more time with your family. Write your ideas down. Finally, try to pinpoint those things that would prevent you from reaching your goal. Are you out of town too much? Are you too busy with other people?

You can be a success in all the *things* in life, but are you allowing other people to prescribe the rules and regulations for success—like holding a certain position with your firm, having the right kind of car, living in the right neighborhood or dressing in a certain way? Is that really your conception of success? Don't allow other people to tell you how you are going to be successful. The one who must decide what success is for you is *you.*

But again, you must be in the right position to find that happiness. If you want to enjoy your children, you have to spend time with them. If you want to enjoy your marriage, you must be willing to spend time with your mate—time to listen, time to share, time to be alone together.

No Excuses!

You must not indulge yourself to make excuses for failing to find the time to be happy. I could write a whole book on excuses for not enjoying life, but I don't think it would tell you anything new or different. You have probably heard them all before.

A farmer once asked his neighbor to let him borrow a rope. "Sorry," said the neighbor. "I'm using my rope to tie up the milk."

"Tie up the milk!" the man exclaimed. "Rope can't tie up milk!"

"I know," replied the neighbor, "but when a man doesn't want to do something, one excuse is as good as another!"

The truth is that at best all excuses are frivolous. You have to forget the excuses and replace them with goals for a happy situation. Then position yourself in that situation.

Does happiness for you mean being with your kids when they win a medal in a swimming contest? If so, you must first be willing to go to the swimming pool to watch the race!

Do It Now!

My daughter once asked me to pick a flower for her. That was simple enough. But when she said, "Now put it back," I experienced a baffling feeling of helplessness I had never known before. How could I explain that such a thing cannot be done? How could I make my child understand that some things that, once broken, can never be mended or replaced?

The same is true for today's chances for happiness. You must be willing to go and give of your time if you ever want to have that as a part of your living experience. But it is *you* who must do it. And the time to do it is *now!*

A little boy was brought before a magistrate and

charged with throwing stones at passing railway trains. "What have you to say for yourself?" asked the stern-faced judge.

"I didn't throw no stones, Sir." said the boy. "I was only *going* to."

"Only going to!" echoed the magistrate. "Well, the intent was there, and in the eyes of the law the intent is as good as the deed. As a deterrent I shall fine you $5."

The father took the youngster by the hand and proceeded to leave the courtroom, but the judge called him back and reminded him that he had failed to pay the fine. "That's quite so," replied the parent. "I should have paid it and I meant to do so. But since the intent is just as good as the deed in the eyes of the law, you're paid."

In life, intent is not as worthy as the deed. So go out and research what you really want. Start thinking about what you would like to happen, and things will start happening.

Maybe happiness to you means owning a new car. If you are driving around in an old car and you never go out and look at the new cars, you will never be able to put yourself in a position to get the car you want. When the opportunity comes to get the car of your dreams, you won't even know about it. If you want that new car, and if you think it is going to make you happy, go out and look at it. Visualize yourself in it. Price it. You might not be able to get a brand-new Porsche, but you might be able to find an excellent resale for a fraction of the cost of a new one.

You can get what you want by placing yourself in the proper situation to obtain it. That's practicing the art of living!

Let me summarize this principle by giving you an example from my own personal experience. I always wanted to go to England. Some of my ancestors were English, and I had a yearning desire to visit that country. I wanted to see Big Ben, the River Thames, Oxford, and Shakespeare's home. I wanted to see what the English countryside was really like, with its thatched-roof cottages. So what did I do? I positioned myself in such a way that I could find the opportunity to go to England.

Well, I did make the trip and my two weeks in England were some of the happiest of my entire life. I had thought about that trip for years. I had dreamed about it. But it was a long time before I took the opportunity to position myself in a place where I could finally find the way to say, "I'm going to go!" and to start placing myself in a situation to make it happen. But once I did I found the funds to go, the time to go, and the strength to make it happen. By correctly positioning myself I was able to savor the art of living.

PART C: FAITH CAN RESOLVE BIG PROBLEMS

Have you ever really wanted to venture into a new project but you just didn't have enough faith in yourself to really get it going? When that happens, when you need that little extra something to get you to the point where you can have the faith you need, look back at some of your successes. Review some of the things in your life, however small and insignificant they may seem, that you were able to accomplish. Look back at those successes and see what formula you used to get them done.

Reviewing your successes will help you bolster your faith by putting your abilities into the proper perspective. In that very critical moment in which you need something to hold on to, to help and encourage you, you can apply those past victories to this new situation in your life.

We take some of the simplest things in life for granted. They require total faith and we give it unquestioningly. Such everyday activites as eating and driving a car are examples of this. Of course, many other examples exist that you can pull out of your own life, times when you have exercised faith and have experienced success. By looking at and reviewing those experiences you will see for yourself that you can apply the positive feedback you received on those prior occasions and use it to ensure success for the new project you're considering.

When you look back at those successes from your past, don't make the mistake of limiting them to big, giant ones. Look at the small ones and remember how you succeeded in them, too. You see, no success can really be called small or unimportant. Every single detail, when put in the proper perspective is equally important.

Have you ever had the opportunity to take a time-management course? If so, you know that the number-one element in such courses is that you learn to prioritize everything that you want to do. Example. In category A you list your top-priority items, in B the things that rank second in importance, in C the third most-important things, etc. If you have a long enough list you may even have items in the G and H categories.

To see how this principle works, let's examine an

illustration. Suppose your best suit needs to be cleaned. You don't really need to have it done for another month, however, because you won't be having an occasion to wear it until then. So taking your suit to the cleaners today is definitely not in the A category. In fact, with the many things you have going on today, it ends up at the very bottom of the list, perhaps in the G category. You do need to get it done, but it's not a top-priority item.

A week passes and you still have not found time to take your suit to the cleaners. And the job is still in the same low-priority spot. Still another week goes by and the job hasn't been done. You have only two weeks left, but since it takes only a day or two to get a suit cleaned, you don't think it's necessary to move it up on your list.

Another week, and now you have only one week left. You are still as busy as ever and you still have many things to do so you continue to postpone this little job. When you are six days from needing that clean suit, with only four days' leeway, you decide to move it up from the G to the D cateogry. Another day goes by and you move it up to the B category. It is definitely gaining priority!

When still another day goes by, you realize that you have got to take your suit in today or tomorrow or you won't get it back in time. It's still a simple little task, but now it's an A category item.

That's the way time management works. You have to put all of your tasks, whether large or small, into proper perspective. A minuscule problem can become a big one!

Where Does Faith Come In?

This same principle holds true when you apply faith to the different problems you are certain to face throughout life. Although one problem may seem small and another one gigantic, when it comes to faith you have to treat them all as though they are equal. For if you can have faith in yourself in one situation, there is no other situation in which you cannot apply that very same faith. It's entirely up to you!

With total faith in yourself at all times and in all situations, you will be amazed at the problems you will be able to handle. For, when broken down into small pieces, no situation will be too big for your abilities.

A famous minister has a saying he repeats over and over: "Inch by inch anything's a cinch. But by the yard, it's hard." That is just how it is with your big problems. Put them into proper perspective. Look at how you can break them down into bite-size pieces. Have faith that each one of them, as you accomplish it, will give you the overall results you want. Bolster your faith and give yourself the support you need by looking at what you accomplished by dealing with your past problems.

With Faith and Common Sense
There Is Always an Answer!

That minister's statement is undeniable. If you have faith in something, you tell your subconscious mind that you are going to do it. Since your subconscious mind knows only what you tell it, it takes your belief as an absolute and then proceeds to find a way to accomplish it.

If you decide to drive across town, for instance, you

tell your subconscious mind where you want to go. You envision the specific place in your mind. Your subconscious mind creates in your brain the necessary plan for action, either by telling you to get out the map to see how to get where you're going or by drawing that knowledge out of your own experiences. It is your subconscious mind that instructs your mind and body to do the things necessary to get the job done. That's why with faith there is always an answer. You're pulling from more than just what you see and what you're thinking at the present time.

At times, however, you must recognize that the thing you are considering is not something in which you should be placing your faith in the first place. How can you tell what is and what is not worthy of your faith? Example. I'm driving from Los Angeles to San Francisco. I would like to take the coastal route that goes along Highway 101 part of the way, then just north of San Luis Obispo switches over to Highway 1. I especially like this route because it offers such a spectacular view of the Pacific Ocean. It goes through Monterey and Carmel, then on up to San Francisco.

I start off on my trip. Everything goes well until I get to San Luis Obispo where I see a sign noting that Highway 1 is closed 50 miles ahead. I can choose to continue on in my planned route, but if I do and if the sign is correct, I will end up going 50 miles up to a dead end where I will have to turn around and backtrack that 50 miles to San Luis Obispo. Even though I want to take the coastal route, discretion tells me that I should go to San Francisco along the inland route of 101. By doing so I will not only arrive at my destination, but I will make good time and I won't have to backtrack.

Sometimes you may encounter a problem in which the facts and your own common sense tell you that you should not do whatever it is that you are planning to do. Before you give full faith to your solution to that particular problem, pause, sit back, and analyze it a bit more. I certainly am not telling you to do foolish things thoroughly.

If I decide to take Highway 1, having been duly warned that it is closed and that I will just have to turn around and come back, I am not using good sense.

Whenever you decide to apply your faith to something, it must be something that has a reasonable chance of success. It has to be a good alternative to the situation you are encountering. Just as insisting on continuing to San Francisco via the closed coastal route does not make good sense, no matter how much faith I have in it, there may be times when you, too, will have to back off your original plans.

There is always an answer when you have good facts, and if there is a way to reach the goal, you will. But don't do foolish, ill-advised things simply for the purpose of proving that you can do them. Look at each of the things you want to do. If you can realistically envision yourself accomplishing it, then you can do it. Just be sure to be realistic and to use good common sense.

Common sense will get you farther in life than just about any other trait. Did you know that managers who have held their positions very long do not choose employees for their intelligence or enthusiasm? It's true.

Many times they will assign the tasks to the person who has repeatedly shown an ability to use good common sense and good judgement in every situation. To advance in your job and to get the recognition you desire, you must constantly demonstrate your ability to use common sense and good judgement in everything you do.

When faced with a problem situation, whether large or small, examine it carefully. If it looks right and if it can be accomplished, have full faith in yourself to carry it out. By using common sense you will not find yourself traveling a dead-end road just because you have determined to go that way. Approach the problem realistically, then go out and do it!

PART D: IMAGINE THE NEW YOU!

Picture in your mind a new you, positive, and in control at all times. Sound good? It is! And I'm going to tell you how to do it. Imagine yourself as you want to be. Whenever a negative thought enters your mind, whenever you are sure that you're going to make a mistake, when you look at your project and just *know* that it is going to fail, rid that negative thought from your mind! Immediately turn it around. Imagine how you—the *new you*—can handle that situation positively. Imagine yourself as the leader, in total control. When you do this, an amazing thing will happen. Suddenly you will find that the whole world looks new and different, bright, and exciting. And do you know who is making the difference? You are! You are doing it by imagining the new you being what you want to be.

This is a vitally important step, one that you must do again and again. Any time you get a negative thought, turn it around immediately and fill your mind with a positive thought. Remember, your subconscious does not know the difference between negative thoughts and positive thoughts. They are all fed into and recorded in your brain on an equal basis. To counter a minus you must put in a plus. Then if you go ahead and put in another plus, you will end up with two pluses to counteract that single minus. You will have tipped the scale on the positive side!

As an example of this principle, let's look at something that each of us faces every day. This is the matter of life's irritating little trivialities. Those small things that so annoy us. For instance, suppose you are being asked to do something you really do not want to do, something disagreeable to you or perhaps degrading. How can you turn such a situation around and make it a positive one? Well, let's analyze it. What is the person's motive in telling you to do that specific thing? Is it to denigrate you, to frustrate you, or make you angry? Probably not. Most likely it was simply that the person realized that the task needed to be done and you just happened to be nearby. That's why you were asked to do it.

Many years ago a general, a brilliant strategist, had successfully conquered nation after nation. He was so well loved that his ruler, the mighty Caesar himself, began to worry. If the general had many more victories, Caesar reasoned, he might end up posing a real threat to the ruler. So Caesar devised a plan to call the popular general home and disgrace him. Bringing him home to Rome, Caesar put him in charge of the Roman sanitation department. The brilliant general was demoted to garbage collector!

But the general was an astute positive thinker. Although he had no idea why he had been put in this degrading position, he realized that if he acted in a negative way he would end up causing more trouble for himself. On the other hand, if he acted in a positive way he could only improve his lot. So taking on the filthy, garbage-strewn, rat-infested city of Rome, the general set out to clean it up. As if it were a battlefield that he was going to conquer, he brilliantly set all of his strategies to work in an effort to make Rome the world's cleanest city.

Well, the general accomplished his task. And he did it with style. In the end the people who considered him one of the greatest generals of their time grew to have even more respect for him because he was able to conquer the garbage-strewn city of Rome. His fame grew, leaving Caesar in an even worse situation than before.

From that negative situation, the general created a positive situation simply by going out and doing the very best job he could do. He didn't argue or pout, he refused to be negative, he didn't disobey. Rather, he went out and proved that he was a better man than the one who assigned him the job.

That's exactly what you can do with any situation in which you find yourself. Even if you feel that a person is intentionally attempting to do you an injustice, you can make it work for you. Go out and do that job so well that it will make him look foolish. On the other hand, if the command wasn't given with such a motive in mind—and most are not—if you do an excellent job of it the person in charge is almost certain to look at you in a positive manner. And in the future, because of his new image of you, he is going to be careful what he asks you to do. He will see you as a person with whom he is interested in working, one who is worthy of more responsibility. You will find that he is assigning more and more important jobs to you, and he will be doing it because you have proved that you are a person who is always going to do the very best you can no matter what job you are given.

Begin right now—today—to experiment with life, to practice the art of living. Use faith to resolve those big problems. Begin to imagine yourself as the *new* you. Whenever you are given a negative situation, reverse it and turn it into two positives. Remember, no one can defeat you. You can be defeated only by yourself. With your new positive image, you will enjoy life as you never have enjoyed it before! You will be the winner!

OLD ENGLISH PRAYER

Work—
  It is the price of success.
Think—
  It is the source of power.
Play—
  It is the secret of perpetual youth.
Read, listen—
  They are the fountains of wisdom.
Be Friendly—
  It is the road to happiness.
Dream—
  It is hitching your wagon to a star.
Love and be loved—
  It is the privilege of the gods.
Look around—
  It is too short a day to be selfish.
Laugh—
  It is the music of the soul.

Philip R. Simenton
4424 San Jose #2
Montclair, California 91786
(714) 621-9875

Philip R. Simenton

Phil's approach to life management is founded upon time honored principles. Anyone can be told to drive their dreams, engineer their destination, and accelerate their results, but, how?

Phil's broad financial background lends itself to all facets of money and estate management.

Phil has taught accounting in the Community Colleges, and has produced and taught seminars in mortgage banking and real estate taxation. In addition, he was issued a Certified Public Accountant license, and has completed numerous postgraduate level courses in federal and state taxation. He is also a member of the National Speakers Association.

Phil received a Bachelor of Arts degree in Business Law, Insurance and Office Administration from Michigan State University, with dual disciplines in accounting and economics. Having served his country as an Infantry Officer, and after graduation from Officer Candidate School, he was heard to quote:

"A self-confident fool has no delight in under-standing, but only in revealing his personal opinions, and himself."

Phil speaks to thousands, including the top management teams of America's greatest corporations, associations, and governmental agencies. He states "I can do all things . . ."

You can too.

Accelerating Money
Simplified Money Management for the Non-Rich
by The Accelerator Phil Simenton

"I don't know about you, pal, but I rank money right up there with oxygen."
— ***Actress Ruth Gordon***

"The Lord delights in the prosperity of his servants."
— ***Psalm 35:27***

If you have too much money, and know what to do with it, do not read any further. But if you do not have enough, or you do not have the knowledge of money management techniques, read on. I will share with you how to keep more of what you earn in your own pocket, and how to make it work for you, instead of you working for it.

Unless you accept welfare, or are willing to work for an employer, or at your business, the only other source of wealth is your money working for you. If I were to tell you that you could have $10,000.00 per month (or whatever that number was for you) and that it would be tax free, and indexed for inflation, what would you do with your life?

You would probably do the same thing that I would do, and go out and enjoy each and every day without having to worry about money. Studies have shown that if people are concerned about their finances, this can become the most stressful situation in their lives. It affects their business, it affects their job performance, and, it affects their relationships. Learning how to properly manage money helps avoid this burden, and if we want to be a winner with our money, we must understand the principle of acceleration.

When I took my drivers education class in Michigan at the tender age of fifteen, I discovered three things about a car. The brake slowed it down, the gear shift was for forward or reverse, and the accelerator made it go faster. I discovered the best way to move ahead was to move the gear shift into forward and to press the accelerator. The car was an old 1949 Dodge, but it went. After the unfortunate incident with the tree in my parents' front yard, I had to learn another lesson. I had to not only know where I was going, but the directions on how to get there. The "verbalize" and "visualize" of goal setting were then apparent to me, (especially when Dad showed up), but still unfocused were the "how-to's." I can press the accelerator, but what are the directions to get me from where I am now, to where I am going?

Goal setting was never easy for me. Being a very shy child in grade school, I had trouble focusing on what I wanted in life. My inferiority complex would repeat the subconscious message that I was not worthy to receive what my self-confident peers received. In fact, I started doing public speaking in high school just to overcome the shyness and lack of self-esteem. To my surprise, (and that of my ego's), I won several speaking contests. That began to reinforce what my parents were instilling in me, that I could be the best with the gifts that had been given me.

Being the oldest of four children, in a midwestern middle-class family, finances were tight. When it came time to go to college, even my parents couldn't help much beyond the academic scholarship I had won, so it was necessary to work part-time during college. I bagged groceries to get to my goal and sold housewares and men's clothing to complete college, in that my next goal was law school. Hard work had paid off when I received my law school acceptance, and my fiancee, who later became my wife, looked forward with me to the challenges ahead.

But, "the best laid plans of mice and men oft go astray." Shortly after graduation I received a draft notice. After three years as an infantry officer, and a newborn son to support, my goal of law school changed to that of finding a job. So goals do change and, in fact, they should change as we change and grow. If there is a simple solution to life's problems, I certainly don't know what it is. But I do know that if we persist, this certainly does help. Hang on. God did not create you and me to see us perish as losers in life, in either our daily activities or our finances.

Accelerating our money actually begins between our ears. Our minds are the architect's drawing board for tomorrow's results. What we put in there becomes what will happen to our winning or losing our future financial security. So where do we begin?

In two words—MANAGING MONEY.

I.   **GOALS—TO PRESS DOWN, PRESS HARDER?**
   A.   Set a specific goal, and write it down. Don't say "I need more money." Make the goal as specific as, "$500.00 per month."
   B.   Determine the amount of time needed to accomplish this financial objective. Is it two weeks or four years?
   C.   Visualize and verbalize the steps as already accomplished. (I visualized that tree in my parents' front yard *after* I pressed down the accelerator. Woe to my bottom and the 1949 Dodge.) Use your other senses—smell, feel, touch, and hear, along with your mouth.

II.   **BUDGETING—WILL I FEAST OR FAMINE?**
   "Budgeting is a distasteful and dirty word. How dare this piece of paper tell me how to spend my money? It will take the fun out of spending what I worked so hard to make. I refuse to have a budget control my life."

Rubbish. If the accelerator wants to be a winner at managing his finances, he starts with a budget. It will help you to save for what you want without the need for borrowing; it will show you where those hard earned dollars are currently going; and a budget will help in the preparation of your tax return. Most importantly, a budget eliminates family arguments. When we decide in advance where the money is to be spent, when the money is spent there is no argument.

A caveat, however, budgeting did not solve my in-law problems, nor is it a proven source of disease elimination.

III. CREDIT—DO I REALLY HAVE TO REPAY?

Credit, obviously, should be used wisely. I believe that everyone should have their own separate credit. The Equal Opportunity Credit Act of 1975 provided equality. This is not simply because you may be single some day, through a death, or a divorce, but it is part of being your own person, especially if you have income, hobbies, or interests of your own And, yes, you do have to repay.

IV. TAXES—DOES THE I.R.S. REALLY HAVE MY NUMBER?

Yes they do. The Internal Revenue Service is one of the most efficient and competent agencies of our government. They oversee most of collections and revenue for the United States, as well as endless adjacent functions. Consider them as a friend.

Current tax laws are designed to help us manage our money, and we have to know where and how to use the laws properly for our personal situations. The four tools that we can legally use to reduce our taxable income are as follows:

1. Convert the taxable income. Take the ordinary income that otherwise may be fully taxable to you, and convert to income taxed at a lower rate. An example would be, taking ordinary income and converting it into capital gain income. which is taxed at a lower rate. Do this by holding the appreciable asset over six months.

2. Defer the taxable income. If you don't have to pay the tax now, use the money that you might have paid in taxes, and invest it. Earn some return on the money. Then, pay the taxes at a later date, even after you are retired and may be in a lower tax bracket.

3. Eliminate the taxable income. While this is the best tax-saving maneuver, it is not always feasible. You might consider saving receipts on capital expenditures on your home to increase the basis, or the use of the once-in-a-lifetime exclusion on the gain of the sale of your personal residence.

4. Transfer the taxable income. When all else fails, and you can't convert the ordinary income into capital gain income, and you can't defer the taxable income, and you can't completely eliminate the taxable income, why not take that taxable income and transfer it to someone else who, hopefully, is in a lower tax bracket than you

are, and who can greatly reduce the tax. There are several tools to accomplish this goal.

Benjamin Franklin said: "Nothing is certain except death and taxes."

My only wish is that they would occur in that order.

V. ESTATE PLANNING—IF I DIE, AM I REALLY GONE?

The answer, generally, is no. You might be gone, as far as you are concerned, but chances are you left behind some smelly old socks. Who gets them?

More importantly, during your lifetime, you created wealth, children, a loving spouse, church affiliations, and good friends, In consideration of them, use a will. A will will pass your estate to whom you want it to go. Does the heirloom furniture go to your loved ones, or Aunt Matilda (twice removed), in Siberia?

Secondly, consider how you hold title to property. This can avoid probate, through the proper use of a will, a living trust, and proper wording of your title documents. You might even reduce the amount of insurance that you are carrying by wise estate planning.

Consider the case of the old and feeble man who called his errant son to his bedside.

"I know that we have fought all these years, but I have decided to make you the beneficiary of my will. I leave you everything—stocks, real estate, and cash."

The son, with tears welling up in his eyes, said, "Dad, I am not worthy to be the beneficiary of your will. We have fought all these years. Is there anything that I can do for you?"

The father replied in a very feeble voice, "Yes, son. Take your foot off of my oxygen hose."

To make a very old joke short, the time to make your will, and to do your estate planning, is right now.

VI. INSURANCE PLANNING — I'D RATHER BUY A MERCEDES.

Life, health, accident, disability; home, car, boat, jewelry; owners, renters, lessors, buyers; Betty Grable's legs. The insurance list is almost endless. Where do we turn?

In a word—the experts. With the advent of new twists and advances in this field, coupled, in some cases, with lower costs, it does pay to shop the market. Your next-door neighbor can discuss this with you. I found that mine referred me to someone I trusted. No joke this time.

VII. INVESTMENT PLANNING—WHAT'S IN IT FOR ME?

The answer? Everything, or nothing, depending upon two things. Are you willing to do investment planning all by yourself, or are you willing to use experts to enhance your own judgement? Of course, there is a third choice. And that is procrastination, in which case everyone loses, and be sure to include yourself.

Investments cover a wide array, ranging from ultra-safe Treasury Bills to risky strategic metals, and not necessarily in that order. A married couple I spoke with shared with me that they were ages 72 and 70, respectively, and he invested in race horses. His wife later found out that he was playing the ponies, and was telling her that he invested in race horses! Such is life.

If there are hundreds of different investment opportunities offered in the marketplace, how does the accelerator find them? When do you press your foot down, and on what?

The key to understanding investments is timing. There is no season for all investments, but there is an investment for each season. Learn to understand each phase of the economic cycle, so that you can know when to buy, and even more importantly, when to sell.

The next key to understanding investments and money management, is to know what to look for in the product being offered. The following four criteria should help.

1. Safety
In the future, will I use it, or lose it?
2. Inflation Hedge
In the future, will I win, with the government?
3. Growth Beyond Inflation
In the future, will I win over the government?
4. Tax Shelter
In the future, can the government help me?

There are basically two categories of investments. The first category is called fixed dollar investments, and includes corporate bonds, municipal bonds, mortgages, commercial paper, savings accounts, and treasury bills, notes and bonds. These investments all pay a fixed dollar amount during the period held. These investments are "loaned" to the issuer of the debt.

The second category of investment is equity investments, where you own it instead of loan it. This category of ownership includes common and preferred stocks, mutual funds, real estate, limited partnerships, and hard assets. The hard assets, often called collectibles, include gold and precious metals, precious stones, art, antiques, old coins, stamps, Persian rugs, and so on. Generally speaking, owning the asset is preferable to loaning the asset, because of inflation and tax considerations.

The question is not whether you invest, but how you should invest to provide a financially secure future and to make inflation work for you instead of against you. Your overriding goal is to preserve and enhance your real wealth on a tax-favored basis.

Before doing anything with your investable dollars, there are three things for you to determine:

1. Your need for income.
2. Your level of risk.
3. Your tax status.

Begin by compiling personal financial statements, including a balance sheet showing your net worth, and budget. This was discussed earlier. Knowing your net worth and cash flow needs will help you answer to following questions, which will better define your investment needs and your goals.

1. Are your insurance needs covered? This includes not only life, but health, property, liability and disability insurance. Single people often reveal to me that they consider disability insurance the cornerstone of their financial plan, in that there may not be someone else to help them should they become disabled.

2. Do you have emergency savings? An adequate fund might be three to six months worth of living expenses in a liquid vehicle, such as a money market account.

3. Are your needs short term or long term? The time frame for buying a new car or taking a trip may be drastically different from saving for college tuition or your retirement.

4. Do you have a need for additional income now, or capital growth for the future? For most people, the need is for a combination of both.

5. Have you opened an Individual Retirement Account or a Keogh plan? These are excellent tax favored ways to provide for your future financial security. The following chart shows an example of the compounding effects of an I.R.A. earning twelve percent. *(See chart next page).*

6. How much time can you find to monitor your investments? Market fluctuations are often dramatic, and choosing a money management team may help you in this area.

7. What income tax bracket are you in? The higher

your bracket, the more critical tax sheltering becomes.

8. Do you have a large anticipated expense? A lot of people I have met save regularly for a vacation, but not for college expenses or retirement.

9. How much can you afford to invest each year? This is where a budget is critical.

10. What investment yield do you want? This must be tempered with your personal comfort zone with risk. Maybe you would sleep better with a money market fund as opposed to futures in pork bellies, even though the rewards may be higher.

COMPARISON: RATES OF RETURN

IRA EARNING 12%

CURRENT AGE	VALUE AT AGE 65	MONTHLY INCOME AT 65	EQUIVALENT INCOME TODAY
20	$3,042,435	$19,623	$615
30	$ 966,926	$ 6,236	$422
40	$ 298,668	$ 1,926	$281
50	$ 83,507	$ 539	$170
60	$ 14,230	$ 92	$ 63

The rapid growth in the number of investment vehicles in the market-place requires strategic planning. As a fifteen year old, learning to drive the car, I also learned to shift gears. If one doesn't work, try another. I experimented and, like you, had many varied results. Now we go into another step— selecting our money management team.

Selecting a money management team can be difficult, costly and time consuming, and you will need expertise from all four fields of money management. These are estate, investment, tax, and insurance. Select as your accelerator one who can draw others, and approaches money management from a team approach. (I can't think of any one person who is an expert in all four fields.) This accelerator is best recommended to you by a friend.

VIII. TO RELEASE, DO THIS

As a final note, ladies often call this "women's intuition," but men have it as well. It's called comfort. You have to feel comfortable with your advisor. There was only one person I ever met who continued to see their family doctor after they realized that they weren't comfortable with that doctor—Bozo the Clown!

If you don't feel comfortable, please change financial advisors. Do not allow your emotions to say "Yes" when your intellect says "No." These people are addressing you on the subject of your money.

Proper use of the tools of money management do work. If you want to go faster than you currently are going, start your engine, find the correct direction, put it in gear, and then do something---

ACCELERATE

If you want to walk on the water of financial freedom, you have to get out of the boat.

Education makes people easy to lead, but difficult to drive. Easy to govern, but impossible to enslave.
—Henry Baron Brougham, 1778

Robert W. Gaber

Robert Gaber Company
P.O. Box 577
2737   77th Avenue S.E. #118
Mercer Island, Washington 98040
(206) 232-7153

Robert W. Gaber

Dynamic, resourceful and entrepreneurial, Bob Gaber is truly a renaissance speaker. A seasoned executive with more than twenty years of experience in banking, finance and real estate, he has served at all levels of the business and corporate world from trainee to Chairman of the Board.

He is the holder of a California lifetime teaching credential, author, lecturer and consultant in business, real estate, investment and financial matters.

Bob is a graduate of California State Polytechnic University with additional work completed in banking and finance at the Stonier Graduate School of Banking, Rutgers University and in Investment Banking at New York University.

He has served as Chairman of the Personnel Board, City of Riverside, California and as Commissioner of Parks and Recreation, City of Belmont, California.

An outdoorsman, photographer and explorer of out of the way places, Bob makes his home on beautiful Mercer Island in the middle of Seattle, Washington's jewel-like Lake Washington.

The Winds of Change
by Robert W. Gaber

*"The winds and waves are always on
the side of the ablest navigators."*
—Edward Gibbon

In the continuing evolution of management, in a business world buffeted by the winds of change, skill and knowledge in business, the ability to forecast and plan accurately; the ability to develop objectives and coordinate the activities needed to reach them; and the ability to provide both authority and freedom for workers all combine to be the hallmark of the successful executive.

No longer can managers live in a shell, where their decisions can be made in isolation and accepted without complaint. Today's manager is accountable to a variety of groups and individuals—from superiors, to peers, to subordinates, to the community at large. The successful manager is able to obtain consent, cooperation and support from all—and still reach his business objectives.

The role of the manager in the business world is continually evolving, responding to both internal and external circumstances. Whereas the traditional view of the manager as an authoritarian autocrat was once dominant, more contemporary thinking places the manager, particularly the middle manager, as more of a "contingency" manager whose actions continually respond to new and different situations.

However, regardless of the exact title of a manager, or the job functions under that title, the manager has one central task, making decisions. The means through which decisions are reached and the effects of those decisions, continually vary; but the bottom line for the manager still must be to make that decision.

In the continuing pursuit of excellence in management, it is first necessary to analyze the successful manager, and to determine what characteristics of personality, or specific style of management, seem to correlate with successful management performance.

The Measure of Managerial Success

Perhaps the first question that must be answered is the definition of success. In some cases, for example, it could be argued that success is measured in terms of company performance. This, in turn, is usually expressed in terms of increased sales, and/or increased profitability.

On the other side of the equation, however, is the concern of some business analysts that human performance is as vital to the success of a business enterprise as is profits. Under this school of thought, success becomes more complex; it is tied to issues such as worker and management satisfaction with jobs, morale, and productivity.

Which of these two extremes is the better criteria? While each has its merits, the truly successful manager must at times employ tactics from both camps; in some cases playing the role of the conciliator and negotiator, in other cases becoming the supervisor and sole source of decision. Therefore, the criteria of success must also be as varied; if a definition of success is to be employed in this analysis, it should reflect the performance of a manager which meets or exceeds corporate goals for sales performance and/or profitability, while maintaining satisfactory levels of worker cohesion and morale.

It's Not Simple—It's Not Easy

Perhaps it would be helpful to first determine just how extensive the role of the manager is, and to review the varied activites performed under the job heading. A recent study, based on an intensive observation of managers in both formal and informal situations identifies both the characteristic of the work itself, and the roles played by any one manager.

Six characteristics of work performed by managers were identified:

- The manager often performs a great quantity of work at an unrelenting pace.
- Managerial activity is characterized by variety and brevity.
- Managers prefer issues that are current and specific.
- The manager sits between the organization and the network of contacts.
- Managers prefer verbal media.
- Despite the level of work, managers appear to control their own affairs.

These characteristics require managers to perform different roles at various times. In other words, managers must be flexible enough to move from one role to another as the situation requires.

Research shows that three basic categories of managerial roles exist; interpersonal, informational, and decisional. Each of these categories seems to be relatively clear-cut; the interpersonal and information categories providing the backdrop for that of decision making (the culmination of any executive activity).

Within each category, there are three types of behavior characteristics for each set. In the area of interpersonal activity, there are figure-head, liaison and leader behaviors; the first corresponds to the workers' need for a figure of authority and advice, and the other two refer to horizontal and vertical communications activities respectively.

In the area of the informational role, the typical managerial roles are nerve center (the focal point for information); disseminator (the distributor of information) and spokesperson (the public dissemination of information). The final category, that of decisional roles, involved the activities of entrepreneur, negotiator, and resource allocator.

Another Way to Look at It

Another means of looking at managerial effectiveness is to examine authoritarian and democratic behaviors. In looking at managerial behavior from this point of view, we can observe that managers will exhibit certain specific styles of management—ranging from the totally autocratic, with no worker input on a decision, to totally participatory, wherein the workers share the responsibility for the decision with the manager. Each style has its own values, and its own sense of applicability to specific situations—but most managers continue to fall toward the authoritarian side of the scale.

However, the effective practice of management requires the judicious application of a set of management skills rather than the utilization of abstract principles. In other words, successful managers live in a real-time, pragmatic world rather than an abstract, theoretical one. In a very real sense, the manager is continually devising his or her own rules as he or she goes. The sophisticated manager realizes that he or she never truly solves problems; they merely displace them with smaller, more manageable problems. Each decision generates shock waves which translate into new problems of communication, coordination, and of decision making itself. The manager's obvious technical skills and business knowledge (reflected in his or her position) must be complemented by interpersonal or leadership skills (again, reaching back to the need to balance the tendency of the manager to make decisions alone with the need to broaden and balance communications with peers and subordinates).

The job of the successful manager, however, goes far beyond that mere coordination. The coordinating skill requires an understanding of the integrative nature of the organization and of how the parts relate to the whole. Management is the encompassing term for a whole set of skills of which coordination is but one part.

Up, Down and Sideways

The complexities of modern business organization demand a certain set of stratified relationships—an organizational hierarchy to ensure that the management function is allowed to function properly. It is from that hierarchical framework that the performance of the typical manager can best be viewed. Following the pioneering work of Peter Drucker and others, it is now commonly assumed that all successful management springs from a definitive plan, a set of objectives which are clearly defined and expressed. They can be in terms of unit sales, or dollar volume, or profits, or virtually any yardstick. The point is, objectives exist for all levels of management and need not be restricted to corporate objectives only. Circumstances may dictate alteration of goals, or even abandonment where necessary; but the essential point is that management by objectives provides any manager with a clearer path of action than by blindly responding to changing circumstances and events. The more a manager understands the importance of objectives and their relationship to his assigned task, the better his decisions will be. He can then relate his decisions to the objectives, discarding those decisions that may serve a short-term purpose but fail to help meet longer-term objectives.

The fact that many managers of all levels fail to heed that advice can be seen in many areas—such as the automobile industry. While the consumer market for automobiles was changing from larger cars to smaller cars, American manufacturers avoided immediate retooling to produce smaller cars; this was reflected in continued profitability at the corporate level. By 1980, however, the influx of Japanese automobiles, coupled with the recession, significantly cut the American share of the market, hurting not only short-term but long-term profitability as well. While it is speculative as to the degree of success we would have enjoyed had we introduced small cars with a flurry before 1980, there is little doubt that the reluctance to sacrifice short-term profits for long-term gain hurt the American manufacturers.

Another major skill of successful managers is the ability to work within an organizational structure—to use the strength of that structure to accomplish certain goals. The purpose of organization is to allow the assignment of specific tasks in the best possible way to achieve the objectives already determined—in other words, the means to reach the end.

The second major problem that managers encounter—and conversely, a problem that the successful manager overcomes—is the inability to work within the organizational structure to accomplish goals. The organizational structure should not be considered something sacred, but rather a means of coordinating resources to meet the company and managerial objectives. The successful manager should be able to alter the organizational structure (within limits, of course) to accomplish objectives. This, in turn, implies a sense of organizational balance, for any formal restructuring of a business organization causes considerable upheaval in the lines of formal and informal communication, and can impact worker morale and effectiveness.

Planning Helps Stay the Course

A third major skill utilized by the successful manager is that of planning. Regardless of the behavior pattern involved, planning is a tool for the manager to use in completing tasks and realizing his or her objectives. Most managers recognize this need for planning but few are truly effective planners. First, most managers do not realize what is involved in the planning process; secondly, the day-to-day operating pressures make it difficult for the manager to find time to plan. Third, the manager's ego often leads him or her to believe that they can successfully solve all problems as they arise; this leads to an *ad hoc* mentality that defies organizational structure, and often robs the individual manager of any potential support and aid provided by subordinates, or through existing channels of information.

Fortunately, new tools have become available to the harried manager in his need for effective planning. Computers, once the domain of mathematicians and specialists, have become available on a mass level to the manager; they can permit extensive modeling and financial forecasting in a matter of minutes, reducing the time formerly needed to plan. While most managers have not yet availed themselves of this new generation of computers, the trend seems to point towards an increasing use of computers as a planning tool for not only the middle manager, but the lower level and top level managers as well. Just how effectively they are utilized will depend in great part upon the inclination and effort of the individual manager—but they do provide a means by which managers can more effectively plan and develop strategies and contingency programs to react to current and future events.

Communicate!

Still another major skill for the successful manager is that of control—not in the sense of policing the activities of subordinates, but becoming the focal point of operating information—the nerve center. While this can certainly be construed to include any disciplinary actions for deviance from procedure or failure to perform to expectations, the overall goal of the successful manager here must be to ensure that the specified tasks—the means by which objectives are reached—are being completed. The direction should be complimentary and conciliatory, as opposed to autocratic.

This requires a feedback loop from the manager to subordinate managers, and from the lower level managers to line employees themselves. It should be noted that more recent thinking on this element of communications indicates that including some form of feedback from the line employee upwards to the manager (as opposed to downwards) is an effective means of increasing the overall level of communication, and providing an outlet for employee feelings. Again, the successful manager will be able to control this process so that a complete picture of company performance is communicated to him—and that his response to that situation is also effectively communicated to all employees. As in all the other characteristics of successful management, however, the actual practice of communications control falls far short of the ideal; what often transpires is a strictly downward flow of information to the low level employees, with the upper manager receiving doctored versions of performance reports so that lower management performance will not be questioned. It is this short-sighted approach that causes eventual problems in the long run. Problems not confronted when they're small are inevitably overwhelming when they're bigger, and it's usually because the lower managers only tell the upper managers what they think they want to hear.

The Human Side of Leadership

The final area of major skills involved with successful leadership and management involves the act of leading itself. This can be further broken down into categories of human behavior skills, and evaluative and appraisal skills.

The former category is perhaps the most-discussed topic within the larger framework of management. It is in the field of human behavior and interpersonal relationships that the greatest change has come about in management theory and practice. As mentioned before, the traditional management style was fairly authoritarian in nature, wherein managers made decisions either alone or with peers, and then merely communicated them to subordinates for execution. The feelings of the workers, or the effect the decision might have on them, was of secondary consideration. What has changed is the degree to which employee behavior and attitudes have been incorporated into pre-planning and management strategies.

In the area of human management, between the polar extremes of total supervision and complete delegation of responsibility, lies the area in which most effective managers and supervisors lie. They elicit participation without relinquishing authority; they exercise command and yet simultaneously permit subordinates' self-determination. The overwhelming body of research indicates that managers as a whole master managerial skills to a much greater degree than leadership skills. This seems to follow from the fact that they are usually promoted to managerial posts on performance and technical knowledge, rather than on the basis of their interpersonal skills.

The change that time has brought to the topic of

interpersonal relationships involves the degree to which subordinates are consulted in the decison-making process. Thus, the pendulum has swung somewhat from the extremes of autocratic management styles to a stance which blends the traditional role of the manager as the final decision-maker with elements of group participation and shared responsibilities. What usually results, according to one researcher, is that subordinates, particularly lower level managers or line supervisors, are incorporated into the input process, but the final decision rests with the manager or department supervisor.

The key, again, for the successful manager is to adopt a flexible stance that permits selection of appropriate modes in any given situation. In some cases, for example, it may be that participatory discussions and planning are not necessary, and the matter can be resolved more efficiently by executive action. In other instances, to ignore the input of lower level individuals may undercut executive effectiveness, and make any decisions seem arbitrary and forced. The successful manager will be able to recognize the demands of a given situation, and marshall his resources effectively to meet the problem and solve it.

Lend a Hand—the Future Depends on It

The final area, that of evaluative skills, plunges even deeper into the area of interpersonal and human relations. The successful manager must be able to identify those individuals working under him who have the skills and desire to advance within a company—and then give them the opportunity to do so. It has been well documented that many younger executives leave their positions with a company because they feel thwarted in their ambitions. It remains the province of the manager to cultivate such individuals, and help advance them whenever appropriate. This, however, involves a certain degree of selflessness on the part of the manager, as well as willingness to lose certain skilled workers who might better be deployed elsewhere in a business., Unfortunately, many executives feel threatened in this situation, and fail to ensure that the workers feel wanted and appreciated.

Psychologists and business analysts also see the "mentor" effect in some executives, in which individual managers almost "adopt" a younger executive (very often a mirror image of themselves), and act as a tutor and supporter. What would be hoped is that this tendency to sponsor certain individuals could be made on as rational a basis as possible—so that the most deserving could receive the support and aid they need.

As was mentioned at the beginning, "success" is a nebulous term in the business world; no one definition appears to answer all needs. But there can be little doubt that the truly successful manager can and must utilize both business and human relations skills to maximum advantage—to extract maximum efficiency and output from his workers, while maintaining their enthusiasm and support. To have either one or the other alone is insufficient. How well the manager can achieve both is the most meaningful measure of his or her success and a precursor of his or her ability to deal with "The Winds of Change."

Anybody can become angry—that is easy; but to be angry with the right peron, and to the right degree, and at the right time, and for the right purpose, and in the right way—that is not within everybody's power and is not easy.
                    —**Aristotle,** Nicomachean Ethics

Speakers Showcase producer Ron Fellows, left, presents a Robert Owen clown print to Robert Henry, President of the National Speakers Association. Bob Henry was the banquet speaker at Ron's Professional Speakers Showcase at Newport Beach, California. The print featured the Robert Owen Clowns and was inscribed to "Robert Henry, Our Favorite Clown."

Ron Fellows, C.M.
2014 Siegle Drive
Lemon Grove, California 92045
(619) 463-2955

Ron Fellows, CM

Ron Fellows is a professional manager. He is Chairman of the Board and Past President of the Rohr Management Association, Rohr Industries, Chula Vista, California. Rohr is one of the world's largest producers of components for aircraft. He holds a lifetime California teaching credential and has taught courses in supervision and management at Southwestern College. He has also produced and administered numerous seminars and workshops at National University and San Diego State University.

Ron is a member of The National Management Association and Meeting Planners International. He has earned the professional designation, Certified Manager, CM, conferred by the Institute of Certified Professional Managers. The designation is evidence that a manager has met challenging standards of education and experience. He is a recipient of the NMA Leadership Award, the Superior Achievement Award, the Free Enterprise Eagle Award (in recognition of the commitment to preserve and strengthen the American Free Enterprise System), and many others.

*It was his background in theatrical production and sales management, coupled with a need for thousands of speakers and trainers for NMA meetings and seminars that led Ron to producing the **Ron Fellows Professional Speakers Showcase,** now the most exciting speaker's platform in the world.*

NATIONAL
MANAGEMENT
ASSOCIATION
2210 Arbor Blvd.
Dayton, Ohio 45439
513 / 294-0421

The National Management Association
Serving America's Management Team
Since 1925
by Ron Fellows, CM

"There exist limitless opportunities in every industry. Where there is an open mind, there will always be a frontier."
—Charles F. Kettering

BIGGER—MORE—BETTER. These seem to be underlying objectives of the Ron Fellows Professional Speakers Showcases. Speakers find the showcase a unique opportunity to personally meet with a great many association executives and meeting planners who employ hundreds, even thousands, of speakers each year. The meeting planners, those who employ speakers, meet and preview a great many platform professionals—from newcomer to superstar; business leaders, economists, motivators, educators, humorists, sales leaders, entertainers, and motion picture and TV personalities. The speakers showcases bring together buyers and sellers with a common interest: to fill the thousands of speaking dates available through the multi-billion dollar meeting and convention industry and a hundred-thousand meetings every year.

Speakers and meeting planners who come from across town, across the nation, and across the world describe the showcases as elegant theatrical productions, professionally managed, and executed with precision and class. Although now acclaimed internationally, their success must be viewed, at least in part, as a result of my training in management skills as a member of the National Management Association and the practical experience in their application as chapter president.

Management As A Profession

Founded in 1925 under the guidance of Charles F. Kettering, famed inventor and industrialist, the National Management Association has become the world's largest organization of professional managers. Today, NMA is a national non-profit organization with a membership of 68,000 managers in 255 affiliated chapters with representatives from more than 1200 companies. NMA members are dedicated to the development of management as a profession and the promotion of the American Free

Enterprise System.

Management chapters in NMA devote at least 75 percent of their activities to the development of the management skills of members. Programs produced by NMA are a major source of educational activity. The national organization draws upon the vast reservoir of management knowledge within its membership and from experts in every field to develop programs that will keep members abreast of the latest management techniques. In addition to providing educational materials, services from the national headquarters include leadership training, educational guidance, counseling, and internal communications between members and chapters.

Overview of Management

Management is often called the newest of the professions. Reflect for a moment upon the range of skills and knowledge of a manager. Not only must he master the technical information essential to his immediate task, but he should also be well versed in managerial economics, business finance, and human motivation. On top of this, he must have or develop some degree of a highly intangible skill called "leadership."

The management process consists of certain management functions, applied to resources, in order to achieve organizational objectives. The process utilizes a manager's skill with results dependent upon the quality of leadership and imagination exercised.

MANAGEMENT FUNCTIONS

The description of management functions; planning,

organizing, controlling, and motivating will establish a basic outline, but management is a very dynamic process. The four functions are very closely interrelated and often difficult to segregate in a specific situation. The whole process of decision making is anything but static. The manager doesn't make one decision regarding a problem, he makes many of them, each predicated upon what resulted from the last one. Conditions constantly change and entirely new premises for the decision come into play. It is precisely because of these factors that managers need conceptual tools and skills to help them go about their task.

Classifying Activities into Functions

Planning is establishing your objective—a broad statement of what is to be accomplished. Planning is determining the specific measurable goals or milestones leading to the accomplishment of the objective. Planning is forecasting future problems and events and determining courses of action to handle the problems and events forseen.

Example: *Deciding the best date to schedule a speakers showcase considering all potentially conflicting meetings and conventions nationally. Scheduling each activity and event leading to that date such as hotel selection, room block required, meeting room layout, promotional activity. The completion of each milestone is a measurable goal leading, step by step, to the accomplishment of the objective.*

Organizing is getting ready to do what has been planned. It consists of getting together, when needed, all of the resources required to accomplish the plans. (Resources: money, people, machines).

Example: *Making sure that all audio/visual equipment will be in place when and where required.*

Controlling is deciding to what degree plans have been achieved, and taking appropriate action when they have not.

Example: *The plan calls for a block of 350 rooms for three nights, but registration indicates more rooms will be needed. Contact the hotel for additional rooms, if possible, or arrange for overflow hotels.*

Motivating is convincing each subordinate to want to do what he has been assigned or directed to do.

Example: *Getting showcase timers commitment to the precise timing of each speaker on the program.*

PLANNING

Of all the basic management functions, planning is probably the most fundamental. An organization structure is designed for the purpose of carrying out a plan. People are motivated to carry out specific plans. It is the work of planning that separates managerial from non-managerial work. The manager plans what, when and how a product is produced or a service performed while the non-manager concentrates on performing the physical task. Yet, everyone plans, even the non-manager. The difference is that the manager plans the work of others while the non-manager plans, primarily, his own activities. The function of planning is the forecasting of future events and problems and selecting courses of action to handle these events and problems. This definition indicates two basic elements in all planning activity, those of forecasting and decision-making or selecting courses of action. There is a third element without which forecasting and decision-making are meaningless. This third element is objectives. No plan can be effective without a clearly established objective in mind. The lack of a clearly defined objective is the source of more planning problems than any other factor.

Planning Objectives

The meaning of the term "objective" is clear enough. Simply stated, an objective is a predetermined goal. Objectives tell us where we want to be next week, next month, next year. Objectives may be classified as follows: primary, secondary and corollary.

Primary Objectives are the basic objectives of the firm or project, its purpose for existence, its reason for being. Many people will insist that the primary objective of any firm is to make a profit. Obviously profit is essential, but is not too meaningful as an objective telling us what the organization is to do or what direction it is to go. Primary objectives must provide a meaningful basis for making specific decisions that will guide the organization.

Secondary Objectives or goals must directly support the primary objectives. They must be clearly defined and measurable. Secondary objectives generally reduce themselves to accomplishing the primary objective efficiently and effectively.

Corollary Objectives have to do with goals that exist alongside the primary and secondary objectives and may be typically personal goals of individuals and such organizational goals as good community relations.

There is one particularly important aspect of objectives—the clearly defined objective, the measurable goal cannot be effective if it is not properly communicated to those who must implement it. The importance of communications in establishing objectives cannot be overstated. Establishing objectives without communicating them represents a job only half done.

Forecasting

Planning is almost synonymous with forecasting—anticipating the future. Since a plan always involves future action, every planner must necessarily forecast. Forecasting is, of course, based upon assumptions. Some assumptions have a greater basis for validity than others. Validity may be greatly increased by collecting pertinent facts and information, thereby reducing the uncertainty of the forecast.

Decision-Making—Selecting Courses of Action

Decision-making is the "action" element of planning. All planning must culminate in deciding upon a course of action among several alternatives. This is not always the case. It may be that a manager has not taken the time to develop more than one particular alternative. The line of least resistance is to go ahead with the first solution that seems reasonably likely to succeed. It may seem that, in a particular situation, there is only one course of action possible. Usually this is not the case. A thorough job in considering several alternatives and evaluating and weighing each carefully will usually result in a course of action that consists of a combination of two or more alternatives. A fundamental test that we can apply in selecting a course of action is the test of objectives— would the objectives be served by the plan or course of action?

ORGANIZING

One of the most fundamental functions of the managing process is that of organizing. The ability to organize has often been associated with the outstanding entre-preneurs. Many famous leaders have won acclaim as "great organizers," those who lead through example or some indefinable ability to motivate large numbers of people. The concept of organization can be misleading, for a process of organizing involves very specific procedures and activities. It consists of getting together, when needed, all of the resources required to accomplish the plan.

Perhaps a more descriptive definition of organizing is provided by Louis Allen, the noted Management Consultant, who defined it as follows: "Organizing is the process of identifying and grouping the work to be performed, defining and delegating responsibility and authority, and establishing relationships for the purpose of enabling people to work most effectively together in accomplishing objectives." Basically then, organizing involves three types of work: Identifying and grouping work; defining and delegating responsibility and authority; establishing relationships between position, units, and resources.

Identifying and Grouping Work

This part of the organizing activity is often called "departmentation" and involves breaking down all of the work to be done into small parts and then grouping them in such a manner that the firm can most efficiently and affectively achieve its objectives and carry out its plans.

Defining and Delegating Responsibility and Authority

This aspect of organizing concerns determining the scope of decision-making and freedom of action needed to perform the work. It also involves establishing the obligation to perform certain tasks consistent with the requirements to achieve the objectives.

Establishing Relationships Between Positions, Units, and Resources

Finally, it becomes necessary to specify who reports to whom, what the relationship between departments should be, and how the line of command should progress. This is the part of organizing activity which has become familiar to most of us . . . the organization structure. The organization chart, however, does not really give us a complete picture of the structure of relationships such as the lines of communication between positions and units. A staff person may have no relationship with a production unit on the basis of authority, but it may be imperative that he have easy communication. In many instances, staff does have a type of authority relationship with production or other line units, usually a form of advisory authority or authority on procedural matters

The organizing process is essentially the same regardless of what level of the organization is being considered. The procedure is applicable to all managers. The differences are generally in degree and emphasis. Good organizing requires both recognizing what to do and when best to do it.

CONTROLLING

We have defined controlling a "deciding to what degree plans have been achieved, and taking appropriate action when they have not."

The controlling function of the manager takes place after the other functions have been performed. The control function consists of determining whether or not actual results coincide with planned results—in some instances, a simple task—assuring that an order was shipped or received on time.

But in most cases, such casual control does not suffice. The production manager cannot rely on simple observation to determine whether or not costs, for example, are in line. He must have a basis for comparison. This comparison, furthermore, must be quite precise. This brings us to a very important concept in controlling; control is largely based on measurement. To compare results means to look at two factors: actual results and planned results. To do this requires some unit of measurement. If all of the material in an area is to be moved to another area, and the original area is empty, the measurement is visual. But if only a certain quantity of the material is to be moved, a more precise method of measuring is required. Furthermore, another unit of measure may be involved in this example. Plans may call for the movement to be completed by a certain time. The time factor becomes a definite unit of measurement and a basis for comparison in judging whether or not the planned results have been achieved.

The function of controlling is very closely related to the other three functions, especially planning. Often it is difficult to separate the planning function from the controlling function. One reason for this is that we "plan" to control.

The Basis of Good Controlling

Most managers are familiar with the comment that "you can't inspect quality into a product." An extension of this idea is relevant to the relationship between planning and controlling. Good controlling depends upon good planning. If the plan is not realistic in the first place, the objective of controlling cannot be achieved.

Often the objectives of the plan itself are either not clear or not appropriate. It may be questionable whether the achievement of a particular plan or program will actually contribute to our ultimate objectives. The prime basis for good controlling is good planning. Control is more effective when it is built into the plan itself. A closed-loop planning and control system can be designed in most situations. When properly done, corrective action can be nearly automatic.

MOTIVATING

No manager will argue against the point that the level of motivation will often be the single most determining factor in how productive an organizational unit may be. You can plan in great detail, organize the objectives of a position and, by describing functions and relationships, establish the boundries and a framework within which an individual performs. But a good planning and organizing job alone is no guarantee that the desired performance will take place. Controlling provides the measurements and the method of measurement by which performance can be evaluated. But controls alone cannot guarantee the kind of performance desired and necessary. Effective planning, organizing, and controlling requires that we give consideration to the motivational factor.

Focus on Motivation

What is a high level of motivation? An individual can be extremely enthusiastic, show great initiative, but be ineffective or unproductive because those characteristics are pointed in the wrong direction. It is not sufficient, therefore, to define motivation in terms of enthusiasm, initiative, and a cooperative attitude. From a managerial point of view, those qualities must be directed toward specific ends. Therefore, the following definition of motivating applies: motivating is thinking, deciding, and acting in a way that causes members of the organization to want to apply their abilities and efforts toward the maximum achievement of organizational objectives. Several points are important. First, we should emphasize that it is how the manager thinks, decides and acts himself that causes the other members of the organization to be highly motivated. Second, we should observe that what we are trying to cause to happen is for people to want to perform. This recognizes that motivation is something internal to an individual. What the manager can do, and all he can do, is to try to cause the attidude, which is internal to the individual, to be assumed and developed by him. Finally, this self-generated level of performance is aimed at organizational objectives. We should bear in mind that organizational objectives include personal objectives—those personal goals which are consistent with the organizational objectives and, in fact, make a contribution to them. An individual may strongly desire to advance in the organization. By helping him to advance in the organization, we provide him with opportunities to grow and develop as an operative employee or a manager, and that is consistent with the organizational objectives. A manager should strive to create the conditions within his unit that are conducive to the positive motivation of the individuals in the unit.

The Behavioral Scientists

How a manager tries to motivate others is deeply rooted in the theory of motivation that he embraces. We should recognize that in psychological literature there are several theories of motivation. Management experts and writers have tended to make great use of one in particular: the so-called "Hierarchy of Needs" theory set forth by A.H. Maslow. This is a useful theory and should be studied, for much that is suggested in motivational practice is based on it. The works of other behavioral scientists should also be examined: Douglas McGregor, Fredrick Herzberg, Rensis Likert, Chris Argyris, and Robert Blake, who (with Jane Mouton), developed the "Managerial Grid" as a framework for increasing the manager's concern for both people and production.

All of these theories seek to explain motivation in one way or another. While each emphasizes a different aspect, there is consistency in the ideas that they present: an individual's motivational drive can be explained in terms of his striving to satisfy needs.

On the job, most people are better motivated when they see and understand clear-cut goals and objectives. One of the continuing functions of a manager should be the constant striving to clarify and pinpoint targets. Of course workers apply themselves better and more diligently to solve problems and get the job done when they feel personally committed to the goals and objectives. Commitment is usually better achieved through significant and meaningful participation in the decision process.

Communicating

It doesn't take much to convince a manager that the ability to communicate effectively cannot possibly be overrated as an important management skill. Communicating has a special significance for the motivating process. While communicating is the transmitting and receiving of information, it is more than that. Communicating is the means by which attitudes and behavior and changed. And that, after all, is exactly what we are talking about when we speak of motivation. We speak of improving motivation, developing positive attitudes toward job and the organization, and facilitating personal development. All this boils down to change—in attitudes and behavior. One way or another, that change is brought about by communication.

We should add that there is more than hard, factual information that is communicated in most instances. Attitudes are communicated. The project manager questions an engineer at length about his work on a project. The project manager's questions convey certain things to the engineer. They convey that the project manager wants to know where things stand. But the nature of his questions and how he asks them may convey something else. They may convey doubt in the engineer's method of solving the problem. They may convey to the engineer some doubt about his personal abilities. This may not have been what the project engineer intended to convey at all, but this is what the engineer heard or, more accurately, this is how the engineer interpreted what he heard.

So we see that communicating is more complicated than sending and receiving information, particularly as it affects motivation. Attitudes and feelings are also transmitted. Furthermore, the communication data are not only heard by the receiver, they are interpreted and evaluated by him.

APPLYING THE INTERRELATED FUNCTIONS

The application of the four management functions does not necessarily mean breaking down one's managerial work in a time sequence sense. This may be possible when we look at one particular project or program, for example. But even here, the breakdown is very general. A more realistic method for applying the functions is to look at a particular problem or situation at a specific time in terms of the planning, organizing, controlling, and motivating elements in that particular instance. It may well be that, following such an examination, the manager will identify the problem as essentially an organizing one, for example. But he is able to identify it as an organizing problem only because he has, at the same time, considered the planning, controlling, and motivating elements. If the manager does not consider all elements, there is a strong possibility that he will not identify the real cause.

Planning, organizing, controlling, and motivating should represent a kind of "picture" of the whole management process. Its value will depend upon the manager's conditioning himself to "seeing" this picture instantaneously and somewhat automatically when he analyzes problems and approaches decisions. Once conditioned in this manner, he may be quite unaware that he uses the four functions in any systematic manner. It becomes, in effect, part of his philosophy of management.

Includes excerpts from NMA course materials.

Troy D. Gill, M.D.

Rubicon International
1587 South Main Street
Salt Lake City, Utah 84115
(801) 485-2317 • (801) 277-6173

Troy Donald Gill, M.D.

*Troy Donald Gill, M.D. is an adult and child psychia-
trist in private practice. His psychiatric philosophy is
eclectic with emphasis on assisting clients in the
development of their inner potential. Clinically, he
utilizes the principles of cognitive and reality therapy
as well as analytical hypnotherapy.*

*He received his Doctor of Medicine degree from
Howard University, Washington, D.C. He completed his
pediatric training in Phoenix, Arizona and his fellow-
ship in adult and child psychiatry at the University of
Utah Medical Center. He has received additional
training in alcoholism, drug abuse, reality therapy,
mental retardation, metaphysics and hypnotherapy.*

*He has held membership on the Board of Governor
of the Salt Lake Area Chamber of Commerce, advisory
board of the University of Utah College of Nursing; has
served as a consultant to Job Corps, Chairman of the
Utah State Board of Mental Health and black history
instructor at Westminster College.*

*He is a Toastmaster and is available for speeches,
workshops and seminars in creativity, motivation,
prosperity, black history, human resources development, communication, negotiations, human behavior
and inspirational rallies.*

"PROGRAMS ARE CUSTOMIZED FOR INDIVIDUAL NEEDS"

Actualizing Your Creative Spirit as a Management Tool
by Troy Donald Gill, M.D.

"The barriers are not yet erected which can say to aspiring talent and industry, 'Thus far and no further.'"
—Beethoven

Life is a miraculous journey; a copious festival of joy, love, beauty and rapturous experiences. It's God's gift of ecstasy to mankind. Paradoxically, living that life can become a nightmare, without the appropriate knowledge. Such were my thoughts several years ago as I sat on a sofa viewing majestic Mt. Olympus contemplating how

I could partake more abundantly in the "festival of life."

Instantly, I decided that I would seek out the answers and I wouldn't be satisfied until I made them mine. I remembered the advice of my grandparents: "Read the Bible and don't forget to pray." Without hesitation I began reading the books of the Psalms and Proverbs and . . . EUREKA . . . I found that I had an education but that I lacked adequate understanding and that my festival of life was fizzling because I was leaning on my own understanding, which was replete with enormous pot holes. "How could I get more understanding?" I pondered.

1. Be ye transformed by the renewing of your mind.—*Romans 12:2*
2. He that believeth in me, the works that I do shall he do also; and greater works than these shall he do.—*St. John 14:12*
3. "Where your life will be five years from now, will be determined by the books you read and the people you meet."—*Charles "Tremendous" Jones*
4. "Life is consciousness."—*Emmett Fox*

With these insights I was on my way to: (1) improved service to my fellowman and (2) a true celebration of my "festival of life." Along the way I learned many things; the thing which awed me most were the capabilities of man's incredible mind. The capability which intrigues me most is man's creative spirit and that is what I would like to discuss with you presently.

What is creative spirit? Creative spirit is an inflamed

mental skill, housed in the whole of mankind, which facilitates the changing of one's environment, via changes in one's thinking and level of consciousness. Creativity is working with the old or present with new insights, which results in a new manifestation. According to Overstreet, two factors are involved in every creative enterprise: The maker's idea, intention or insight and the material he uses, and his technical skills in the handling of that material, which results in a creation or product. Although, one feature of creative thinking is that it is triggered by specific problems; problem solving is not always creative action. Ingenuity is not creativity! This article will focus on the obstacles of the manifestation of creative spirit and how to overcome them; then a profile of the creative person and manager.

Letting the Barriers Fall . . . Now

As a psychiatrist oriented to the amazing creative powers within *all* of us, I am alarmed by the plethora of people who are not mindful of their creative talents. Their thinking is that "others" are creative (artists, musicians, architects, writers, etc.) while the rest of us (the majority of people) are "normal, common, uncreative and un-gifted." Would you believe that your author used to wallow in such ignorance?

ACTION STEP

All humans possess more creative power than can be used in a lifetime. Every newborn infant has, at the instant of birth, a higher potential creative force than Albert Einstein or any other "genius" ever used.

Therefore, if *you* and I have it, why aren't we using it more abundantly? The reasons are multiple and varied; but can be categorized under one word ... BARRIERS. The thought of a barrier in relation to ourselves is something we do not like to consciously accept; we associate barriers with restrictions, no's, limitations and preventing us from doing what we want to do. Since we feel that way about barriers, let's work on leaving the barrier baggage behind and going forth with the force of creativity. How do we accomplish this? We accomplish this thusly:

1. We define and comprehend what a psychological barrier is and how it diminishes our creative personhood.
2. We learn what our barriers are and we study how those barriers affect us.
3. We accept where we are presently.
4. We set goals to work on eliminating each barrier one at a time over a specific period of time.
5. We give ourselves praise for our accomplishments *everyday*. Praise works wonders.

Now, let's get going.

What is a barrier? A barrier is a piece of "software," it's a learned program of repetitious stimuli, thoughts and attitudes which are housed in a computer ... the human brain. Since the software directs, controls and limits what the computer can do and how effectively it functions, it determines how creative your behavior will be. The bottom line is that barriers are automatic, irrational, complex behaviors that are in your subconscious, are usually out of your control and, most importantly, prevent you from moving from your present position (limited creative power) to your goal (abundant creative person).

Here are some of the barriers which you should overcome towards becoming a creative manager:

1. WHY CAN'T AN ADULT BE MORE LIKE A CHILD?

I remembered as a child looking forward to becoming an adult. Finally adulthood came and I noticed that the more I acted like an adult the less fun I experienced, the more limited my perception of life became and the less creatively I thought. Then I read the poem, "I'd Pick More Daisies" and I thought about childhood. I read the scripture, "For the children of this world are in their generation wiser than the children of light." I began to learn that the child within us is where the creativity is, where the wisdom is and where the gifts of life are.

When we think of our childhood, that was when we were most creative. When we study children we observe that they have fun doing what they are doing (playing— we should all play more, really play), they are spontaneous and uninhibited, they are not rule oriented, they believe that anything is possible (they think of *how to* . . . instead of *that will never work*), they take risks, they are curious, they like themselves and believe that the world is theirs, they ask and ask and ask, they experiment, they see nothing as serious, they love life, they ponder situations (not worry about them) and they not only ask but seek, knock, demand, affirm and never give up on their desires. In addition to these traits, a child believes in himself and believes that he shall have his desires met. Most importantly, children love unconditionally and when you love unconditionally you overcome all, including your parents and the "obstacles" in life because when you love as a child you turn obstacles into love objects and they cooperate with you and give you that which is good.

ACTION STEP **Study children, learn from children, reflect on your childhood, listen to children, present your obstacles and problems to children, play with children, play more, get in touch with the child within and love unconditionally. BE MORE LIKE A CHILD, LESS LIKE AN ADULT!**

2. FIXED INNER IMAGES

Until recently, my inner image and, as a result, my outer image was that of a physician-psychiatrist. Subsequently, I learned that by having such an image I was limiting myself, limiting my services to clients and limiting my involvement with life. So I changed by changing my inner image to that of a student of life, releasing my thoughts of being just a physician. I worked on being a person in the flow of life, being of service to others. So can you!

As you read this work (of labor) your inner image is broadcasting that you have a title, a position in society, a trade, a profession or some kind of restricted and sanctioned title. As long as you retain this image you restrict your creativity; as long as you think of yourself in terms of a title or position you can never rise above that level of thinking, thus you can't see things from a different perspective, i.e., if you are in business you see things from a business perspective instead of from a humanities or spiritual perspective.

Therefore, to activate your creative force you must strip your mind of your title, lose yourself in life, become a student of life and begin walking in the other person's mocassins, thus acquiring a variety of ways of thinking about conflicts, issues and obstacles. A potent way to do this is to *ask and listen* to people from a variety of life styles (welfare recipients, cooks, prisoners) . . . you will be surprised how much they can enhance your creativity. A good example is the concept of the elevator on the outside of a building, which came from a janitor. In addition to this, begin studying subjects that are unrelated to your occupational field. By doing this you will create a holistic life, your approach to problems expands and your creativity index zooms.

ACTION STEP

Change your inner image from *whatever your title is* to a student of life, get out of your present world and venture into the world of others, study "alien" subjects and rise above your current level of thinking. Instead of digging deeper in the same hole, dig new holes.

3. CONFORM AND BE DULL

Have you ever considered your conformity profile? Believe it or not, most of us are conformists. Worse than this, have you ever thought of yourself as a ROBOT? You probably haven't, but ponder the question. Do you do things the acceptable way? Do you imitate others? Do you follow most of the teachings of authority figures? Do you seek advice often? Are you consultant addicted? Do you function mainly within the realm of what you learned during your formal education? Are you functioning in your work, marriages, interpersonal relationships, financial affairs as you were 1 to 10 years ago? Such is the behavior of a robot until he is reprogrammed.

The important point is not that I advocate the elimination of authority figures, formal education, or that you become anti-social or even a non-conformist just to be different. What I am advocating is that you rise above the "old wineskins" and pour the wine of you into "new wineskins." You must be you—a unique, creative individual, and you become that by rethinking and reshaping your approach to life; by so doing you become more creative. If you don't you become dull of spirit and less of a force in life. You begin to feel less powerful, ambitious and excited about what life is all about—living. The "alive" person is the creative person. Remember that your human potential will never evolve appreciably until you ignite your inner resources and flow with life peacefully. When you obstruct your creative force you limit inner growth and subsequently outer performance.

One of the major obstacles to using the creative force is persistence with old knowledge, old attitudes, old behaviors and worn out thinking. The more and the harder you approach life in this manner, the more you bury yourself in the hole of restricted creativity. The success principle which will bring you out of the darkness of limited creativity to the sunshine of peak creativity is adoption of the principle of persistence with experimentation. Yes, the more you apply the formula of persistence plus experimentation, the more creative you will become.

ACTION STEP **Start visualizing and thinking of yourself as a positive, creative, non-conventional person. Never accept life or things as they are; always think of how they could be better. LET GO OF CONFORMITY— GRAB THE CREATIVE FORCE.**

4. POVERTY OF HEALTHY MENTATION

Composing this section reminds me of the words of Shakespeare: "The fault, dear Brutus, is not in our stars, but in ourselves, that we are underlings." The reality is that until we alter our mentation we are underlings in utilizing creative spirit. The art of arts is learning how to clear the mind of its enemies. In developing the creative process, who are the enemies? They are anti-creative attitudes, habits, emotions and thinking patterns.

Attitudes which are limited, negative and bias are thieves of creativity. Here's the line up of attitudes that strangle creativity:

1. A cynical, malevolent sarcastic attitude about life and people.
2. A narrow, shallow and apathetic perspective.
3. A believer in ethnocentricity. According to Mike Vance ethnocentristic people feel superior to

others.
4. Comfortability and apathy.
5. Not looking for the good in every situation and person.
6. A deprecative self-image.
7. Accepting facts as the last word.
8. Thinking that you are educated when you really are "trained," not educated.
9. Reluctance to change.
10. Authoritarian attitudes.

Habits can be flowers or weeds growing side by side, they can make us beautiful or unattractive. Habits are learned behaviors and thus can be changed. Since we are desirious of being creatively oriented, let's hoe the following "weeds" out of our garden of behaviors:
1. Not using your imagination.
2. Not taking the time.
3. Squelching the art of daydreaming and fantasizing.
4. Failure to question and research facts.
5. Reading without studying, thinking through or applying what was read.
6. The habit of perfectionism.

It's been said that "nothing is good or bad, save thinking makes it so." How we think is critical to survival; yet we increasingly allow our thinking to be done by others. Thinking puts "life" into living, gives you dominion over living and converts potential brain power into great brain power. Thinking is a learned talent which requires daily nurturing and continual upgrading. As

Alex Osborn said: "Your mind needs bread to feed on and bones to chew on;"selective and active studying (not reading) is a way to do this. Have you fed your mind lately? Thinking well and learning how to think may be hampered by:

1. Having an inferiority complex about your thinking capability; believing that others are better thinkers than you.
2. Perceiving thinking as passive behavior; preferring to be active or entertained instead.
3. Avoiding the hard work and time commitment required to enhance "how to think" habits.
4. Formal education which formalized your thinking; feeding you information but not teaching you how to think.

As a mortal and as a psychiatrist I have learned to be attentive and respectful to the benevolent and sinister effects of emotions. Emotions are Herculean in the impact which they exert on the life experience; a blissful emotional state is precious, while a pernicious emotional state can be cataclysmic. Emotions govern what you will accomplish in life! In the unfolding of one's creative spirit emotions are cardinal; facts are secondary. The creative person must pay attention to and maintain a state of mental healthiness; thus he must eliminate the following emotional traits:

1. Taking life seriously.
2. Worry, worry, worry.
3. An impoverished sense of humor.
4. Regurgitating the past and thinking of "if only."

5. Conditional love.
6. A competitiveness orientation to life.
7. Emotional dependency on people and things.
8. Fears of all types, especially fear of failure, fear of criticism and fear of risking.
9. Self-consciousness.
10. Over reacting to situations via anger, psychosomatic illness or vengefulness.

ACTION
STEP

Take inventory of your attitudes, habits, thinking pattern and emotional status. Then plan to work on changing one weakness per month.

5. COMMUNICATION AND PERCEPTUAL BLOCKS

To enhance one's communication skills is to boost one's creative adroitness. In management situations no other single factor even approaches the importance of communication. Communication involves more than output (talking, writing, etc.); it involves seeing, asking, listening and feeling. The result of positive communication is action; something happens when we communicate effectively.

A creative person needs "seeing power;" he needs vision. With vision he sees beyond his present circumstances and thinks about and prepares for the future. Vision triggers the imagination and empowers the creative spirit to accelerate.

Asking aids your creative spirit by giving you a

different perspective, stimulating your thinking and providing you with additional information; this is increased when you ask a variety of sources. When you ask you learn, when you learn you think and when you think creativity is enticed.

Without exception, listening is the cornerstone of effective communication. The benchmark of an astute communicator is that he is an active listener. Dr. Earl Koile says that listening is a way of being; a way of being sincerely involved with the world, with others and with yourself. When listening we must overcome all barriers to listening as well as all biases. Listening is a reciprocal event; you bring something out of the other person and they bring something out of you. Listening is improved when we do not dwell on one another's motives for being the way we are, when we are nonjudgmental and when we are supportive instead of critical. We also become better listeners when we are not distorting or editing what is being expressed or overpersonalizing what we hear. The risk of listening is that by listening actively our thoughts may be changed. In a creative vein listening helps us to clarify problems and derive solutions. Since listening is germane to communication mastery, why aren't we better listeners? Here are some reasons:

1. Inadequate respect, love and interest in the speaker.
2. Poor concentration skills.
3. Our minds are already made up about the person, situation or issue.
4. Lack of knowledge of the importance of the concept of understanding.

5. Biases towards certain types or groups of people (members of the opposite sex, those you consider to be inferior to you, people whose thinking is divergent to yours, those who are not in your social circle, etc.).
6. Thinking of defending yourself or contradicting what the other is saying.

ACTION **Ask, watch and listen creatively.**
STEP

6. INADEQUATE KNOWLEDGE ABOUT BRAIN FUNCTION

This is the most significant part of the discussion; it deals with what makes all that we have been talking about work. Our subject is the brain; the storehouse of man's most powerful inner resources. To excel in the utilization of our creative spirit we must activate the power of the inner, not the outer. Emerson believed that man becomes weak to the extent that he looks outside himself for help. All the help we need is within and has been there since conception; our challenge is to positively express our potential to the maximum. A hotel tycoon summed it up well when he said: "When a man ain't got no education, he's forced to use his brain!" Educated or not, in order to survive and create, brain power is of the essence.

Psychologically, we separate the mind into the conscious and the subconscious. Mostly we use the conscious but the power is in the subconscious. The conscious part of your mind is the smallest part; ninety percent of your mental life is subconscious. Thus, when you make active use of only the conscious part of your mind you are using but a fraction of your ability. The conscious mind remembers nothing beyond what is held in it's thought. It must extract all of it's information for all actions from the subconscious.

Therefore to augment conscious creative productivity, reprogram the subconscious mind to deliver creative information to the conscious part of the brain.

In order to make your subconscious mind your servant, all you have to do is remove undesirable information from it and replace it with new desirable information. When you do this, and later give the subconscious mind a fact or problem, it works it out to a logical solution; making it available to the conscious mind. When you master this process, creativity is enhanced.

Another functional division of the brain is right/left. The left brain's functional areas are logic, language, judgment and mathematical skills; while the right brain is used for visualization, feeling, dreams and intuition. Our formal education has taught us mainly how to use the left brain. The most effective approach to becoming more creative is to develop right brain functions more, then employ both sides of the brain to bring new thoughts to old problems.

Other ways to increase creative spirit is to use visualization, affirmations, dreams, biofeedback and alpha wave techniques. Also pay closer attention to hunches and intuition. Contact professionals, study books and attend seminars for further assistance in developing these skills.

ACTION   **Vow to become the pharaoh of your mind.**
STEP

Characteristics of the Creative Individual

All people are born with creative spirit. To the extent that this special gift is expressed is determined by hereditary, social, educational and other factors. A University of California study demonstrated that those who express their creative potential best have recognizable traits. The creative person is:

1. The one for whom life is a continuity of purposes, who is unoffended by the requirement that he match these purposes with skill in the handling of materials.
2. One who enjoys the creative process as well as the created product.
3. Psychologically astute about self.
4. Usually an introvert; however, those who are extroverted score high in creative potential.
5. Not especially conscious of what others think of them; thus they are less susceptible to social restraints and inhibitions.
6. Independent concerning his ideas.
7. More independent and less conformed.
8. Uninterested in supervising his own image or impulses or those of others.
9. Verbally oriented and highly communicative.
10. More concerned with meanings and implications of facts, than with just facts.
11. Emotionally responsive and accepting of others,

including those with opposing views.

12. An information seeker.

Skills of the Creative-Oriented Manager

Managing is a challenging experience, requiring the development of a variety of skills, the most important of which is the development of human resources. To adequately develop human resources a creative-oriented manager should master the following skills:

1. Encourage independent thinking and support a credo which inspires creativity.
2. Open minded and accepting change.
3. Masterful communicator; avoiding discouraging and threatening remarks.
4. Capacity to praise in abundance, even when the job is not done perfectly.
5. Welcome and support employees who "rock the company boat" instead of demanding conformity.
6. Delegate with support, positive expectancy and a specific due date.
7. Establish and maintain high company morale.

Cross the Rubicon

Two thousand years ago Caesar made a great decision; to conquer the heart of the world. He acted, never thought of retreating and crossed the Rubicon. Since that time, the expression, "crossing the Rubicon" has meant making a great decision and not turning back. I challenge you to cross the Rubicon, destined to maximize your creative spirit, never to turn back to less than your highest potential.

I'm hurt, but I'm not slain.
I will lay me down and bleed awhile.
Then rise and fight again.
                    —Ancient Scottish verse

Charles G. Armfield

Delphi Consultants
7300 West Rim
Austin, Texas 78731
(512) 345-8240

Charles G. Armfield

As a graduate of Hampden-Sydney College, Charles Armfield began his professional business career in the wholesale industry in 1971. He started Delphi Consultants, Inc., a communications and management consulting company, in 1983.

As President of Delphi Consultants, Inc., Charles has spoken to representatives of such companies as AT&T, Xerox and IBM; and many others.

Charles is a member of the National Speakers Association, an alumnus of Leadership Austin and a former member of the board of directors of Leadership Austin. In addition, he is a member of RepublicBank-NW Austin Board of Directors, a past Chairman of the Board of the Capitol Area Branch Arthritis Foundation and current Central Texas Chapter Chairman for the Arthritis Foundation.

Delphi Consultants, Inc. has a six-week training course on change and creativity. This program has been sold from California to New York and comes complete with a 118-page manual and four cassettes, so it can be completed in the privacy of your own home.

In addition to change and creativity, Charles has spoken on and published articles on decidophobia, which is the fear of making decisions. Realizing that few people ever achieve all they want in life, and fewer still use their potential to become self-fulfilled and autonomous, Charles changed his career to one of helping people "bridge the gaps" between decidophobia, the fear of making decisions, to autonomy, the realization of independence.

19

Management by Creativity
by Charles Armfield

*"What lies behind us and what lies before us
are small matters compared to what lies
within us."*
—Emerson

Today, we are looking at a whole new approach to management—a whole new approach to the leadership styles of the 1980's and the 1990's. The traditional way of managing people with delegation from the top down, prevalent in 1945 because of World War II, is now becoming archaic. We are looking at a new breed: students from new and higher levels of education. We may read countless articles lamenting how these students are less educated, less skilled in mathematics, reading, and simple letter writing due to our schools settling for and encouraging mediocrity; but this in no way can predict their final level of achievement, for these students can still be trained and, more importantly, *want* to be trained. They learn these and other critical skills once they get on the job—and *once they get committed.*

The problem facing management, then, is getting that commitment. Let's take a quick look at the young people of the 80's and compare them to the children of the 50's and before. The former have grown up having basically everything they want. Many people growing up prior to World War II did not have what they needed, much less what they wanted. Some wore hand-me-down clothes, lived in smaller homes, and "made do" with what they had. A man then probably had two suits and two pairs of shoes. Today we have walk-in closets, dressing areas and bathrooms the size of earlier bedrooms and living rooms. Also the modern dwelling may have work-out areas to accommodate the need for physical fitness and personal indulgence. Women may wear a dress one or two times as fashions change drastically from year to year. Our young people have grown up with color coordinated Calvin Klein's and polo ponies, while the children of yesteryear were thankful for a new outfit. Clearly, we have moved from an era of self-denial to one of self-indulgence.

Times Are Changing

Times are changing, and we're having to adjust to these changes. At the turn of the century, 97% of the population worked in agriculture, or the distribution of food. During the 1920's industry evolved and the rural population started to move to the cities creating the urbanization of our civilization and culture. These people then experienced the depression and, ultimately, war. They left their farms and cities and went to fight in foreign countries. When they returned, they were no longer willing to "walk behind the mules" as they had broadened their view of the world. The farmers, now without their usual labor force, had to become creative. They had to develop better farm equipment in order to maintain production in the face of a lessened labor force. The cities and the manufacturers had to become creative to handle the influx of people moving to the city. This mass movement was a mass commitment to change—a commitment to "creativity by necessity," which marked a major shift in our culture.

Following World War II, employees needed direction, and this was expressed in leadership styles. At this point, educational levels were low; technology and engineering experience was minimal because it was not necessary. To many, the main reason for existence was survival, and they wanted someone or some company to give them direction—someone to tell them what to do. Understandably, the leadership style of delegation from the top down was very appropriate. Then, the workers had just come back from fighting in a war where they were accustomed to being told what to do and valued such direction as their very lives depended on it. They were familiar with being in situations where they had to follow orders, so it was a very logical step to continue this pattern in the work place.

However, the young graduates of today are coming into this system with no military experience and little value for responding positively to being told what to do. They have been in schools which encourage a progressive style of leadership where the students are taught to make their own decisions; to evaluate the situation, the alternatives, and then make a *conscious choice* to choose their own way.

The traditionalist leaders do not understand this. They are accustomed to giving orders; they have worked hard to be in a position to give orders. When this new group of graduates does not follow their directives, management is frustrated and does not know where to turn. Money and security are not major problems for this generation. They want to have *fun* in their careers. At the same time, they want to be committed and challenged. This generation wants responsibility, wants it now, and gets frustrated when management does not move fast enough.

This generation can have commitment. They are already committed to the "search" for a better quality of life. Learning, growing, experiencing change are already a part of their nature. They not only expect change, they look for change; they look for ways to express their freedom and unique personality.

However, in the bureaucracies and hierarchies of big business, they are not finding this freedom. Consequently, they are challenging the system. They want participatory management. If not promoted fast enough, they simply move and become the entrepreneurs of tomorrow. So how does modern day management cope? *They, too, must change.*

Normal Evolution

Let's look at an evolving company. There are four distinct stages—the *beginning,* the *implementation,* the *democratic approach* of group involvement, and finally the point where *"the system"* takes over.

With each stage people exhibit a distinct style necessary to assure the success of the company's development. One style assesses and creates. In observation of objects or concepts, this individual can look at material and interpret it in different ways. By rearranging old concepts into new ideas, they exhibit creative thinking, which is the *"beginning."*

Once an idea exists, it must be expressed by a person of action—*"implementation."* This person has capital, influence, or the where-with-all to act. This person is generally direct and authoritative, while the first person is contemplative and more mentally oriented. These two styles together create the entrepreneurial spirit which gets new projects and new businesses off the ground. As businesses grow, they need people to carry out the plan—*"the democratic approach,"* and these people must be very adaptive. This third type of person listens to instructions well and communicates well. They organize and coordinate activities to make the business grow. However, in order to keep things in control and the company on track, a "system" is needed. This requires a very analytical person who is reserved, structured, and methodical to keep everybody in line and going in the same direction.

Interaction among these people is essential to success. In the beginning, the consulting person is very self-directed and self-reliant, has a lot of self-confidence and is innovative, but also is somewhat indirect in his dealings with others as he is always open to change and new ideas. The autocratic person is very assertive, very straightforward and authoritatively direct in dealing with others. The democratic person deals with groups and is very persuasive. He is a team builder—he looks for involvement and is very flexible and understanding. Finally, the bureaucrat is the one who is systematic and procedure oriented, always consistent. He looks to methodology to overcome problems, enjoys working with details, and is structured. Typically this person does not deal well with others. He is more reflective, and is convergent in his approach. Thus *he does not pass on information and knowledge of details to those within the system who can assess and improve the company.*

The person in this last position is crucial to the survival of the company. If management cannot pass on its experiences and its knowledge to company youth in such a way that they can learn from it, accept it, and use it to further the business, the business dies. It is this constant cycle of birth, learning, maturing and gaining wisdom that is the underlying process that man goes through at all levels of his development. It happens to us as individuals—it also happens to companies and businesses. Nature is always in a constant flux of beginnings and endings. With each beginning there is hope and excitement; with implementation there is enthusiasm. There is enjoyment in the success, both within the individual and within the group, as more and more people get involved. Finally, there is enrichment as management shares its talents with the employees of the company. If the cycle stops before knowledge can be shared, then there can be nothing on which to build a new beginning. The company stagnates and the excitement is over.

Productivity to Creativity

So what do we do to encourage excitement with companies? The following diagram shows the flow from the old style of management, which concerned itself with production and bottom line results, to a new style which is oriented toward creativity and stimulation.

As depicted by the diagram on "management by creativity," we see that production by itself is simply not enough.

Production

Production deals with the negative. Management expects young graduates to be right—expects the educational system to teach its graduates all they need to know, or expects perfection after a period of in-house training. Twenty-five years ago, this may have been acceptable; then it took eight days to do what can be done today in one. It seems logical, then, to think that since we are doing eight times more work in a single day, we do not

Management by Creativity

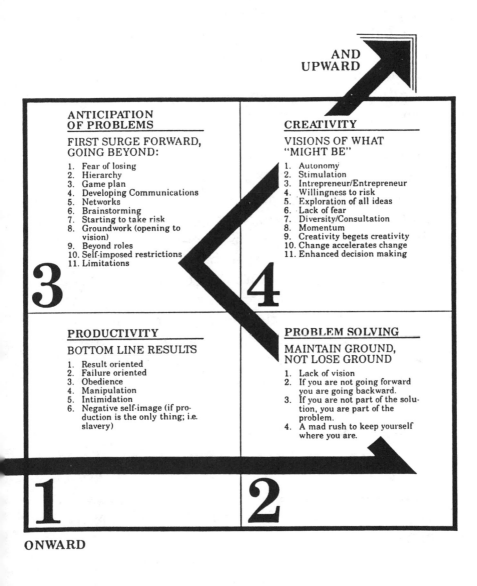

AND
UPWARD

**ANTICIPATION
OF PROBLEMS**

FIRST SURGE FORWARD,
GOING BEYOND:

1. Fear of losing
2. Hierarchy
3. Game plan
4. Developing Communications
5. Networks
6. Brainstorming
7. Starting to take risk
8. Groundwork (opening to vision)
9. Beyond roles
10. Self-imposed restrictions
11. Limitations

CREATIVITY

VISIONS OF WHAT
"MIGHT BE"

1. Autonomy
2. Stimulation
3. Intrepreneur/Entrepreneur
4. Willingness to risk
5. Exploration of all ideas
6. Lack of fear
7. Diversity/Consultation
8. Momentum
9. Creativity begets creativity
10. Change accelerates change
11. Enhanced decision making

3

4

PRODUCTIVITY

BOTTOM LINE RESULTS

1. Result oriented
2. Failure oriented
3. Obedience
4. Manipulation
5. Intimidation
6. Negative self-image (if production is the only thing; i.e. slavery)

PROBLEM SOLVING

MAINTAIN GROUND,
NOT LOSE GROUND

1. Lack of vision
2. If you are not going forward you are going backward.
3. If you are not part of the solution, you are part of the problem.
4. A mad rush to keep yourself where you are.

1

2

ONWARD

have time to make mistakes. Because of this fallacy, when management expects perfection and does not get it, it becomes frustrated. Managers deal in the 5 or 10% of things that go wrong when training their employees. They deal in the negative, instead of reinforcing the positive. Typically, management, which stresses production, becomes manipulative, intimidating and motivates by fear, creating negative self-images within their employees.

Problem Solving

Since employee self-images are low, personnel and administrative departments spend most of their days *problem-solving*—"putting out fires." In this situation there is no vision; there is no forward movement. Management does not always study the alternatives and get to the second or third or fourth best answer. They do whatever solves the problem with the least amount of resistance at that particular moment, not realizing that they may be making bigger problems for themselves and the company down the road. This situation is one which is best described as "a mad rush to keep ourselves where we are".

Anticipation of Problems

The Japanese approach, which anticipates problems, goes beyond hierarchial management which relies on traditional game plans and rules. Modern management has accepted many of the tenents of the Japanese approach:

    1. We develop communication lines.

2. We network with other people in management and with our employees.
3. We brainstorm to determine the best solutions.
4. We study the alternatives to make choices based on second level decision making.

Now what management needs is a solution that solves long range problems and creates better working conditions along with more profits. There are no restrictions in this approach and there are no limitations. We make a choice based on what we, as a group, want to happen, not based on what is expected to happen from either higher or lower management.

Creativity

We can even go beyond Japanese Quality Circles by establishing Creative Thinking Circles. Japanese Quality Circles deal in problem-solving and production problems; Creative Thinking Circles allow people to decide in their wildest imaginations what it is they want, and how to make it happen. Creative thinking becomes visions of what "might be."

By encouraging autonomy from employees, companies enjoy management by stimulation. They are willing to take risks by sharing decision making responsibilities with their employees. At the same time, once employees see that management is giving them the opportunity to be in the decision-making process, the employees are more inclined to be *committed* and to get involved in helping the company grow. With this momentum, creativity begets creativity and change accelerates change.

By dealing only with bottom line results and profits, productivity alone causes employees to feel frustrated and receive negative feedback. What they find out is that they cannot be right 100% of the time. There is always going to be a time when they make mistakes and are reprimanded. This reinforces the negative cycle of conflict, separation, defensiveness and fear. Ultimately employees become unable to recognize and trust other people. If this continues they become destructive to the organization and possibly to themselves. They start assigning blame, become self-righteous, and may even get to the point of getting revenge with employers or employees. Employers need to encourage commitment at all levels through positive meetings where the goals and the means to accomplish these goals are clearly stated and understood. With this communication level, there exists trust, recognition, and a harmlessness which allows employees to concern themselves only with the success of the project. With everyone working together and committed to common goals, there is little "water fountain" or "bathroom" talk where the employees sabotage management.

New Styles of Leadership

This sets the stage for the different styles of leadership. In any situation a leader has to evaluate the objective, the structure and the information available to determine what style of leadership best fits the situation. No one style is always appropriate. If a quick decision is required and the manager has sufficient information, the group need not be consulted, and an autocratic type approach may be the choice. On the other hand, if involvement by and commitment from the group is needed, then a group style approach is the choice. If a leader makes a decision without getting group input, then the group may or may not implement the decision.

In between, there is a consulting style of leadership which allows the leader to ask questions and get feedback before making a decision. In this way the leader maintains responsibility for making the decision. In the group process, he must turn over that responsibility to the group—an envisioned threat to many traditionalists. Many leaders do not trust the group style because they do not want to lose control. What they do not understand is that this style takes away their responsibility to be "right" *all* the time, yet does not change the leader's responsibility for the final outcome. At this point the leaders are involved with the success of the project, the training of their personnel, and the involvement of the employee; not with personal satisfaction and personal advancement within the organization.

What Happens to the Bureaucracy?

So, what are we seeing here? We are basically seeing the elimination of the fourth quadrant in our diagram of *managing by systems* or *bureaucracy*. What we are seeing is a new style of leadership of managing people. This new generation wants the responsibility and the challenge of being a part of the company. We are seeing where the systems are not necessarily the solutions. The younger generation will create a new set of challenges and responsibility for management, requiring even more change from the leaders of today. Their young minds will be programmed to change, instead of once every ten years, to perhaps once every five years or less. There are projections as high as 100% change every three and one half months, by 2020, because of improved technology, improved computer programming, and improved education.

But one thing is clear, there will be change. There will be change at a much faster rate than we are accustomed to today. And it is going to be the creative people, Carl Jung's "intuitor" the people who are willing to act, those who are open to change and understand it that are going to be best suited to adapt and develop when change occurs. Those people who are analyzing, bureaucratic and priority conscious are not going to have the luxury of *time* to make these decisions.

The new style of leadership is going to be one of accessing and adapting. There will be failures and mistakes, but the new leader will learn from those mistakes, instead of being disappointed and internalizing the failure. It becomes a learn-learn-win situation, in which they are constantly growing, changing, and asking themselves, "Now what? Where do I go from here? What have I learned which can improve my career choices and interpersonal relationships?"

Mental Blocks

In addition, we are going to see a breakdown of the mental attitudes which do not allow us to be creative. We no longer will have to have the "right answers" or "logical answers," because we will be open to suggestions, open to growth, and, open to different ways of doing things. Rules, although they will have a time and a place, will be changing at a rapid pace, because they will have outlived the purpose for which they were intended. The rules will be necessary for the implementation stage but not for the creative stage. Also, we need to look at material things and concepts and see them in different ways. The younger group, since they are looking to have a "good time," will be less structured. They will be more open to change and they will see things in different ways; they will realize that they do not want to feel badly when they make mistakes. They will want to learn from mistakes and do a better job next time. People like to stay in environments where they are mentally stimulated. If they are not being creative and learning, they will want to leave. The higher the level of learning attained in an environment, the greater the degree of creativity, and the greater the personal satisfaction; thus the smaller the percentage of employee turnover.

What I am suggesting is that we start looking for ways to open up to creativity, open up to possibility thinking, open up to group development, dynamics and understanding. We should avoid the problems of bottom line thinking, manipulation and intimidation which cause stress and frustration within our employees and interpersonal relationships. Our jobs as managers, leaders, or parents, is one by which we encourage and guide others, assisting them as they develop. By understanding what is important to help each individual achieve their highest potential, we establish the "quality of life" that everyone seeks.

Today, 80% of us are uncomfortable with our career choice and current success level. In the 70's people discussed the possibility of only getting 5% more energy from each employee, saying, "Just think how much more productive they would be." I feel that with 80% of the people not liking what they are doing, 5% does not make any difference. We could probably get 3 or 4 times the amount of energy from all employees if we motivated them by values and obtained their involvement through commitment. What I am talking about is the "quality of life;" producing quality products and quality services. I am talking about developing companies in which people are comfortable, where people feel they are a part of the growth of that company, that they are contributing to their future; and that their employers are genuinely glad to see them at work and to see them productive. In other words, they really care.

New Energy Levels

People have all the energy they need to develop their lifestyles and vocational careers. When they are getting the rewards and reinforcement they need at work. If they are always concentrating on what they are doing wrong, or on the ways they are making mistakes, then they have plenty of energy too; but it is to run, to get away. If they cannot choose to get away, because what they are doing vocationally solves most of their problems, they are in a "rut of hopelessness," and are unhappy with their positions—thus the 80%.

So, it becomes our job as managers and leaders to establish a quality of life that encourages growth, encourages people to be all that they can be, to learn from their mistakes. We must start managing by values— looking for a leadership style which promotes a creative climate where people can be self-motivated and can contribute to the successful achievement of long term goals which are understood and agreed to by all employees. It becomes an environment of mutual respect, and positive feelings of self-worth. The employee develops a self-confidence while the company establishes an atmosphere that is conducive to achievement, without excessive policies and restrictions inhibiting growth.

The creative climate occurs because we deliberately develop it, encourage it and foster it. Leadership is the ability to establish and manage a creative climate in which people are self-motivated. It is the ability to create an environment where everyone can express their unique talents and have compatible personal values. In *management by creativity,* people are important, not the systems. We are meeting the needs of all our employees— intellectually, physically, psychologically, as well as financially.

Delia Villarreal-Stewart

Villarreal-Stewart Enterprises, Inc.
10930 Whisper Valley
San Antonio, Texas 78230
(512) 492-7828

Delia Villarreal-Stewart

Delia is Chairperson and Chief Executive Officer of two California companies: Villarreal-Stewart Enterprises, Inc., and Silhouettes of Beauty, Inc. The range of her business activities include classroom training, seminar training, and personal one-on-one marketing efforts. The thrust of both of these companies is concentration in Spanish speaking and Far Eastern Markets.

She has matriculated at: (1) Del Mar College, Corpus Christi, Texas, in Marketing and Business. (2) Graduated from Bauder Fashion College, Arlington, Texas as an Interior Designer and Professional Model. (3) Graduate of Joe Blasco Makeup and Prosthetics Center in Hollywood, California.

Delia loves working with people and is obsessed with the desire to approach the emerging men and women of the middle classes with the realization of self awareness, pride and dignity of the individual world wide. Her motto: "One must give for one to receive, but give in such a manner that each recipient retains his/her personal and special image."

Her professional and business experiences include: Several public relations projects involving high level diplomatic groups from China, Hong Kong, Nigeria, Liberia and Mexico. Delia has worked in various movie and location shootings with many famous stars and Japanese commercial film producers.

She is a Fashion Editor for a chain of Spanish-language newspapers, headed by Miniondas, in the Los Angeles, Orange County area.

As a Fashion Editor and Consultant, she teaches color and fashion as they relate to the people and their surroundings. She teaches people: "When you look good, you feel good about yourself and other people around you."

Managing the Radiance of Your Own Style
by Delia Villarreal-Stewart

"You are a child of the universe, no less than the trees and the stars; you have a right to be here. And whether or not it is clear to you, no doubt the universe is unfolding as it should."
—Desiderata

I began working with color when I was in high school. There I learned to combine and see color. When I graduated I went to college and became an Interior Designer and Professional Model. By combining the skills I learned in high school and as an Interior Designer, I began to understand that the use of color and fabric should either make or break the look, whether it was in decorating the house or building a wardrobe. My career as a Professional Model in Dallas was very rewarding because I could use all the knowledge of color, fabric, and body proportion and combine them to make the statement for which I was looking.

What started me on the road of fashion was my intense desire to learn how to dress. I grew up in a Mexican-American home of six children. My parents did not have extra money to clothe us. The clothes I usually wore were 2 or 3 sizes too big and were 4 or 5 years behind fashion. So you can imagine my going to school in a dress that came down to my calves and with shoulder seams dropping off my shoulders. The armholes were sometimes big enough for both my arms. It was really bad! The worst thing about it was that this was during the time mini skirts were in fashion! I also noticed that the majority of the Latin people didn't have the money or the knowledge to dress properly. When I was in elementary school, I decided that I was going to learn everything about fashion and I was going to teach others.

Years after I had finished college, I studied to be a makeup artist in Hollywood. I worked on location for various shootings. Some of the many stars I worked with were Priscilla Presley and Tanya Roberts of *Charlie's Angels.* I learned that even the most beautiful stars radiate a more gorgeous presence when using the right color cosmetics.

From there I went on to study fashion at different

Institutes and learned how important wardrobe management is for our self-esteem, budget, appearance and career. Did you know that there is a direct correlation between the economy and fashion? There is! When the economy booms, the hemline goes up, and when the economy goes down, so does the hemline. In our present times the hemline is "take it as you like." The reason is mass confusion in our economy! However, prices in clothing keep going up! Designers can no longer drop a hemline and the world will follow. When it comes to fashion you, the buyer, no longer take dictation! You do what's right for you. How you look is an extension of how you feel about yourself and what you want the world to see. You use clothes as a way of self-expression and enjoyment.

We are in a time when ready-made clothes, hanging on a rack, can cost as much as we once paid for a small car. We are in an environment of discipline; any waste, excess, or self-indulgence is out. Clothing investments should be thought out as clearly as stock investments in order to reap good, steady, long-term rewards. The better your thought investment, the more self-confidence, elegance and overall style you'll radiate. A small, flexible, select wardrobe composed of top-quality apparel is 100 times more effective and easier to manage than a colossal collection of mediocre clothes. Before you go out to purchase any item over $75 dollars, you should have a precise plan.

A garment or accessory that has at least 5 of these 6 classifications can be considered a wise investment:

1. Superior quality

2. Classic style
3. Flexibility (Can be worn with other clothes)
4. Proper fit
5. Durability
6. Correct Color

Style is very important to consider in the management of your new wardrobe. Stay within the realm of the classics. In my travels to different parts of the world, I have noticed that the best dressed people are the ones that are attired in classic outfits. Trends are very "of the moment." Some can be quite creative, but do not withstand the test of time. Classics are fashion perpetuals. Line and design are simple and neat. I will give you a few guidelines to help you start managing your wardrobe.

Buy Fewer Pieces! Buy the Best You Can Afford!

Some of the most ingenious American designers are helping with their emphasis on separates. This is a system unbeatable for giving a wardrobe maximum versatility. Designers and manufacturers know that consumers can not afford expensive fad items that will be too gaudy to wear in another year. It would be in poor taste to make our wardrobe obsolete at a time when people have less money to spend. Stores are now featuring clothes with classic styles that will last and that can be worn with a tailored shirt or sweater for the office and for a woman, a ruffled silk blouse or a sequined camisole for dinner. A man can change to a silk or more colorful shirt for evening. One way to cope with higher prices is to buy basic separates that are convertible and can be worn in different ways. Each season, try updating these basics with a new purchase, such as a Bill Blass blouse or shirt for a skirt or pair of slacks you already own.

Another thing to consider before purchasing an item is the cost per wear, not only the initial price. What this means is, take the price that you paid and divide it by the number of times you expect to wear the item. Always buy with that in mind.

Use Color to Structure and Enlarge Your Wardrobe!

When I went to the Orient to speak about color, I found that people there were in great need of learning about the use of it. People in the Orient use color very openly. They use 3 or 4 different colors at the same time. Understanding the strategies about colors, many Far Easterners as well a Westerners can select the colors that best suit them.

Both men and women are very conscious of how their clothes harmonize with them. Harmonization is very important in today's society, in all areas of our everyday life, yet many people don't know how to make it work for them in their favor.

If you could find a way to harmonize and use color effectively, you would like to know more about it, wouldn't you? Well, a new concept has been developed by Mr. Robert Dorr—THE COLOR KEY PROGRAM™— which does just that for you. It enables you to be your own color professional and allows you to have confidence in the choices you make in regard to all color related tasks.

THE COLOR KEY PROGRAM™, as it is called,

selects and separates all colors into two different color groups. The color groups are identified as Key 1 Colors™ and Key 2 Colors™. Each color group has been selected so that all colors in each group harmonize with each other.

Everyone responds to colors and has color preferences. Extensive testing has shown that color influences our everyday lives. By preferring one color group over the other, you have a better chance of looking better and being more at ease with your selections and surroundings.

Whichever color group you decide to use will most likely be the one that is most suited for your personality, but having a professional Color Key® representative to assist you in correctly identifying your correct color group may be exactly what you need to make you feel confident about your choice.

All colors with a prominence of blue undertone are considered Key 1 Colors™ and all colors with yellow or golden undertones are considered Key 2 Colors™. Knowing which color group you prefer will enable you to expand your wardrobe by allowing you not only to mix and match the clothes that you already have, but also to help you select, with more authority, the clothes you buy from now on.

As you start your wardrobe management, it's important to remember that the contents of your closet should not resemble a rainbow, but rather your clothes should have a concentrated color scheme. The whole idea in planning your wardrobe is to buy clothes with colors that do something for you. Colors should be exciting and also have a purpose. It can open up a whole new life for you and help you express your inner feelings.

Choose a basic color from the Key 1 Colors™ (blue undertones) or the Key 2 Colors™ (yellow undertones) that you like and can be used as a pivot of your wardrobe. A good choice of neutrals and basic colors that can be found in both keys are: brown, navy, gray, beige, white, black or red. When purchasing your major pieces—a suit, a blazer, or a skirt—I suggest you concentrate on subtle, sophisticated shades. Make sure the colors you buy are in your chosen group so they will all harmonize. You can start with the neutral colors, then add colors to complement your choice. Those neutral colors, which go with everything, should be the basis for your wardrobe.

Before I chose my color scheme I asked myself which were my favorite colors and which colors made me look my best. That was not a very hard question for me, because without a doubt I knew that black and red were my favorite colors. I prefer Key 1 Color™, so the blue reds and jet blacks look great on me. Now my wardrobe color scheme is red/black and white. I use other bright colors as accents, such as blouses, scarves, belts, hats, and jewelry. Once your basic wardrobe is set, you may want to add to it. Your wardrobe can contain an infinite number of pieces based on a "two color" scheme, or it may be composed of different "two color" schemes, which interrelate. For example, if after I have built my first wardrobe in the color scheme of red/black, then maybe my next choice would be gray/blue. These two groups may be combined within my wardrobe since the four colors can all work together. But, be sure to start with one scheme, and then go to the next, only after the first has been built. **

Choose Natural Fabrics and/or Good Synthetic Blends!

Natural fabrics look better and wear longer than most synthetics. How can you tell when it is a rich fabric? "You can feel it!" Natural fabrics have texture and depth. Just by putting your hand on soft cashmere, mohair, angora, smooth silks, and crunchy knits, you can get a feel for these natural fabrics. To this list you should also add wool, cotton and linen. Natural fibers are best because they can breathe and absorb moisture, which makes it more comfortable to wear all year around. It's softer to the touch, more supple to drape, and lighter weight. Polyester, because of its new variety, is now more readily accepted. It comes blended with small percentages of nylon, cotton, or wool. Synthetic and natural blends are great for us that travel because these fabrics resist wrinkles and survive packing

Be Certain of Fit! Be Aware of Proportion!

No matter how expensive or exquisite an outfit, it will look terrible if it does not fit properly. A jacket should lie smoothly across the back, and should not buckle in the front. The look is always smooth. Look for plum straight leg pants and make sure the crease is sharp. Also, anything that fits you tightly is not right. The look today is "any way you want it." But, the right, always fashionable look, is basic or baroque, but never modest. It's often eccentric, but never dull. Any style you choose should have ample room around the armholes. Look for jackets that are lined since they will hang better on your body. It's important to learn the signs of good workmanship and shop with them in mind.

Let's teach the eye to judge proportion. This is what assures that clothes look great on us. To wear a longish skirt with a brief jacket is good for short women. Short men choose slimmer pants with a jacket that does not fall below the break of the leg. A shorter skirt with a longer blazer is best on a tall women. Tall men can wear baggier pants with longer jackets. Women with long skirts choose a low heel and, as the hem goes up, the heel height should rise. Proper proportion is an important consideration for your wardrobe management, because it can camouflage figure flaws. The petite man or woman, by keeping top and bottom in the same color and fabric, can add to their height because there are no breaks to make them appear short. Women, avoid spikes or flat heels! Medium heels work best for this long and lean look. Men and women that wear large sizes should avoid shirts or blouses that have extra bulky fabrics. For example, the dolman sleeve top should be chosen over the batwing sleeve top because of the excess bulk of fabric. Wear simple stylish shoes with big tops. Heels can be high or low.

Anything, regardless of cost, worn in excess looks tacky and negates a monied look. Simplicity is the key to chic! "Less is more," is definitely the rule. Flashy is very declasse. The point is, too much of anything can spell disaster: too much fur, too many ruffles, too many details, too much makeup or too much jewelry.

Learn to Recognize Quality!

No matter what the price tag or label of a garment, you should be well equipped with your own personal built-in quality detector to guarantee that you will get your money's worth and to recognize quality when you see it. First, study the fashion magazines and check good stores to see what clothing is being shown. Then put on some low, comfortable shoes and start shopping around. Go to discount stores and look through the racks. Another good place to find some fabulous buys is at thrift shops and consignment stores. Some very rich people give their almost new clothes to their favorite charity and they, in turn, sell them for a few dollars. If you have a trained eye for quality clothes, you will be able to find some very expensive clothes at the thrift shops. Consignment stores are a little different. There you will find nicer clothes. People turn their clothes over to the store and they, in turn, sell them on a percentage basis, like 50/50 or 40/60. Find a consignment store that is in a very nice area and see the kind of clothes they carry. Many wealthy people go from time to time to see if anything fabulous is for sale. So don't be ashamed to go into places like this. Everyone does it. They just won't admit it. It's OK! This is a little more time consuming than going to a department store, but you will get better bargains.

Don't buy a garment that is on sale just because of the low price! Make sure that it is the same style as the rest of your wardrobe. Also check for proper color, fit and workmanship. When you buy from a private label you can save and get good quality. Stores are offering more variety of style, color, and price, through their exclusive private label merchandise. It is a good deal for them and for you also. By developing clothing exclusively for their inventories, stores create a distinct image. Customers save because they buy in large quantities, directly from the manufacturing source. Some of the ways to detect a well made garment are:

1. The garments have zippers dyed to match and completely concealed in perfectly sewn plackets.
2. You will never see a metal eye in a well finished garment. A hook and eye is the preferred fastening whenever it is apt to show.
3. Snaps are usually avoided whenever they might show. If a large snap is necessary, it should be covered with a material of the same color and wherever possible, the same fabric as the garment.
4. Buttons should always be functional. Purely decorative buttons often down-grade a garment. Buttons should be stitched only through the outer layer of the fabric, not the lining. For heavy fabric the button should have a stem that is the same thickness as the material. The stem is made by attaching the button loosely and then winding the thread around between the fabric and the button. However, if the fabric is delicate, the underside of the spot where the button is attached should be reinforced with a small square of matching fabric and interlined with muslin.
5. Hemline stitches should not show from the outside of the garment. If the garment, because of the fabric, can not have a hem, it should be well finished by hand-rolling.
6. Well-made slacks and skirts are fully lined with dyed-

to-match silk.

7. Seams and stitching are even and without puckers.

All of these suggestions and guidelines will help you get started in managing a more radiant wardrobe. There is no need to be afraid of getting started. Just go over all the suggestions again and have fun! Shopping should be fun and rewarding! Go on and get started, you will surprise yourself and those around you! It is important for your self esteem. That person you're trying to impress will see a radiating confidence coming from you. They will respect you for it. As you know, your clothes will make a statement about you to the world!

**Note: The Color Key Program, Color Key, Key 1 Colors and Key 2 Colors are registered trademarks of Color Key Corporation, a member of Grow Group, Inc.*

Oliver L. Niehouse, President

Niehouse and Associates, Inc.
Speakers • Seminars • Consultants
109-23   71st Road
Forest Hills, New York 11375
(718) 544-7552

Oliver L. Niehouse

Oliver Niehouse workshops consistently receive high ratings and rave reviews from participants.

Why? First, because he structures them to solve problems managers face. Having been there himself, he knows their typical day. As a former company president in the U.S., Canada and Great Britain, he "knows what it means to meet a payroll."

Second, participants learn by doing. They are involved throughout the program in completing tasks, in management games, in making executive decisions, in small group problem solving and other experiential learning. So they leave with both knowledge and the understanding that comes from hands-on experience during the workshops.

And third, Ollie Niehouse employs creative and unique use of films—all the way from early, silent Laurel and Hardy shorts to recent full length Hollywood classics. For these simulate the real world better than anything else that could be used in workshops, and participants reinforce new concepts by applying them to these situations.

The result: Participants are stimulated and motivated to reach out, acquire new skills and develop comfort in their use. Thus Ollie Niehouse is invited back repeatedly to give programs for such clients as General Motors, DuPont, W.R. Grace Company, Long Island Lighting Company and many more, including medium and small size companies and for major associations here and abroad.

Leadership—The Proven Key to Team Success
by Oliver L. Niehouse

"Give us a leader, and we'll follow him through Hell."
—A line from a folk song by Tom Paxton

When was the last time someone was willing to go through on-the-job Hell for you? If it's been a while, then you have arrived at this final chapter just in time. That's because I'm about to discuss, in practical detail, the most important aspect about team management—the manager who leads the team!

Now, you may be wondering, "What does leadership have to do with teamwork?"

The answer is everything, especially if you want to improve productivity. You do not have to take up the way of the samurai or go running around in quality circles to learn this. Instead, you can learn a valuable lesson about productivity—and, what leadership has to do with teamwork—by looking within yourself.

A Lesson from Within

The human body is composed of various systems, which are like divisions or departments in organizational terms. Each system has its own functions and goals. For example, the digestive system takes in raw materials and disassembles them, directing precious nutrients to other systems. Some of these other systems re-assemble the nutrients in order to achieve their goals such as skeletal strength or muscular maintenance. Meanwhile, the digestive system passes on what's left to the intestinal and excretory systems.

The net results of all of these interactive systems is that the body, as a whole organization, lives. It simply exists in a state of rest. If the body is to engage in some activity, its various systems must go from a state of rest to a state of output sufficient for what is to be done. In short, improved productivity is necessary—and that's accomplished through a team effort by all systems, each system contributing to, rather than competing with, the body's goal.

Thus, the human body is the purest example of effective teamwork. And it all takes place within a very complex organization—one that is far more complex than any business!

What makes this teamwork possible and, occasionally, contributes to team disfunction? The answer is the brain which conceives, desires, and sets into motion the body's goals. It also evaluates the results. The brain is the command center, the seat of management. The brain is the body leader without which there simply is no truly effective team effort!

The Nature of Leadership

Leadership is an active skill wherein one person attempts to influence the behavior of one or more other persons in efforts towards accomplishing a task or specific goal. For example, George Washington influenced his army to defeat the British at Yorktown, while Martin Luther influenced his followers to reform Christianity.

No two situations for exercising leadership are ever exactly the same. The details of a situation, the times, the people involved, and other factors can all be different. As such, what works in one situation will not necessarily work in another because there is no one right way to lead.

Instead, leadership needs to be flexible. That is, a manager needs to vary his or her behavior relative to the situation. This is why a manager who never varies his/her leadership style because of a desire for consistency or some other reason can fail as a team leader—he/she may be using the wrong behavior for a specific situation.

Achieving Leadership Flexibility

A manager can vary his/her behavior by choosing a style

of leadership from a range of styles, each of which is a blend of two factors, task behavior and relationship behavior.

Task behavior is the amount of input and focus a leader gives in order to achieve a specific task. Such input and focus can involve explaining who is to do what, when, where, and how a task is to be done. Relationship behavior is the amount of two-way communications a leader provides through supportive actions, "psychological strokes," and facilitating behaviors. These can involve active listening, giving reasons why, and being sensitive to the stroking needs of individual followers.

The results of various combinations of task behavior and relationship behavior can be divided into four quadrants as shown in Figure 1. Starting from the lower right-hand corner and moving counterclockwise, each quadrant represents a basic leadership style.

Let's look at an example of a manager who has just hired a secretary. Initially, that secretary will need a lot of direction about company policies, office procedures, and other things in order to do his/her job—and do it right! This is high task/low relationship, quadrant 1 behavior. As the secretary gains familiarity and on-the-job experience, the manager can use more relationship behaviors while still being somewhat directive. This is a quadrant 2 leadership style of high task/high relationship. It's a "selling" style of leadership because it enables the follower to "buy into" the decision implicit in the manager's directions. In time, the secretary will reach a point where he/she can meaningfully share in the decision-making process for relevant specific tasks. This

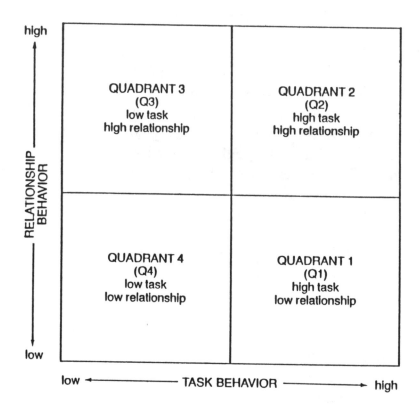

Figure 1. The three factors involved in flexible leadership.

would mean more effort by the manager to get the assistant involved (high relationship) but less direction (low task), which is quadrant 3 behavior known as "participating" style of leadership. For example, the secretary may participate in deciding which new computer workstation would best fulfill his/her needs while still being relatively easy to use.

Finally, the manager recognizes that the secretary can accomplish specific tasks without any direction such as replying to certain types of correspondence. The manager thus "delegates" responsibility and is simply kept informed rather than involved. This is low task/low relationship, quadrant 4 behavior.

Deciding when to use which style is a matter of recognizing when a follower has reached a certain level of competence and willingness. This is the follower's level of readiness, which has two aspects. First is job readiness, which concerns the skills and competence of a follower to fulfill an assigned task. Second is psychological readiness. This deals with a follower's capacity to set a high but attainable goal, and a willingness to assume responsibility.

Through readiness, flexible leadership acknowledges individuality in terms of each person's strengths and weaknesses. It recognizes that all workers do not develop to the same level or at the same rate for the same task. Each follower's readiness can vary from one situation to another and can change over time, forward or backwards. It also recognizes that some followers may never be ready. That is, that because of personality, beliefs, past experiences, and other factors, a follower may never mature beyond a certain level of readiness for a particular task.

Selecting an Appropriate Style

To select an appropriate style of leadership for any situation, a manager can do the following:

1. Determine the task.
2. Determine the follower's level of readiness for that task.
3. Draw a vertical line from the determined level of readiness to the bell-shaped curve in Figure 2, which is a mechanism for tieing the follower's readiness to the leader's task/relationship behaviors. The quadrant where the vertical line meets the curve is the style of leadership with the highest probability of being both successful and effective—of accomplishing the task and doing so in the best manner possible!

Note the use of the term, "highest probability." It's there because one can not absolutely guarantee results. Leadership involves people, who are neither always predictable nor controllable. In addition, if a manager is not continually sensitive to the shifting readiness levels of an individual, he/she may fail to see a sudden change caused by a non-working influence such as an impending divorce.

How to Determine Readiness

The essence of flexible leadership is the manager's ability to determine a follower's level of readiness. Now, while

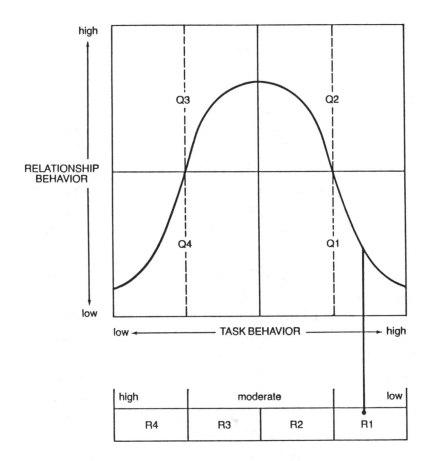

FOLLOWER'S LEVEL OF READINESS

Figure 2. The bell-shaped curve is a mechanism for tieing the follower's readiness to the leader's task/relationship behaviors. The quadrant where a vertical line (drawn from a determined level of readiness) meets the curve is the style of leadership with the highest probability of being successful and effective.

there are several ways to do this, the simplest method is to view each of the four levels as follows:

R1—The individual has little or no task-related ability and is seldom if ever willing to assume more responsibility.

R2—Some task-relevant ability and a willingness to assume responsibility on occasion.

R3—The individual has quite a bit of task-related ability. He/She is also often willing, almost eager, to assume responsibility.

R4—Possesses a great deal of task-relevant ability in terms of knowledge and skills, and is usually willing to assume responsibility because of self-confidence and commitment.

Sometimes, it can be difficult to distinguish between two levels of readiness for a specific task. When that happens, a manager should choose the lower of the two levels in question and closely monitor the effectiveness of his/her choice. Why the lower level? Because, should one need to, it is easier to adjust one's leadership style upwards than downwards. Moving downward has a tendency to take away responsibility from a subordinate and can thus be viewed as a criticism of his or her capabilities. In short, moving downward unnecessarily could create additional problems with that individual.

One can easily master this and other aspects of flexible leadership with time and practice. And it's worth the effort because it works not just in individual efforts, but also in team efforts. Flexible leadership is in fact that key to team success.

Leadership—the Key to Team Success

What makes flexible leadership the key to team success is the understanding of the mutually dependent relationship that exists between a leader and his/her subordinates.

On the one hand, a manager can not do everything alone. He/She is dependent on workers to get a job done, no matter how difficult or hellish the job may be or how few the number of workers. On the other hand, workers are dependent on the manager as a leader to provide: knowledge and direction for their weak skills (quadrant 1 leadershp or Q1); understanding about the tasks they are to accomplish (Q2); a sense of involvement in what they are accomplishing (Q3); and, ideally, opportunities to demonstrate their developed strengths and talents (Q4). Ultimately, these are the measurements for their movement within an organization.

The flexible leader knows this and acts upon it, creating a self-motivating environment where workers know that their efforts will pay off for them. Pay off both inwardly in terms of satisfaction and more earned responsibility, and outwardly in terms of promotions and financial rewards. A worker's self-interest and need for achievement thus work in the manager's favor, and a stronger team is forged as a result because a team is only as strong as its weakest member. The more they all pull together, the more they collectively—and individually!—achieve. That, in turn, can lead to a maximization of individual potentials as well as a maximization of human resources for measureable productivity gains. And when that happens, the team is a success.

Incidentally, because of this self-motivating environment which can maximize individual potentials, flexible leadership inspires loyalty. Loyalty that as Milton once wrote "can make a Heaven or Hell."

A Closing Proof

What makes flexible leadership the proven key to team success is what I have encountered as a management consultant to the public sector and to private industry. Time and time again over the last ten years, company-specific leadership seminars and public workshops on Improving Managerial and Leadership Effectiveness have produced unsolicited comments such as this one:

"I've attended many seminars and workshops; but I've never seen one that ended like this. Everyone went around shaking hands with each other, exchanging business cards, and agreeing to keep in touch. This was a remarkable team building experience."

What's really impressive is that this participant's experience occurred within a public workshop consisting of individuals who were all strangers to each other. And, it is by no means an isolated comment. They all hint at or remark on one essential point: just as a learning process, flexible leadership fosters teamwork even among total strangers!

These comments are not so much applause for my consulting skills. Rather, they are testimonials or proofs that, in practice, flexible leadership can go beyond just building team efforts and lead to team success. It really can, for those managers willing to try it.

We may not always see eye to eye, but we can try to see heart to heart.

—Sam Levenson

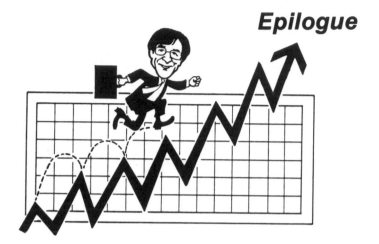

Epilogue

The Essence of Management
by Burt Dubin

*"If you could see what I see—
the brilliant future of America—"*
**—John Adams, second President
of the United States**

Management is defined as "planning, directing, organizing and controlling the activities of others." That's true. Literally true. Yet, not essentially true. Your subordinates have so much to give. They have so much that they want to give, long to give, yearn to give, ache to give—if only we, their managers, will liberate and give wings to all of their encapsulated potential.

An old approach to managing people included the "us" and "them" view. We would use every manipulative technique at our command to secure more yield of work performed, more productivity from subordinates. The cost to those subordinates in physical, emotional and mental health—as well as in depletion of their spirit—was of no concern to us at all. Return on investment, ever higher dividends to the shareholders, beating the same quarter last year—this was what mattered.

People were there to be used up, consumed, thrown away like an old shoe when their usefulness to us was over.

That *modus operandi* doesn't cut it any more. Today's subordinates, especially those under 35, are generally bright, articulate, aware, far better educated than their parents were. What's more, they care. They care a lot.

And—they want you, their manager, to care a lot, too. They want you to care about them as human beings first—and as units of production second.

Being more inner-directed, they require a feeling of OK-ness at the level of essence—in the place where they live. Their inner spirit now demands connectedness and closeness. They want to make a difference. They need to know that they matter.

We, as their managers, have a priceless opportunity to engage not just their bodies and minds, inducing them to complete so many technical activities that add up to profit contribution and growth for the company.

We have that rare chance today to touch the hearts of our subordinates, to provide them with an indefinable psychic satisfaction that they crave so much. The result is far more productivity, profit contribution and growth for the company.

How do we do this? What do we do to release the true potential sleeping within our subordinates, to inspire them to give us their best—and then to go beyond themselves and give us more.

We satisfy their inner needs—that's what we do. We provide them with a mission to share, a sense of transcendence. We grant them permission to go beyond perceived limits and to be greater than they are.

To Create a Better Team of Subordinates, Do These Seven Things:

1. Let your subordinates know of the meaning within their work. Empower them with understanding.
2. Be fully committed to your purpose—and you'll automatically attract your people to partnership in that commitment.
3. Endow your people with a vision to share.
4. Trust them all the way. Have no secrets. Lay truth on the line.
5. Give your people a reputation to live up to.
6. Let them do the work their way. They're closer to it than anyone else, including you.
7. Finally, share the glory, the recognition, the rewards, with them. Give them all the credit. They will love you for that.

I'm sure you've guessed, by now, that this stuff is what I teach and share in my management workshops. This is my mission. I feel a sense of deepest gratitude to have the privilege of touching lives healingly—and enhancing productivity, profits and company growth at the same time.

On behalf of all the "Management Team" authors— I hope that you've been inspired to reach beyond yourself in your management practice so that you will help others reach beyond themselves, to tap their highest potential— as they produce the results you want.

> *"You've asked me the way, and I have shown you the way—and, in so doing, I have reached beyond you, and far beyond myself."*
> *—George Bernard Shaw*

About the Publisher
DOTTIE WALTERS, C.S.P.

Dottie Walters' mother almost lost her at the seaside one day when the little girl disappeared from sight. After lifeguards, police and friends had searched for an hour, she was discovered sitting up on the boardwalk. In front of the five-year-old was a stack of pennies and a large quantity of "sand dollar" seashells.

"Why are you mad, Mommie?" Dottie beamed with joy. "I am so happy to be giving these people *dollars for pennies!*"

Dottie sold bouquets of wild flowers during the depression, had a doughnut route, organized a baby sitting service, ran ads and hired other teenagers, was advertising manager for her high school newspaper, then went to work, on the day after graduation, at the *Los Angeles* Classified Department. When the recession hit her family, she bought space from a small weekly newspaper in Baldwin Park, California and walked to sell ads, pushing her two little children in a rickety old stroller. When the wheel kept falling off, Dottie gave it a whack with her shoe. But she never gave up. Local merchants knew her as a promise keeper who had fresh ideas for advertising copy. She finally earned enough to buy a Model A Ford. (A chunker, not an antique.)

She began a newcomer welcoming service . . . used public speaking to promote her business; expanded it until she had the largest such service in the Western United States; wrote the first book on sales for women, the pioneer *Never Underestimate the Selling Power of a Woman;* created cassette albums; has spoken all over the world; began a publishing company; organized a speakers booking agency and publishes and edits the largest newsletter for professional speakers in the world, *Sharing Ideas for Professional Speakers.*

Dottie has spoken all over the United States, Asia, Canada, England and other foreign countries. Dottie and Bob Walters are parents of three fine children: an attorney, a teacher and a graphics art expert who leads the top Gymnastic Vaulting Team in the world—National Champions. The Walters have four grand-children. Dottie is President of four corporations, and serves on the Board of Directors of other companies and organizations. Friends think of her as an inspiration, a mentor, a dynamic worker, poet and as Dottie often says herself, the most important, "an inspiration."

**# 11: HOW TO ENTER THE WORLD OF PAID
SPEAKING by DOTTIE WALTERS, C.S.P.**
Rally speaker tells you now to
start, what to charge, and how to find paying
customers. Rated TOPS by Cavett Robert. How to
begin where you are, how to ask for the right fee.
How to sell products from the platform, how to
promote yourself at no cost. How to locate those
paying audiences. What to do if they have no
money—to make more than ever.
■ *4-cassette album $59.00*

**# 12: SEVEN SECRETS OF SELLING TO WOMEN
by DOTTIE WALTERS, C.S.P.** One hour cassette.
After listening to this cassette, you can sell ANY
woman ANYTHING! . . . so they say! Amazing!
■ *Cassette, single, $9.95*

#13: *SELLING POWER OF A WOMAN* by *DOTTIE WALTERS, C.S.P.* Big six-hour cassette album, full course, six cassettes. Dynamite! This is IT! Top course sales!   ■ *Cassette album, $69.00*

#14 *SHARING IDEAS*
Newsletter for Speakers
includes list of 150 booking agents

■ *$35.00 1 year, $60.00 2 years*
Sample copy, $3.00

(Foreign countries add $10 annual postage)
SEE ORDER FORM

SUCCESS SEMINAR SERIES
ANTHOLOGIES

#1: SUCCESS SECRETS! How 18 everyday women became builders and famous speakers! Role models! Beautiful hardback. Stimulating, inspirational, how to build your business and your life. ■ *$11.95*

#2: POSITIVE POWER PEOPLE. Men and women of achievement radiate positive attitudes, inspire readers to greater success. Foreword Cavett Robert. Book, hardback. ■ *$12.95*

#3. THE PEARL OF POTENTIALITY. Are you ready to catch it? An anthology of women of achievement from a woman. Train engineer to inventors, to speakers a wealth of inspiration! Hardback, beautiful gift for women beginning their careers. ■ *$11.95*

 # 4: HERE IS GENIUS. Men and women tell the stories of achievement and inspiration by opening the *genius channel.* Foreword by Dr. Norman Vincent Peale. Book, hardback. ■ *$11.95*

 # 5: THOSE MARVELOUS MENTORS. Amazing stories of the influences on their lives of top notch speakers and business people. Hardback. Foreword by former Arizona Congressman Somers White. Outstanding! **■ $13.95**

#6: STAR SPANGLED SPEAKERS. Here are stories of the Space Shuttle, the Statue of Liberty, Americans who have overcome. Hardback. True stories of the people who won the battles of life. **■ $13.95**

 # 7: THE SUNSHINERS. Secrets of humorous speakers. You'll laugh, you'll learn, you'll love them. Hardback. The speakers who light up your life. **■ $13.95**

 # 8: THE GREAT PERSUADERS. Sales and sales management. The top managers in the United States give you their best information. Hardback. A treasure trove of how-to and when-to by the very top people. **■ $16.95**

 # 9: *NEVER UNDERESTIMATE THE SELLING POWER OF A WOMAN by DOTTIE WALTERS, C.S.P.* The FAMOUS bestseller. The best sales book ever written by a woman for women in sales. Used as a textbook by many national sales firms. Easy to read, full of power. The classic! Hardback, book. ■ *$13.95*

 # 10: THE MAGNIFICENT MOTIVATORS. Inspiring collection of motivational techniques revealed by some of the country's foremost speakers. Learn how these same methods can inspire you to greater achievement. Hardback ■*$14.95*

#11: THE SYNERGISTS. Exceptional achievers focus on qualities that help you develop a healthful, secure, successful lifestyle. *$16.95*

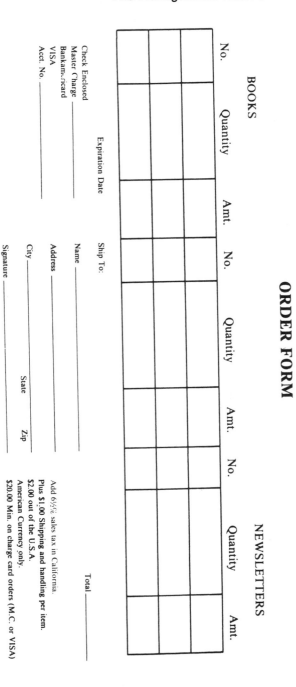

ORDER FORM

BOOKS

No.	Quantity	Amt.

NEWSLETTERS

No.	Quantity	Amt.

Check Enclosed
Master Charge ———
Bankamericard
VISA
Acct. No. ———

Expiration Date ———

Ship To:

Name ———

Address ———

City ——— State ——— Zip ———

Signature ———

Add 6½% sales tax in California.
Plus **$1.00 Shipping and handling per item.**
$2.00 out of the U.S.A.
American Currency only.
$20.00 Min. on charge card orders (M.C. or VISA)

Total ———